SUBVERSIVE DIALOGUES

SUBVERSIVE DIALOGUES

Theory in Feminist Therapy

LAURA S. BROWN

BasicBooks
A Division of HarperCollins*Publishers*

Designed by Ellen Levine

Library of Congress Cataloging-in-Publication Data
Brown, Laura 1952–
     Subversive dialogues : theory in feminist therapy / Laura Brown.
          p. cm
     Includes bibliographical references and index.
     ISBN 0–465–08322–6
     1. Feminist therapy—Philosophy.   I. Title.
RC489.F45B76   1994
616.89'14—dc20   94–18185
                                                                      CIP

94 95 96 97 ❖/RRD 9 8 7 6 5 4 3 2 1

In memory of my grandmother,
Pauline Landau Schwartzberg, and for
Miriam Vogel, sine qua non

Contents

Acknowledgments

FIRST, THANKS TO MY EDITOR at Basic Books, Jo Ann Miller, and her assistant editor, Stephen Francoeur, who pursued me at just the moment when I needed that stimulus for writing a book. They have given me superb, clear, and unblinking editorial feedback of the sort I rarely encounter and always need. Copyeditor Nina Gunzenhauser transformed my compound, complex, jargony phrases into lovely, clear form. Jane Judge, my project editor, responded calmly with good humor to my various attempts to obstruct the final production process by doing too much on the computer at the wrong time, and graciously accommodated my travel schedule to get the manuscript finished.

My research assistant, Laura Anderson, was of invaluable help in preparing the reference section of this book. Without her work, I would have had no winter holiday in 1993.

My aunt, Thelma Pierce, was a source of information and reality checking about certain events in my family history that appear in this book. She and her husband, Bill, have stood *in loco parentis* for me with love and respect, and have been an important healing force in my own life.

Faithful Staffordshire bullterriers Boychick and the late Chazer gave me many opportunities for long walks where I could develop some of the ideas floating around in my head.

My friends and readers Ken Pope and Maria Root have contributed much to the quality of this work through their incisive comments and their words of support and encouragement. No work happens in a vacuum, and they filled my writing environment with air and light.

Introduction

EVERY SPRING, Jews around the world celebrate the holiday of Pesach, or Passover, as it is known in English. In thousands of Jewish homes, people meet for the Seder meal and the recitation of the Haggadah. The story is one of a journey of liberation, the freeing from bondage of Jews who had been oppressed as slaves in Egypt and the transformation of an entire people from a band of individuals into a nation with cultural values and identity. The service reiterates throughout that this millennia-old story is not simply historical but instead is happening to each person sitting around the Seder table and sharing in the telling. Each one of us experiences the liberatory process in that moment, and each one also acknowledges how she or he has been, and continues to be, enslaved to some degree, literally or figuratively. Throughout the service, the participants review and reopen the discussions of ancient sages about how we can, today, demonstrate our dedication to and involvement in the movement from slavery to freedom; we explore the costs of freeing ourselves, the emotions that emerge when our oppressors are revealed as human and in pain themselves, the fears of freedom that intrude when the safety of strictures is no longer available. This ritual defined the springtimes of my childhood; it was a rich experience in which past and present were drawn together over and over again.

The telling of the story of liberation begins with a short ritual, performed by the youngest present (usually a child), who asks a series of four questions about the subtle symbolism of the Seder meal, beginning with *Ma nishtanah halaila hazeh mecal halailot?* "How is this night different from all other nights?" These are lines that, as a child, the firstborn of my generation, I chanted yearly. The questioner notes that while this is a meal like any other meal, there are small but potentially meaningful differences between the practices of daily life and the processes by which liberation from oppression is symbolized in the Seder: special foods are eaten, and the meal is taken reclining in comfort rather than sitting upright. The telling of the Haggadah is in fact a response to these four questions, a careful exegesis of how liberation from oppression and delivery into freedom are manifest and symbolized. The story tells us that while certain acts of liberation may not seem especially different from daily life—for example, eating bitter herbs rather than simply any vegetable and unleavened bread, Matzoh, instead of the usual risen loaf—each such act carries a subversive significance that serves to undermine the assumptions of oppression that are inherent in the enslavement of any group or individual. Each small transformation reminds us that we were and can again be freed.

This book is written in the tradition of the Haggadah, a story about the process of liberation. It is about answering the question of *ma nishtanah*, about how feminist therapy is different from all other approaches to psychotherapy. It is about identifying the sometimes small and subtle markers of feminist theory and analysis that are evidence of a powerful process of liberation from oppression that is occurring during the telling of the tale that is psychotherapy. As does the Seder service, this book dwells in detail on the various ways in which liberation and revolutionary social change manifest themselves, but here, the focus will be on those healing relationships founded in feminist practice. In this book, I will explore the means by which each participant in feminist therapy, therapist and client alike, relives a journey of liberation.

My own feminist journey to this book began more than twenty years ago. In 1972–73 I was working as a nurse's aide on a psychiatric inpatient unit, biding my time until I could make a second attempt at getting into a graduate program in clinical psychology. Hanna Pavilion was considered a very good psychiatric hospital, a teaching setting in a university, with no back wards or untrained attendants. It was the best that inpatient psychiatry could offer in Cleveland, Ohio in the 1960s and 1970s, and I felt lucky to have landed a job there.

But something happened to change my view of this place and of my work there. In that year when I temporarily stepped out of academia into the world of hard work for low pay, I had become active in what was then called "women's liberation," the second wave of the white feminist movement in the United States (after the first wave of the suffrage movement). I was seeing and hearing everything in my life through new senses. All my casually taken-for-granted realities were shattering around me. I found in the women's movement the shared names for feelings and experiences I had always thought were unique to me. In the midst of this awakening of feminist consciousness, a book arrived on the shelves that seemed to demand that I take it home. Reading it changed the direction of my life and started me on my journey.

The book was Phyllis Chesler's *Women and Madness.* It brought together pieces of awareness about my work in mental health that I had not until then allowed to come to the surface with any authority. Chesler, peering through a feminist lens, argued that the mental health professions were not benign sources of comfort for women in distress. Her passionate and thoroughly documented work on women's experiences as psychiatric patients led me to the uncomfortable insight that my chosen profession of psychotherapy, which I had planned to enter since I was very young, was a source of oppression to women, a tool, witting or not, of a culture that needed to keep women in their place.

I knew that what Chesler was writing was true, because I was seeing it at work every day. I had been attempting to justify what happened there by citing my own inexperience; I thought I was uncomfortable with what I witnessed because I lacked the training to appreciate its worth. I had not yet learned to trust my own gut reactions to situations that made me uncomfortable. I still needed an expert to support my perceptions, and to my great good fortune, Chesler's book became the expert authorizing my own voice. I realized that I was present at the scenarios described by Chesler for the eight hours of every day that I spent on the third floor of Hanna Pavilion: depressed women being told by their male psychiatrists to put on makeup before they would be considered well enough to go home, whether they preferred to wear it or not; an incest survivor (although we didn't have that name for her then) labeled "hysterical" because of her rage at learning that her father/perpetrator had now offended against her own daughters, bringing the violation to a second generation; the profoundly depressed women given drugs and shock therapy, the reality that they were being beaten at home ignored. I noted the absence of women from the ranks of psychiatrists and psychologists and the preponderance of women who sat, day by day, in the chairs on our politely grim ward hallways. (The nursing staff were, of course, mostly female; we were valued for our caregiving, but the profound expertise of the women on the nursing staff carried less authority than the dangerous fumblings of male first-year psychiatric residents.) I heard the discourse defining our patients' realities and could no longer deny that something important was missing from the conversation. Chesler's book made it impossible for me to avoid what I knew or to discount my perceptions on the grounds of naivete. I was transformed forever at a critical point in my professional development, no longer simply the good student and curious listener. My feminism and my potential career collided.

I emerged from that revelation knowing that the only way I could proceed with my career plans was to bring the insights that I was gaining from my participation in the women's movement into that career. In feminism, I was finding truths that excited and energized me when they did not leave me limp with rage. By the time I was accepted in graduate training in clinical psychology and—with new ambivalence about my chosen occupation—started graduate school in the fall of 1973, I had begun to describe myself as a "feminist therapist," because this was what Chesler and other women who were pointing out the problems in psychotherapy were calling themselves. I knew they were on to something, and I wanted it.

Then, like most of the other women who were using this term, I had no specific idea what I meant by it other than that I was a feminist who was a therapist (albeit a new and not-very-skillful one). I knew mostly what I did *not* mean; I did not mean the traditional, sexist, misogynist approach to psychotherapy, the silencing of women, the adjustment of women to patriarchy that had been standard practice for decades, according to writers like Chesler. I knew that being a feminist therapist meant that I was choosing to ask questions that would be difficult and challenging to the mostly white male faculty who were training me and to the mostly white male leadership of my profession. I knew (by the way the faculty at my graduate program responded to my extremely impertinent questions) that my embrace of this label put me on the fringe of my profession. I also knew that I was most at home on the margins, conceptually and professionally, because things made sense to me there in ways that the assumed wisdom of my discipline often did not. I did not know yet how powerful an approach to therapy this would be. I could not, from that vantage point, foresee the places I would go conceptually and in my practice by attempting to understand what it meant to be a feminist therapist.

In the twenty years that followed my moments of consciousness raising in the pages of Phyllis Chesler's book and the halls of Hanna Pavilion, the culture of psychotherapy and the lineaments of society have both been transformed by the emergence of the second wave of North American feminism. Feminist therapy practice grew by geometric proportions. Organizations of feminist therapists came into being at the local, national, and international levels. Feminist therapists wrote books and articles, circulated papers about what we were doing, trained ourselves and one another, and mentored students. We grabbed hungrily for every experience we could find that might contribute to our becoming feminist therapists and to our contacts with one another.

Together with the entire North American women's movement, we uncovered in the process of consciousness raising many of the silenced and sometimes nameless realities of life in patriarchy: rape, the sexual abuse of children, the beating of women in the home, sexual harassment, violence against gays and lesbians, institutionalized racism. As these aspects of oppression became more visible to us, feminist therapists applied our ideas to practice in each of these dimensions. They were exploring their own experiences critically, and defining reality to include them. Feminist therapists did not objectify themselves; instead, they expanded the dimensions of their understanding of humanity with a broader view of both suffering and triumph.

I, meanwhile, was discovering that rural southern Illinois was a great place to go to graduate school undistractedly, but not an environment in which I would long be happy living. I completed my training, moved to Seattle as my clinical internship site, and in 1979 entered full-time practice as a feminist therapist and one among many women who had chosen this direction for reasons often not different from my own. In the early 1980s, I began to write about feminist therapy in a growing series of book chapters and journal articles. The appearance of the personal computer in my life speeded up this process, freeing me to argue with myself in the middle of an article without having to retype the whole thing painfully. Each piece spurred on another, and I found myself wanting to say more.

This book initially evolved from a desire to write about my experience of participating in the growth and development of feminist therapy, to attempt to say something in a connected and cohesive fashion about how feminist therapy has excited me and changed my life. It brings together in one place many of the ideas that I have been writing and speaking about to my colleagues in feminist therapy and mainstream psychology for the last ten years. It is an effort at an integrated statement about what it means to be a feminist therapist. I want to explicate here what our discipline has to offer that is so unique among approaches to the healing arts of psychotherapy, to say what it is that is specifically feminist about feminist therapy.

In almost every workshop that I have given about feminist therapy, I have said something to the effect that feminist therapy is a philosophy of psychotherapy, not a prescription of technique. By this statement I have meant that feminist therapists can be identified by how we understand what we do—the political and cultural meaning of our work—rather than by the actions we take in a therapy session. While this depiction of feminist therapy as centrally theory-based remains true for most feminist therapists of my acquaintance, the published literature of feminist therapy has not for the most part borne out this philosophical emphasis. What we do have is a very valuable and important body of writing about how feminist therapy is practiced, techniques for applying feminist therapy in work with various specific populations of people or certain types of problems, especially those that are common in the lives of women. This was an absolutely necessary literature because it filled profound and dangerous gaps in practice. But by itself, it has not been sufficient to define feminist therapy.

The feminist therapy literature has been surprisingly short on the explicit delineation of theory, even though feminist therapists tell ourselves that it is theory that binds us together across other technical and disciplinary boundaries and even though theoretical notions have been implicit in much of what is now available. My desire to talk about theory and about the philosophy that is feminist therapy and that informs my work, to fill this hole in our discourse about who we are as a theoretical orientation, has been a powerful motivator for writing this volume. It is an opportunity to examine the epistemological and methodological uniqueness of a feminist therapy perspective and to illuminate our collective understanding of what is meant by a feminist voice and vision in psychotherapy practice.

The Importance of Theory

I believe that theory is fundamental to any psychotherapy practice, because it offers therapists a coherent strategy for thinking about what they are doing, across time and situations. Theory both allows and requires therapists to delineate the conceptual boundaries of their universes, to explicate those notions that are congruent with—or, conversely, inconsistent with—a particular understanding of human behavior and personal and social transformation. Psychoanalytic theory, which constitutes an attempt at a complete and universalistic theory of human growth, development, and healing, derives some of its power both to persuade and to provoke from its presumed capacity to define the universe of reality in just this complete and thorough way. In the universe generated by psychoanalytic theory, there *is* an unconscious mind, an ego, mechanisms of defense. By assuming that such structures exist, the therapist operating with a psychoanalytic epistemology can know, name, and comprehend everything that happens in therapy in an integrated, coherent, and consistent manner.

Feminist therapy needs such a foundation and needs it to be explicit and coherent rather than implicit and fragmented. Without theory, progress in feminist therapy becomes overly dependent on an oral tradition that worked well when our numbers were small but is less useful as we grow, and as some among us die and can no longer pass the traditions along. In order to be able to state with confidence that "feminist therapists do X as a specific expression of feminist practice," we require a theory that leads to X across situations and persons.

To put forward theory in feminist therapy, however, has always seemed a daunting task. We are a tradition without official leaders or gurus (Brown & Brodsky, 1992); we do not have a Freud, a Jung, a Perls, a Beck, although we have a plethora of "mothers," women like Phyllis Chesler who were among the first to ask the hard questions about sexism in psychotherapy. This absence of leaders reflects the feminist commitment to authorizing knowledge from the grassroots instead of granting authority only or primarily to knowledge delivered by a designated "expert." Much feminist therapy practice has developed as a convergence of the work of many women attempting to apply feminist political principles, as we understand them, to the practice of psychotherapy.

This convergence has been present from the very first; Hannah Lerman, one of those founding mothers, tells a story of how she and two other women, Ella Lasky and the late Adrienne Smith, volunteered in 1971 to offer a symposium on feminist therapy at a psychology convention. Although the three had never met, all said nearly identical things about what constituted feminist practice, even at this very early moment in the development of feminist therapy. This meeting of minds across the divides of age, profession, and geography has been a consistent, startling, and affirming aspect of most feminist therapists' experiences. Even when we come from very different traditions in our field (I, for instance, trained as an individual therapist, have little in common with family therapists in general but resonate entirely to the work of feminist family therapists), our underlying and implicit feminist theories have created connections. Writing in 1993 after the first National Conference on Education and Training in Feminist Practice, where I spent four days in the July heat of Boston doing theory with nine other feminist psychologists, I know that this convergence toward shared meaning has persisted, even as feminist practitioners have explored diverse directions and have moved some distance from the places where we began. In our group, filled with excitingly different women, we explicated our theories of feminist therapy in ways that were chillingly similar and informed by one another's visions.

Feminist therapy's identity as a child of many mothers has nevertheless made the development of an articulated therapy theory difficult. Unlike many other psychotherapeutic traditions, in which practice arose from or was crafted to fit theory, feminist therapy has been so taken with the need to respond to the wounds of patriarchy that practice has emerged first and foremost. As Hannah Lerman (1986) stated in her proposed criteria for a feminist theory of personality, such a theory would be feminist only if it remained true to the data of clinical experience. This is also a necessary criterion for a theory of feminist therapy; without the experience of clinical practice, it would be impossible to develop feminist therapy theory. None of us could have easily proposed such a theory two decades ago when we began to create that feminist clinical practice. Yet because each of us, practicing as feminist therapists, has often had to be her own expert, it has been difficult to overcome the years of patriarchal socialization that have taught us to undervalue the authority of that expertise. While we have trusted our experiences clinically, I and many of my feminist therapy colleagues have been less comfortable in generalizing broadly from those experiences in a way that would elucidate underlying theoretical principles.

In order to free my own voice to emerge on these pages, I have reminded myself that my writing takes place within a philosophical and political context, one that for me is heartfelt and not perfunctory. I take seriously the precept of feminist therapy that declares that each of us is expert and of value as a source of information and authority. This book embodies my expertise, reflecting my experience, my thoughts and ideas, and my opportunities to learn and interact with clients and colleagues. And with it goes my encouragement to challenge it, disagree with it, and play with it.

Some Defining Parameters

Mine is thus a very particular and limited experience, as is that of all humans. To avoid universalizing my life story, I have adopted a feminist standpoint epistemology in my work. Standpoint epistemologies assume that there is no universal reality, but only that informed by one's position in the world and relationship to it, literally by the point at which one stands in the social matrix. "Reality" is constructed in the social discourse between oneself and one's emotional and interpersonal environment.

I also believe that there are basic feminist standpoints defining the ideas in this book. A core of the standpoint of feminist therapy theory is that the personal is political. This means that individual experience is consciously deprivatized and holds potentially universal meaning. But the personal is also unique and delimited by who I am; it is not universal. Thus, standpoint methodologies require an attention to the variability of human experience. In the feminist therapy communities of the United States, attention to diversity of experience has consequently become another plank of the theoretical platform on which feminist therapy theory rests.

This is a central and basic notion, that a theory of feminist therapy must balance the deprivatizing instinct of feminist politics against the tendency to overgeneralize and universalize the individual experiences of a given feminist therapist and her clients. Feminist political philosophies, which attend each in its own manner to questions of gender and power in social arrangements, mold the embrace in which personal experiences are held and understood in feminist therapy. Those personal experiences, while prized and respected, cannot be mistaken for universal ones; this has been one of the chief errors of many mainstream theories in the eyes of their feminist critics. For white feminist therapists such as myself, there is an especially thorny and necessary awareness regarding the limits to which white people can make our personal experience everyone's political experience; as members of the dominant racial group in U.S. culture, we have the unfortunate tendency to assume that our lives *are* life, just as the male theorists we have criticized assumed that men's lives represented the generic human. In presenting what I perceive to be a theory of feminist therapy, I offer what I hope will be the necessary irritant to stimulate the reader's own theorizing. Feminist therapy theory arises as a conversation among the practitioners and clients, the trainers and supervisors, the admirers and the critics, of our work. This is my contribution to that conversation, a step in the dance, a *pas de beaucoup*, but not the entire minuet.

Because I believe that it is important to understand the factors delineating my conceptual frameworks, I am very specific about those factors informing my observations of feminist therapy and generating my theoretical constructions. My epistemological process and methodologies reflect my relationship with the world around me as a white-skinned, Ashkenazi Jewish, upper-middle-class lesbian woman, doctorally trained as a scientist-practitioner in clinical psychology, born in 1952, raised by the U.S.-born children of immigrants, quasi-able-bodied, licensed by the state (and therefore to some degree complicit with that institution) in the private practice of feminist therapy and feminist forensic psychology with a focus on trauma survivors. I prize the intellectual and conceptual, while valuing knowledge that arises from so-called nonrational sources as well.

My visions, opinions, and experiences of the reality of feminist therapy come through the lenses of my own life experiences, where and how I practice, and with whom; this book is one feminist therapist's image of how we can understand at a theoretical and conceptual level what we do in the practice of feminist therapy. I believe that this willingness to search for and know the nature of these lenses is necessary to a feminist theory-building process. The theoretical structures I propose here are not meant as the final word or the most correct one. They do constitute a vision and voice that I find exciting, transformative, and empowering for myself and the people I work with. I hope that my readers will find them similarly arousing at times, if only as a source of motivation leading to their own clear theory. Our products reflect the process of their creation; feminist theory arises in a feminist process, a respectful encounter in which no one person is the only expert.

My experience also reflects my immersion in one portion of the twenty-year heritage of feminist therapy, the world of feminist psychological practice. That heritage is such an important emotional and intellectual context for my theory that I will be sharing stories from it as a way of helping readers trace the steps I have taken toward my theorizing. These stories reflect my profound debt to my context and also, I hope, illuminate how my thinking has careened off the edges of the therapy context in a manner that will aid the reader's progress through this land for which we have had no maps because we refused to use the ones drawn by patriarchy, which had said, "Nothing here in this territory anyway."

In this volume I have chosen to refer to feminist therapists as women. This decision reflects the realities of feminist therapy practice. I believe that men can be profeminist and antisexist therapists (Ganley, 1988), but the domain of feminist therapy itself is still the territory of women practitioners. While feminist therapy is not about therapy *with* women, it is therapy practiced *by* feminist women whose insights are profoundly informed by living in diverse female realities. I recognize that this is a contradictory message regarding the gendered nature of feminist therapy and that my position, while shared by many feminist therapists, is not shared by all. It is something of a radioactive issue for even the most certain of feminist practitioners, and I am certain that some of my readers will disagree profoundly with my stance. The use of the generic female pronoun to describe feminist therapists is in keeping with the practices of those feminist therapy organizations that have provided my intellectual home for the past two decades and reflects my strong allegiances to those settings.

Because I am trained to work with individuals, even though I situate each person within concentric circles of social contexts, most of the images of what happens in therapy described in this volume reflect the one-to-one relationships that emerge from my experiences with this approach to treatment. This particular perspective, does not, however, assume that feminist therapy happens only in this way. Feminist therapists work with couples (as I occasionally do), with families (where some of the most brilliant work in feminist therapy is happening today), as consultants to larger systems such as workplaces, and in the legal system, another place where my own practice takes place.

My discussions of theory in this book assume some prior knowledge of work done on feminist therapy practice. Readers who are not familiar with this literature are referred to *The Handbook of Feminist Therapy* (Rosewater & Walker, 1985), *A Feminist Approach to Mental Health* (Ballou & Gabalac, 1985), *Feminist Psychotherapies* (Dutton-Douglas & Walker, 1988), and *Diversity and Complexity in Feminist Therapy* (Brown & Root, 1990) for background material. These four volumes constitute an excellent review of many of the fundamental issues from which my work on theory has been derived; they will also acquaint the reader with a number of the sources to which I will be referring in this book.

A Preview of Coming Subversions

This book is structured in a manner similar to the development of feminist therapy theory, working upward from the roots. I begin with an exploration of the core epistemology of feminist therapy theory and examine how the ways of knowing and understanding that arise from feminism inform the practice and understandings of feminist therapists. I introduce as well some of the critiques of therapy, feminist and otherwise, that have been advanced by feminist theorists inside and outside of the so-called helping professions. I then move to a review of feminist political theories and explore the manners in which each stream of feminist politics can be seen to inform different phases of the development of feminist therapeutic practice. I also explore in depth the importance of multicultural knowledge claims, epistemologies, and methodologies to the development of feminist therapy theory and practice as well as the strongly interlinked oppressions whose understanding is central to feminist theorizing.

I next move directly to certain aspects of feminist therapy practice, examining how each is theorized. I explore the thorny and often misunderstood territory of the egalitarian relationship in feminist therapy, examining the implications of the asymmetries of power in therapy for a feminist methodology. I next move to an examination of case conceptualization and diagnostic thinking. Here, I criticize mainstream approaches to both of these ways of knowing and naming the recipients of therapeutic services and propose how to utilize feminist therapy theory to strategize more complex and liberating ways of understanding the distress that clients bring into the therapy process.

Because feminist therapists must function in the milieu of patriarchal culture, I address some of the critical questions deriving from living and working in the "real world" and consider how to theorize feminist responses to the dilemmas that emerge from dealing with agencies, institutions, and legal requirements for therapy practice. Tying all the previous chapters together, I then address the question of ethics and boundaries in feminist therapy, proposing a conceptual framework that moves away from rigid rule-bound behaviors to a theoretically sound and politically derived stance on ethics in psychotherapy. The book concludes with a look at the future of feminist therapy and questions about where feminist therapy must go in its development of theory and practice if it is to survive, thrive, and continue the task of promoting social change, justice, and liberation into the next century.

Some Words of Thanks

This book owes its existence to many people who have been the nurturers of my work and thinking. While I have expressed my thanks to some in the acknowledgments section, I believe that naming my sources here is important to making my epistemology transparent. My thinking and writing would not exist without the vast complex relational matrix in which I work. To the women and men who have been my clients, I can never offer enough thanks. Each of them has taught me, and continues to teach me, about the central aspects of what it is that I do and reflects to me the power of a feminist analysis in therapy. There have been moments in my work with each of these people when the meaning of a feminist analysis has rung resonantly in the air between us, moving us both beyond the pain and hopelessness bequeathed by life in the patriarchal warzone.

Some of those moments will appear in somewhat changed form throughout this book; all the case examples have been modified to obscure the identities of those involved, and some represent amalgams of several peoples' experiences. All appear here with the knowledge, consent, and at times active participation and encouragement of my clients, who have also been amused to notice when I was especially absorbed with a particular topic in this book (leading to comments such as, "So this is what you're writing about *now?"* delivered with a knowing grin). I have not yet been able to challenge the norms for writing about the experience of psychotherapy sufficiently to take some of them up on their willingness to have their lives described, names and all, in this book, but they know who they are. Each one of them has moved me and shaped me into the therapist and theorist I am.

The field of feminist therapy and feminist psychology has also been a sort of family in which I have felt privileged, from almost my first month in graduate school, to be a loved and mentored sister and daughter (and apparently, to some, a mother of sorts; I am still struggling mightily to accept *that* vision of myself). The organizations that have nurtured me and offered platforms from which I could launch my ideas—the Association for Women in Psychology, the Division of Psychology of Women of the American Psychological Association, and the Feminist Therapy Institute—have all have been foundational to my ability to think and write about feminist therapy. These groups have created experiences in which I could know myself as a source of viable concepts that could then be worked into a theoretical model. Many of the ideas in this volume first saw light as papers presented at feminist psychology and feminist therapy conferences sponsored by these organizations or in books and journals that they published.

Several people who have had major influence on my thinking and on the writing of this book deserve mention here, although their names will be encountered throughout these pages. Hannah Lerman, a feminist therapist in private practice in Los Angeles, was my first intellectual mentor in feminist therapy, and she continues to be a source of profound stimulation for me; without Hannah's persistence and scholarship, feminist therapy as a field would still be in search of intellectual roots. Hannah was the first among us to be willing to risk defining the criteria for a feminist theory of personality. Her thinking has had profound impact on my work and on that of other feminist therapists who are exploring the difficult terrain of theory-building. Those criteria inform my theorizing today.

Lenore Walker, a peripatetic scholar and feminist expert witness on behalf of battered women, has encouraged me to have chutzpah and to expand into the realm of forensic psychology, where I have learned exceptionally important lessons about how different a feminist therapist is from a dominant culture evaluator and expert witness. In that role, I have had the chance to observe how theory must inform every aspect of the work of feminist therapists, no matter what settings we find ourselves practicing in. I have also had the chance to know how powerfully feminist theory transforms the outcome of psychological assessment. From this perspective I have learned to see the meaning of diagnosis in a new light and to find a fresh view of the word "expert." Without Lenore's work on battered women and her willingness to sit in courtrooms week in and out for many years, it is unlikely that this arena of feminist practice would have existed, much less been so clearly founded in feminist thought.

Carter Heyward, who is a lesbian feminist Episcopal priest and theologian, engaged me in thinking about the difficult and complex territory of relational mutuality in feminist therapy and got me to push my limits on this matter where my own conservativism lurked. Her unique blend of feminism and theology has led me into the murky and nourishing waters of the spirit as it manifests itself in our theory and practice. Maria Root, my colleague in feminist therapy practice in Seattle, and herself a brilliant theorist of multicultural feminist theory, has been a source of inspiration to me in thinking about the subtle meanings and manifestations of culture and trauma as a source of strength as well as distress. She also got me to take the time off from my practice to go to Hawaii, where I had the time, rest, and sufficient exposure to reef fish to get this book underway. She has been a "fellow traveler" in both the literal and figurative senses of the term; the tensions and connections created by our commonalities and differences have been extraordinarily fertile resources in my intellectual development. She has also read this book as it has emerged from the hard drive and been an invaluable source of feedback and mindfulness regarding the fact that not all patriarchies and not all feminisms flow from white people's experiences.

My many Feminist Therapy Institute colleagues in Seattle have provided peers with whom I could organize conferences, meet, talk, and be challenged to examine how my whiteness and class background acted to limit my vision. This consciousness raising on race and class has been completely necessary for me to generate this book. One of the saddest lacks in feminist therapy theory and practice in North America has been an inattention to the power and meaning of race, culture, and class, because of the spurious authority some of us derived from our white skin and/or middle- or upper-middle-class status. Being part of a group where I could safely make my errors and then learn to change them allows me to appear courageous and risk-taking. This group also helped to sustain me through a difficult period of illness and convinced me that even though I temporarily could not speak I still had something to say. To these women—Else Bolotin, Carla Bradshaw, Anne Ganley, Christine Ho, Ginny NiCarthy, Denise Pritzl, and Bobbie Stewart-Larson—go many thanks.

My dear friend, fellow faxophile, and Star Trek fan Ken Pope is that rare bird, the profeminist man, who has been another reader and editor of my work. To him go thanks for noticing the awkward turns of phrase, the assumptions of intuitive obviousness. Ken has urged me to be more radical in my verbiage, more active in my metaphors, and more willing to take risks with my thinking. By the vigor and enthusiasm of his response to feminist theories of therapy and his willingness to call oppression in therapy by name, he also reminds me why this book is written to be read by women and men alike.

In the middle of writing this book, I had the enormous good fortune to be a participant in the first Conference on Education and Training in Feminist Practice, sponsored by the Division of Psychology of Women of the American Psychological Association. My four days at that meeting were precisely the stimulus I needed to move on past places where the book was stuck and refresh my perspectives. I had the chance to say out loud some of the words that had been sitting in the C drive and discover that I made sense and resonated with the other women in the room. I particularly want to acknowledge the women with me who were members of the theory group and whose insights, confrontations, and good humor sharpened my thinking and energized me anew: Mary Brabeck, Louise Christian, Rachel Hare-Mustin, Oliva Espin, Dusty Miller, Elaine Phillips, Alexandra Kaplan, and Ellyn Kaschak.

More than anyone, my partner in life and work, Miriam Vogel, helped midwife this book, first by teaching me that I could write original ideas and then by reminding me that it was worth the risk to write this book because she believed that I had something worthwhile to say. When I first met her in 1979, I recall telling her that I did not write because I had nothing original to write about and was at best a good synthesizer of other people's ideas. She pushed me to prove myself wrong and propelled me into my career as a writer of feminist therapy theory. It is impossible to create theory when you believe that everything you know is both unoriginal and intuitively obvious to the rest of the world; Miriam informed me, persuasively and repeatedly, that this was not the case and that it was essential to unburden myself into the computer of whatever I was spouting out loud around the house. Her urgings have been a model to me of what is best in feminist therapy: our refusal to accept any self-deprecating utterance as a form of truth and our passionate commitment to giving voice to that which has been kept in silence. She has patiently listened to my freshly hatched notions, bemusedly smiled at my middle-of-the-night attacks of anxiety and inspiration, and tolerated my tearing her away from her own beloved computer when I was too impatient to wait another minute for feedback on what I had just written. To her also go my thanks for constantly reminding me by her stubborn Dutch presence that there is a world outside the boundaries of North America, and for moving me to a more international perspective on feminist therapy. To all these people I offer my thanks; what is of value in my work arises from and reflects the context of my relationships with them.

CHAPTER 1

Toward a Subversive
Dialogue with the Reader

FEMINIST THERAPY is the practice of a genuinely revolutionary act in which both lives and society are changed. It is a discourse that subverts patriarchy, which it identifies as a major source of damage in human lives. *Subversion* best describes a process in which the power of the patriarchy is turned upon itself, to revolution and healing, a revolution that, because it is subtle and not frontal, can be effective even in the face of formidable obstacles. Feminist therapy, as one aspect of the feminist revolution, functions to subvert patriarchal dominance at the most subtle and powerful levels, as it is internalized and personified in the lives of therapists and their clients, colleagues, and communities. Unlike other expressions of feminism, which address themselves to external and overt manifestations of patriarchal oppression, feminist therapy also concerns itself with the invisible and sometimes nonconscious ways in which patriarchy has become embedded in everyone's daily life—in our identities, our manners of emotional expression, and our experiences of personal power and powerlessness—to our profound detriment. Unlike other approaches to psychotherapy, feminist therapy concerns itself not simply with individual suffering but with the social and political meanings of both pain and healing. It has as its goals the creation of feminist consciousness and a movement toward feminist action. The first and most important "client" of feminist therapy is the culture in which it takes place; the first and foremost commitment of feminist therapists is to radical social transformation.

This book focuses on epistemology: on how a feminist therapist thinks about the work of therapy and on the varieties of questions evoked by specific ways of knowing, intuiting, feeling, and comprehending engendered by feminist analysis. It is an occasion to learn a way of being in the world that serves as the foundation of feminist therapy practice. This developing level of knowledge is an experience in which feminist therapists are constantly challenging themselves to understand how to become free of the dominant structures of patriarchal discourse informing the cultures, educations, and mainstream professional communities in which many were trained and in which most still practice. This epistemology leads toward new language, new sources of wisdom, and new meanings. While mine will be the most obvious voice in our exchange, this book can become a dialogue in which readers respond with excitement, anger, disagreement, resonance, and action to my ideas. I want to subvert, to undermine, their beliefs in a patriarchal hierarchy of value, to bring out those previously unnoticed beliefs and hold them up for scrutiny, and to foster an understanding of how feminist vision illuminates the practice of psychotherapy. I invite my readers to "do theory" with me, with themselves, and with the people with whom they work.

Confronting Patriarchy

Feminist therapy is practiced—and the lives of feminist therapists and their clients are lived—in the context of the individualistic patriarchal cultures in Western societies today, in which male gender and activities associated with masculinity are privileged. Patriarchy is a system in which the value of women and women's voices is obscured and diminished (Lerner, 1993); gender-based inequalities and the devaluation of women are the norm. Depending upon the specific culture, this imbalance may be expressed in both subtle and obvious ways. Sometimes patriarchy is manifested as the purposeful exclusion of women from valued activities or occupations. Sometimes it emerges in "little" things: the higher cost of women's clothes, the pressure on men to dissociate eros from emotion, the association of humanness with maleness in generic masculine language, as in *mankind*. Sometimes patriarchy takes the form of violence and the threat of violence targeted at girls, women, and often gay men. Even in cultures outside the West, in which patriarchy takes a more collectivist form, the devaluation of women and all associated with women emerges, although in forms that may be unfamiliar to Western observers who mistake collectivist cultures for nonpatriarchal ones. In whatever shape it takes, patri-

archy leaves its psychological marks in the form of distortions and limitations to everyone's capacity for well-being and personal power. Although
the dangers to women appear more obvious, it has meaningful and
painful costs to men as well, for when gender is a locus of oppression,
almost every human difference is viewed as a form of "less than"-ness.
Patriarchal modes pervade all intellectual and philosophical systems to
the point where such notions appear to be "the truth" when not closely
examined.

Feminism is the collection of political philosophies that aims to overthrow patriarchy and end inequities based on gender through cultural
transformation and radical social change. Feminism defines gender-based
inequities as a problem and understands women as a valid class or group,
with experiences held in common because of their shared sex. Feminist
therapy approaches the task of ending inequities by addressing patriarchal
oppression as it is manifested as distress in people's lives. It attends as
well to prescribed "normal" patterns of being with which people may be
comfortable but which are ultimately destructive to their integrity.

This liberation from the patriarchy around and inside of us constitutes
both a necessity and a dilemma of feminist therapy practice for which theory provides possible answers and directions. It is difficult, if not impossible, for people to imagine what they might be without the oppressive
experience of living under patriarchy, as both the inheritors of those who
have suffered there and as participants to one degree or another in patriarchal realities and rituals. Even when feminist therapists come together to
think out loud, they find themselves struggling to avoid defining themselves within or against the models of reality emerging from the dominant
culture.

Sandra Webster, a graduate school friend and feminist social psychologist, has pointed out to me the usefulness of science fiction as a source of
theory in feminist psychology, because it allows women to be seen as they
might be outside of today's apparently fixed and immutable realities. Her
comments remind me why I love feminist science fiction and find lessons
in it almost more frequently than in any other type of material I read. In
speculating about life as it might be lived in the framework of various
drastically different social arrangements, this literature provides help in
formulating the questions of feminist therapy. A vision in which anything
is possible—new worlds, new genders, new technologies, new life forms
who have never lived in patriarchy, much less had to overthrow or transcend it—allows me to attempt to imagine myself and my work as they
might be if I were not always looking over my shoulder and into my heart
for the ghosts of patriarchal mindsets. The ways of thinking about therapy

explored in this book reflect my attempts to get myself and my work into those alternate universes that are best described by such authors as Marge Piercy, Ursula LeGuin, and Joanna Russ—places in this and other worlds where gender as a category for organizing experience carries a meaning very different from its meaning in late-twentieth-century North America.

In developing a theoretical base for feminist therapy, I and others who have approached this task are challenged by the difficulty of doing so without referring to or reacting against dominant theoretical perspectives, the work of white men. So much of what we take for granted in the world of the intellect is based on constructs inextricably bound up in patriarchy that it can make one's head hurt to try to do without those assumptions. Terms that I will use in this book, such as *self, consciousness,* and even— and most importantly—*psychotherapy*, reflect decades, and sometimes centuries, of masculinist thought. I plan, here and throughout this book, to work toward an image of psychotherapy practice in which feminist assumptions about reality become its core, its assumed wisdom—the second nature of human experience—and patriarchal values begin to stand out as the erroneous or dangerous stuff that they are. But I will probably be inconsistent in this effort, and when I stumble, I hope that my missteps will serve to illustrate how deeply embedded such patriarchal "realities" are in our epistemologies.

There are certain processes in a therapy relationship that make it feminist, an expression of a politics of gender and power. These processes may superficially resemble nonfeminist modes of operating, but in fundamental ways they diverge markedly from the processes of other psychotherapies. The development of theory clarifies these core differences that make therapy *feminist.* Although many of the interpersonal dynamics seen, heard, and felt at work by feminist therapists are also observed by mainstream practitioners, a theory of feminist therapy provides a perspective for seeing and hearing these dynamics, and in turn naming what is observed, that is quite different from that of therapists who take the dominant culture as a norm. These feminist realities are subversive, "disloyal to civilization" in the words of the poet Adrienne Rich; in them lies the lengthy answer to "Ma nishtanah," how is this therapy different from all other forms of therapy?

This theory of therapy as a subversive act requires a clear definition of what is meant by feminist therapy. Until recently, many writers and practitioners in the field assumed that feminist therapy meant simply women therapists treating women for a variety of "women's issues" such as incest, eating disorders, difficulties with assertion, and the like (see Brody [1984] for an example of this trend). A practitioner was a feminist therapist because she called herself one, whatever degree of feminist thought and analysis had actually gone into her work. Some feminists in psychology have debated whether there exists a litmus test for feminist therapy (Caplan, 1992; Perkins, 1991b), and a certain liberal tendency among feminist therapists, left over from strenuous training not to be judgmental, has impeded collective willingness to define its boundaries more precisely. But such tighter definition is necessary for explicating theory and is occurring as theory is made clearer. As the British lesbian feminist clinical psychologist Rachel Perkins (1991a) has noted, "women's issues" therapy without feminist theory may in fact be counterfeminist.

Why is it important to define feminist practice? It is because in such instances as Perkins relates, the goal of "women's therapy with women" often becomes the adjustment of the client to dominant patriarchal norms. In the absence of a critical feminist analysis of both process and content, the private and unique pain of the client will not likely be tied by the therapist's analysis or interventions to the public and political realities that the pain expresses. The woman therapist teaching her woman incest survivor client that it is necessary to forgive the offender, not honoring some women's need not to forgive until amends have been proffered or until society as a whole rises up in protest against this form of everyday violence, is not doing feminist therapy. She is helping to protect patriarchy as surely as any of the male therapists critiqued by Phyllis Chesler two decades ago (Chesler, 1972). She may be even more dangerous than they, because she is masquerading as a "women's issues specialist."

In addition, feminist therapy is not simply about women. The paradigms for understanding human experience proposed here are just as useful at many other points in the social and political matrix at which oppression occurs; race, class, culture, sexual orientation, age, size, and disability, among others, are common variables in which patriarchal dichotomies of value operate to diminish quality of life and well-being. Moreover, the experiences of the dominant, the oppressor, are as transparent to—and in need of—feminist analysis in therapy as are those of the oppressed. While it may be more difficult to see the costs of patriarchal privilege, the losses attendant upon the struggle to stay on top are real and sometimes life-threatening (Stoltenberg, 1990).

What Is *Feminist* Therapy?

Because of this potentially dangerous confusion, I begin this explication of theory by attempting a comprehensive definition. *Feminist therapy is the practice of therapy informed by feminist political philosophy and analysis, grounded in multicultural feminist scholarship on the psychology of women and gender, which leads both therapist and client toward strategies and solutions advancing feminist resistance, transformation, and social change in daily personal life, and in relationships with the social, emotional, and political environment.* What makes practice feminist is not who the clients are but how the therapist *thinks* about what she does, her epistemologies and underlying theoretical models rather than her specific techniques, the kinds of problems she addresses, or the demographic makeup of the client population. Feminist therapy requires a continuous and conscious awareness by the therapist that the apparently private transaction between therapist and client occurs within a social and political framework that can inform, transform, or distort the meanings given to individual experience in ways that must be uncovered in the process of the feminist therapeutic relationship.

This definition of feminist practice is as true when the client is a child with a chronic illness (not the stereotypical image of the client of a feminist therapist) as when the client is an adult struggling with a minority sexual orientation (very much the stereotypical image of the client). It holds fast when the practice is not therapy per se but rather supervision, expert legal testimony, training, research, or writing about therapy. Feminist therapy aims to deprivatize the lives of the both therapists and people with whom they work by asking, out loud and repeatedly, how each life and each pain are manifestations of processes operating in a larger social context. At the same time, feminist therapy requires that each life experience be treated as valuable, unique, and authoritative, an expert source of knowledge regarding both the individual and the culture as a whole. Because it gives weight to individual standpoints while still attending to the meanings that emerge from larger social contexts, feminist therapy theoretically straddles the gap between subjective (postmodernist) and objective (positivist) views of human behavior and change, owing allegiance to neither.

This definition helps us move toward delineation of the essential components of the practice of feminist therapy and begins the task of describing in detail those phenomena that differentiate feminist therapy from other theoretical orientations. These basic characteristics of feminist therapy theory address the contradictions inherent in framing such a highly individualized act as therapy in the political perspectives of feminism. As I have identified them in my reviews of feminist practice over the past two decades, these components of a feminist therapy theory are:

1. an understanding of the relationship of feminist political philosophies to therapeutic notions of change;
2. an analysis and critique of the patriarchal notions of gender, power, and authority in mainstream approaches to psychotherapy;
3. a feminist vision of the nature and meaning of psychotherapy as a phenomenon in the larger social context;
4. concepts of normal growth and development, distress, diagnosis, boundaries and relationships in therapy that are grounded in feminist political analysis and feminist scholarship;
5. an ethics of practice tied to feminist politics of social change and inter-personal relatedness;
6. a multicultural and conceptually diverse base of scholarship and knowledge informing this theorizing.

Hannah Lerman (1986) has described eight "meta-assumptions" under-lying feminist therapy theory-building as criteria for a feminist theory of personality. They are (1) clinical usefulness, (2) encompassing the diversity and complexity of women and their lives, (3) viewing women positively and centrally, (4) arising from women's experience, (5) remaining close to the data of experience, (6) recognizing that the internal world is inextricably intertwined with the external world, (7) not confining concepts by particularistic terminology or in terms of other theories, and (8) supporting feminist modes of psychotherapy. While Lerman's criteria re-center theorizing on women, they do not define feminist therapy theory as about women alone. Rather, Lerman's criteria suggest a standpoint, a lens through which the world can be viewed, and in which the seer and knower are not members of the dominant group. These criteria are embed-ded in the essential components of feminist therapy theory. They are not assumptions whose primary characteristic is internal consistency, a qual-ity by which psychotherapy theories have often been evaluated. Instead, a theory of feminist therapy recognizes that there are gaps in the under-standing of human behavior and behavior change, gaps that derive from patriarchal, apolitical models currently available, and applies a different set of tests to define its parameters.

The chapters that follow review the various approaches to political fem-inism that have informed feminist therapy practice, present a theory of relationship development in therapy that arises uniquely from the applica-tion of feminist analysis, and describe a model of diagnostic thinking as an essential aspect of feminist therapy practice, radically different from stan-dard approaches to diagnosis. I will demonstrate that feminist therapy requires a multicultural base, theoretically and in practice, and will explore the applications of knowledge from the margins to comprehension of the mainstream. I then show how comprehension of the interplay between the external social context and internal phenomenological experience is an essential, defining component of feminist theories of normal and abnormal development. A discussion of feminist images of the nature of good and evil, of beneficence and oppression, redefines the meaning and nature of ethics in psychotherapy. The relationship of the feminist therapist to the real world of mainstream psychotherapy business and the challenges of maintaining integrity in the face of patriarchal seductions are also discussed. This book leads to more questions than answers if I succeed in empowering readers with knowledge that gives them a better understanding of and trust in their own epistemologies.

These components of feminist theory help to elucidate the many ways in which I believe it is possible to behave subversively while simultaneously offering clients strategies for personal change that respect their uniqueness and diversity. Feminist therapy can be subversive and have political meaning, as therapy commonly does not, largely because of that mixture of revolution and respect; the client need never identify with feminism in order to ask feminist questions or to arrive at solutions that advance feminist goals. The white middle-class homemaker who comes to see me because she is persistently unhappy may not recognize that there is something feminist about the way she is increasingly questioning the assumed norms of her life or about her newfound interest in what other women have to say as she learns to take an interest in her own words. But this deconstruction of the dominant discourse and bonding in solidarity with other women are both profoundly feminist endeavors.

Subversion is a mode of resistance that may be invisible to that which is resisted; as I have described, much of what happens in feminist therapy is not immediately identifiable as a revolutionary act to the casual observer. Feminist therapy is a speaking of truth to power in a voice rarely listened to by patriarchy. The following discussion offers a look at some of the important values and characteristics underlying feminist philosophies of therapy and change and sets the stage for understanding the role of therapy in a feminist reality and for evaluating the contributions of feminist politics to feminist therapy theory.

Resistance and Subversion

Central to a feminist theory of psychotherapy is the idea that the models of personal change must promote resistance. This resistance is *not* the traditional "resistance" of psychodynamic theory, the conscious and unconscious attempts by the patient to avoid the truth and evade change. In feminist theory, resistance means the refusal to merge with dominant cultural norms and to attend to one's own voice and integrity (Gilligan, Rogers, & Tolman, 1992). A feminist theory of psychotherapy, rooted in the call for radical social change, seeks to bring a better understanding of such personal resistance, and of how to identify and strengthen it, reframing it as a positive and healthy act within the feminist political context. Feminist theory postulates that because every aspect of life in Western culture is imbued with the patriarchal notions and values of those at the top of the hierarchy, not only our definitions of the self but our very sense of self have been domesticated and corrupted to patriarchal realities, even in those whose particular culture is not that of the dominant group. Women and men of color struggle to see their beauty in the face of white racist aesthetics of attractiveness; white men are constantly required to reaffirm their masculinity by denying tenderness, vulnerability, and love for one another. "Self" is seen as worthy only if it matches the criteria proposed by dominant authorities as a separated, individuated phenomenon. The referential and relational selves of cultures of color are consequently defined as lesser, or ignored and unrecognized by dominant institutions and psychologies. Shame, the experience of self as something to be hidden, something bad, flawed, and undeserving, is a pervasive result of this constant corruption and domestication. We have been encouraged not to know ourselves, not to speak the truth, but rather to engage in lies of silence and disclaim that deception. Each of us, woman and man, white and of color, lesbian, gay, bisexual and heterosexual, has been taught to participate in patriarchy. While we all resist to some degree, knowingly or inadvertently, even our resistance may not be free from the strictures of thought and deed which permeate our very existence.

Each act of feminist therapy, each relationship between feminist therapist and client, must have as an implicit goal the uncovering of the presence of the patriarchy as a source of distress so that this influence of the dominant can be named, undermined, resisted, and subverted. In feminist therapy, awareness and transformation mean teaching of resistance, learning the ways in which each of us is damaged by our witting or unwitting participation in dominant norms or by the ways in which such norms have been thrust upon us.

Such a learning process allows the participants in therapy to understand how the solutions and strategies that seem intuitively obvious because they are made available under patriarchy may instead be further lessons in powerlessness. Knowing that patriarchal wisdom on how to live life is quite the emperor without clothes can be a valuable component of the development of successful resistance strategies. Feminist therapy conceptualizes the capacity to resist as a form of truth-telling about what actually happened and truth-telling about what is possible and available to each person as avenues for change. Rooting awareness and change in political realities strikes a blow at shame and self-blame. Feminist therapy illuminates how much the restrictions of patriarchal rules limit our visions of possible realities and ways of being for ourselves and our societies.

People commonly enter therapy experiencing themselves as "failures"; when we explore this label, my clients and I often discover that it means they have not achieved the sort of power, status, and control over their distress that they should have "if only I tried hard enough." Feminist analysis can strip bare the assumptions informing this and similar perceptions. It replaces the illusions of equality and power embedded in patriarchal discourse with clear and more honest visions of the self in a social context where power is unevenly distributed and value is parceled out according to arbitrary characteristics rather than effort or talent. Feminist therapy involves the process of finding, in the face of such realities, the ability to engage in "individual or collective acts of courage, strength, and integrity in response to violence, threat of harm, wrongdoing, or untruth" (Fredlund, 1992, p. 7), as well as the ability to know when one is participating in such an act, so that we can give ourselves credit for our courage.

How Patriarchy Can Undermine Resistance: An Example

To understand how complex it may be to achieve these goals, it is helpful to stop and explore some common assumptions about useful ways to resist patriarchy and the complex outcomes of choosing these paths. Since our images of resistance are themselves often contaminated by spurious notions of heroism promulgated by dominant cultures, the feminist therapist beginning to think about resistance must look carefully at the basis for her assumptions and reeducate herself about how to identify resistant acts. One approach is to review some models of resistance that come easily to mind. For example, the notion of justice and how to get it in our lives reveals something of the manner in which the apparent avenues for resistance can be contaminated by patriarchal realities.

Justice is a very important notion in U.S. cultures; those of us raised here grew up reciting "with liberty and justice for all" every day as an expression of our beliefs and expectations about life in our country. Obtaining justice in the face of oppression is a common image of heroic resistance that goes back to the official story of the American revolution. Yet justice is an ill-defined concept, and hidden beneath the clichés are real limits for those not in power. As a forensic psychologist, practicing in legal settings by offering expert testimony, I frequently meet plaintiffs or victims and witnesses in cases involving sexual or physical violation or discrimination. For many of these people, the motivation for their foray into the legal system is their desire to have justice done. They are attempting to engage in a socially sanctioned act of resistance, refusing to "lie down and be a victim." Their resistance would appear to resonate more than superficially with feminist notions of personal healing as social change.

Their visions of justice take many forms: financial reparations, a jury verdict confirming that wrong was done, an order requiring someone to apologize or make amends. Yet almost invariably these people who are attempting to resist their personal experience of oppression, to make it public and to call someone to account, describe to me their feelings that there has been no justice done, no matter what the outcome of the case.

This sense that the pursuit of justice engenders injustice emerges for many of these resisters because the process by which a person pursues justice within the formal legal system is often profoundly revictimizing. The victim is commonly put on trial during the proceedings in place of the alleged offender, exposed to the scorn of the opposing attorney and expert witnesses. The question in the case is transformed from the statement of charges brought by the victim to the victim's credibility. Nothing in the system as it exists allows for the assumption that the targets of oppression may be telling the truth; laws of due process, which appear fair on the surface, do not take into account the profound underlying disbelief encountered by the victims of interpersonal violation. The questions resound: Why did she stay? Why didn't he fight back? Was this a reasonable response or a hysterical overreaction? Why did you leave the bar with him in the first place? Such disbelief is rarely aimed at the victim of a property crime (the prototypical victim whose experience informs the assumptions of the criminal justice system). It emerges primarily when a person of lesser power is accusing one of greater power of engaging in acts that are marginally tolerated in patriarchy because they help to maintain the status quo of power arrangements, acts such as racial and sexual discrimination, sexual harassment, and some forms of sexual and physical violence.

The scales of justice are balanced against the tellers of these tales that expose the underlying root of patriarchal dominance and violation; those who speak such truths must experience further assaults on their perceptions of reality and experiences of distress. No mandated reparations appear capable of truly healing the fabric of lives torn apart by violence and violation when the path toward a verdict is strewn with these land mines of disrespect. Winning a lawsuit against one's incest offender does not make one whole again, no matter how much money is taken home—especially when the settlement comes wrapped in a gag order forbidding one to ever tell what really happened.

The realities of what happens to people whose resistance is framed in this stereotypically heroic manner are instructive. They reveal certain underlying truths; for anyone except the white male property owners on whose behalf English-speaking jurisprudence was developed (Robson, 1992), moral justice, a true calling-to-account on moral terms, is nearly impossible within the patriarchal legal system (although this is not to say that the ruling class necessarily gets justice either). The jurisprudential system does not take the lives and realities of most human beings into account in its formulations; the feminist legal scholar Ruthann Robson (1992), who describes what happens to women in the criminal justice system when they attempt to defend their lives against battering, points out that many people are technically or legally nonexistent in that system (for example, women, African-Americans, aboriginal peoples, lesbians, and gay men), or have been so at some moment in time. (For a detailed description of how women's right to self-defense has been distorted by the exclusion of women's experiences from self-defense laws, see Walker [1990].) The heroes of revolutionary America, from whom the heritage of "getting justice" and the discourse on personal rights evolved, were, carefully deconstructed, simply one set of white male property owners outraged that anyone would make decisions about their holdings without consulting them first.

Victims of violence are often revictimized in this system for not being a "perfect victim." I was the expert witness in a case in which a number of women had been raped in their homes by a man in a work release program. They were suing the state for failing to return him to custody when he violated his parole by not remaining drug-free. But one of these women was a lesbian and another was a devotee of an Eastern mystical tradition that seems odd to many in the mainstream. Rather than addressing the real damages to soul and self suffered by these women when they were raped, the state and its mental health expert developed a discourse about these women implying that they could not possibly be as damaged as a "good" victim would have been, because they were already deviant from dominant culture. The wounds that these particular women suffered in their legal battles were in some ways longer-lasting than those deriving from the rape itself. They were re-raped by the system from which they sought justice when they learned that they were less eligible for protection because of the dimensions of their lives.

This illustration, and my attempt at understanding the limits to resistance inherent in patriarchal heroic modes, is not aimed at devaluing the efforts of those taking such paths, since in feminist theory any and every form of resistance is of value (and none of this is meant to be interpreted by attorneys on the other side of cases to mean that I think there is no merit in participating in the legal process, since the presence of these plaintiffs and the work of feminist forensic psychologists is helping to make the system more truly just). Such analysis functions, instead, to remove naive and cherished illusions from our theorizing, to illustrate how every act of courage and change under patriarchy is in some manner affected and given unwished-for meanings by that social context. Failure to take this process into account can lead to victim-blaming, of the sort that feminist therapists encounter in themselves and their clients in self-accusations of insufficient effort or courage. Feminist visions of psychotherapy must thus be capable of seeing beyond the options presented by dominant culture and able to identify and support paths of resistance and subversion that are not authorized, valued, or easily visible in patriarchy (Noble, 1994).

Therapy as a Disruptive Force

This theory of therapy as a school for struggle against oppression differs radically from the tasks of psychotherapy commonly proposed in dominant culture. The purpose of psychotherapy, in this view, is not to soothe, but to disrupt; not to adjust, but to empower. Rachel Perkins (1991b), a critic of the culture of psychotherapy, is especially troubled by those therapeutic approaches that assume emotional distress to be prima facie evidence of pathology; she notes how such a viewpoint will inevitably lead to the use of the therapist's power and expertise to undermine some forms of political anger and outrage that may be necessary for feminist analysis and social change. For therapy to be feminist, it cannot smoothe over experience, and it will often lead to an enhanced awareness of painful social realities, a defogging, as it were, of the lenses by which therapists and their clients come to view their shared existence.

Sometimes feminist therapy, when it is working well and truly subverting some of the soothing forms of patriarchy in the lives of more privileged clients, will temporarily induce distress where formerly there was comfort and acceptance. Feminist therapy with a white heterosexual man who comes for treatment of his problems with intimacy will probably leave him more unhappy about pervasive male violence against women than he was before treatment, because his "problem" will have been understood as occurring within, and affected by, that social and political context. He will know that every woman to whom he relates will have been made at least somewhat more distant from him by this social phenomenon, and he will no longer be able to be complacent about its existence. Understanding himself will lead to understanding and relinquishing male privilege. To proceed with this description of feminist therapy, it is necessary to question whether therapy is something that can be of value to feminism, or can even exist within a feminist discourse of meaning. I believe that feminist therapy is a possibility, not, as some would argue, an oxymoron. To develop a clear model of psychotherapy as political action, therapists must explore and respond to important criticisms of therapy put forward by feminist thinkers. In feminist therapy theory, clients leave treatment with *more* awareness and distress about certain destructive social realities than they may have had when they first arrived, and those forms of distress are construed as a good outcome of the therapeutic relationship.

Feminist therapy requires a theory that defines therapy as not simply a healing art, although healing is likely to take place. Therapy must also be a conscious and intentional act of radical social change, directed at those social arrangements in which oppressive imbalances of power hold sway. Such social change is not simply about electing more women to office or getting more men to do day care. It involves questioning fundamental values and assumptions about gender-based phenomena across the power spectrum. In this framework, therapy with a troubled heterosexual couple cannot simply be training in communications or working out contracts about his doing more housework in exchange for her having more sexual intercourse (a common example deriving from mainstream marital therapy teachings). Instead, to be feminist, therapy with such a pair must also address the distribution of power in the relationship, exploring how the culture at large has devalued the voices of women and overvalued those of men, asking how that meta-phenomenon affects the communication of this one woman and one man. Feminist therapy explores the relative values placed on housework and sexual intercourse in the social construction of a healthy intimate pair bond. It treats the couple as not simply two adults with dysfunctions but as participants in larger social forces that express themselves in their marital conflict.

Can Therapy and Feminism Co-exist?

Integrating political perspective with a client's individually lived experience can be a tricky business, and it is the invisible obstacle on which our desires to theorize feminist therapy are most likely to stumble in attempts to be feminist, as opposed to being simply a female version of the therapeutic status quo. To proceed with a description of feminist therapy, it is necessary to address questions of whether therapy is something that can be of value to feminism, or can even exist within a feminist discourse of meaning. As I begin this book, I believe that feminist therapy is a possibility, not an oxymoron. But the process of theory development must explore and take into account those points of view that would suggest that feminism and psychotherapy are mutually exclusive. Without a theory to define feminist therapy, the arguments against psychotherapy may have greater merit. Any theory enunciated must anticipate these arguments and contain adequate responses to the important and troubling questions regarding the politics of psychotherapy.

Because therapy as practiced in the dominant culture is a tool of patriarchy, used to maintain the status quo and further stigmatize those who would deviate from or question its rightness, any exploration of the value of therapy in a feminist reality must include an unblinking look at the risks of therapy itself and a consideration of whether any feminist analysis can remove such pitfalls. Doing so thus defines one of the important parameters of feminist therapy: the willingness to question the worth of therapy itself and to continue to identify its risks as well as its presumed benefits.

In fact, the linking of a social movement with an approach to psychotherapy is not a very common phenomenon, and the unusual prominence of therapy within feminism should give us pause to question and reflect. While Wilhelm Reich in his earlier years attempted to draw connections between the social and economic oppression of the working class and their psychological difficulties, for the most part there have not been immediate and assumed links between progressive movements for social change and schools of psychotherapy. In the past, one paid homage to Marx or Freud, but rarely to both.

But no sooner did second-wave North American feminism appear on the scene than feminist therapy began to emerge as well, often dominating the feminist landscape. For many of the white, middle-class women at the forefront of second-wave feminism, the places where oppression of women was most clearly located were internal and psychological, couched in terms like "low self-esteem" or "fear of success." We feminists in the mental health professions moved very quickly from critiquing our own disciplines to channeling therapy into apparently feminist forms or transforming feminist projects into therapeutic exchanges. Many feminist action projects that began as political actions against oppression, such as shelters for battered women and rape crisis hot lines, have been changed in a few short years into new employment settings for therapists and have often lost their feminist identification and politics in the process (Schechter, 1982). Consciousness-raising groups, quickly reframed as a form of therapy (Brodsky, 1973) and reclaimed by the professionals, have for the most part disappeared; by contrast, women's support and therapy groups, in which woman-blaming ideologies masquerading as self-help are common (Brown, 1990e), have multiplied. Consciousness raising led from anger to action; women's therapy groups, while of value in a particular way, are a refocusing inward. Feminism appears to have been good for therapy, creating both more business and more practitioners, while no one could make similar statements about feminism improving the health of other patriarchal structures such as marriage or academia. It is unclear as yet whether therapy is good for feminism.

This turn of events troubles many feminists, including feminist psychologists and therapists. It is troubling to me. It is a source of serious challenges to the feminist nature of what has been called feminist therapy. While a feminist therapist may bravely describe herself, as I have above, as engaged in acts of resistance and revolution, it is entirely possible that all we are witnessing is a feat of verbal legerdemain in which heroic-sounding justifications are advanced by a (usually) white and middle-class woman about the manner in which she makes her living.

The Risks of Repathologizing the Political

One of the serious risks inherent in therapy considered from a feminist perspective is the tendency toward transformation of political realities into psychotherapeutic constructs. As Rachel Perkins has noted, "Oppression becomes psychologized as a pathological entity" (1991a, p. 326) as the discourse is changed from one of external social context to one of internal structures and distress.

Why is this transformation of meaning from political to psychological of concern to the understanding of therapy within feminism? After all, is not the concern of psychotherapy the realm of internal experiences? A theory of feminist therapy defines the universe of therapeutic concerns as embracing both the inner and the outer worlds; in fact, it questions the divisions of private and public. One of the lessons of feminism and other work against oppression, such as anti-racism, is that naming is a profoundly powerful act; to name an experience or phenomenon as psychological and internal as differentiated from political and social can transform one's relationship to reality in a manner subversive to feminism rather than to patriarchy. Rachel Perkins (1991a, Kitzinger & Perkins, 1993) and others (Cardea, 1985; Dyer, 1992) have argued that such a change is dangerous to the goals of feminism because the client in therapy is being persuaded to "understand her experience in personal, private, psychological terms." Perkins goes on to state, "Whilst politics debates and considers issues of morality, right and wrong, social change, therapy nudges, interprets, seeks 'true' meaning in terms of its own framework, seeks individual change and aims to enhance adjustment to a . . . patriarchal world" (1991a, p. 329). In other words, therapy can easily take the political and make it highly private and personal; a political stance of anger about discrimination can quickly be transformed by a therapist into a "dysfunctional cognition" or a sign of "issues with parents."

These charges regarding the antipolitical nature of therapy practiced atheoretically are often accurate and not infrequently describe the sort of "women's issues specialist" approach to therapy described earlier. It is possible to utilize feminist-informed scholarship on the psychology of women and gender in such a manner as to undermine any feminist enterprise whatsoever. One can take knowledge about what happens in many women's lives as a rationale for learning to make peace with such "realities" and abandoning visions of feminist social and political change.

For example, one self-help book for women on dealing with verbal abuse by partners takes the feminist approach of truth-telling and consciousness-raising about the pervasive and damaging nature of this sort of violence against women, citing data gleaned from feminist scholarship and activism. The author then explicitly warns the reader (presumably a woman) against making political interpretations of what she is experiencing or joining movements that seek political solutions to the problem of this and other forms of violence because doing so will distract her from her healing process, a highly internal and individual event.

In another example, Andrea, a woman I assessed in the course of her sexual harassment complaint, told me that the "women's issues specialist" to whom her physician had referred her for therapy had advised her that because research found sexual harassment of working women to be so common, she should learn better ways to tolerate it and stop "over-reacting"; she should consider that she had a very good job for a woman and would have a hard time finding as good a job if she were to move ahead with her complaint. Andrea, who was angry and outraged at what had happened to her at work, had the presence of mind and sufficient trust in herself to withdraw from this therapy, but she came to me for her forensic evaluation less certain of herself and her decision to resist than she had been before meeting this "expert" in women's issues.

Paula Caplan (1992) suggests that some therapists may even call themselves and their work "feminist" not because they are informed by feminist political analysis or scholarship but because doing so will make them more attractive to potential consumers of psychotherapy services. While some inaccurate representation may be ascribed to a confusion of meanings regarding what constitutes feminism (see chapter 2 for a detailed discussion), some of the problem may also indicate a failure of feminist therapy to define its own boundaries adequately, leading to the sort of misuses of therapy, under a false feminist flag, that Perkins (1991a) has described.

Psychotherapy: What Can Be Saved?

In the process of attempting to define the boundaries of their discipline, feminist therapists have tried to understand what, if any, structures and ways of relating could be salvaged from the mainstream practice of psychotherapy. For example, could feminist therapists maintain the traditional role structures of client and therapist, or should they be attempting to develop a more peer-oriented approach to solving problems in which both parties shared to some degree their pains and solutions (Wyckoff, 1977)? How is the work of therapy to be conceptualized: Is it treatment? education? healing? What other structures and assumptions does each term imply, and how do the realities emerging from each fit within a feminist vision of social change and political action?

One strategy for dealing with this dilemma has found various feminist therapists experimenting with getting rid of or modifying those aspects of therapy practice that seemed to be the most potentially oppressive or the least rooted in women's experiences and replacing them, when necessary, with structures that seemed more likely to produce an outcome compatible with feminist political principles. Lacking a theory to define the parameters of feminist therapy, each feminist therapist has identified different danger zones in the psychotherapeutic status quo, resulting in a variety of descriptions, often conflicting, of what constitutes feminist practice. Some of these attempts at transformation have been spectacularly successful, to the degree that they now represent good mainstream therapy practice. When feminist therapy strategies are severed from their original feminist context as they enter the mainstream, however, the potential exists for their being co-opted for patriarchal purposes.

The "therapy contract" is an excellent example of a feminist strategy that has been embraced by mainstream practitioners. What became of this idea illustrates the risks that the feminist goals of a strategy will be lost in the absence of an underlying theory for the strategy. A therapy contract is an elaboration of informed consent, initially proposed by feminist therapists in the 1970s as a radical step toward empowerment of the client as a consumer of psychotherapy services. Such contracts, which typically spelled out the proposed therapeutic approach and the mutual expectations of client and therapist, were perceived by nonfeminist practitioners as detracting from the mystery or neutrality of the therapeutic experience (Hare-Mustin, Maracek, Kaplan, & Liss-Levinson, 1979). But to feminist therapists, these contracts were an expression of a feminist politic of greater equality for clients, confirming the client's power to determine goals and outcomes and right to know about the therapist's assumptions and techniques.

By the early 1990s, informed consent to treatment had become the mainstream norm, taught to students in graduate training programs and occasionally required by law of mental health professionals. But the goal of informed consent and the therapy contract has been transformed in the mainstream from the empowerment of the client to the protection of the practitioner from lawsuits; therapy contracts are now considered good "risk management" strategies by malpractice attorneys. The importance of empowering the client as an informed consumer of therapy has withered in the transplantation of the strategy from its feminist seedbed to patriarchal soil. As we will examine at greater length in a later chapter, even the notion of "informed consent" carries patriarchal assumptions that require feminist disruptions to make it fit within the work of feminist therapy.

Other feminist attempts to purge patriarchy from psychotherapy have often been equivocal, reflecting the difficulties inherent in the attempt to bend feminist constructions to the frameworks of patriarchal theories on which everything resembling psychotherapy is built. The short history of feminist therapy has seen a number of piecemeal attempts to modify surface structures without adequate attention to the underlying theoretical assumptions. The imbalances of power in therapy have proved to be especially thorny problems that have not been responsive to partial attempts at a cure, and because an analysis of power dynamics is so central to feminist theory, the solution to the puzzle of power relationships in therapy is a central theoretical challenge for feminist therapy. Many feminist therapists have attacked what appeared to be the overt manifestations of power imbalances in therapy, such as getting paid for therapy, not forming friendships with clients, and so on, without going more deeply and questioning whether these surface phenomena were simply the masks behind which the power problem really existed. At times, particularly early in feminist therapy practice, we feminist therapists acted as if we were equal to our clients simply because we were all women—a "consciousness-raising group of two," to use the words of one early article on feminist therapy (Kravetz, 1978); this attempt to reframe consciousness raising as therapy failed to address the more profound power dynamics in the relationship and the expectations evoked when it is called therapy. These problems of power, which will be addressed at greater length in succeeding chapters, exemplify the difficulties inherent in an attempt to merge two quite different epistemologies. One, political feminism, sees individual lives within a social context of political meaning and is concerned with the rearrangement of social and political power. The other, psychotherapy, has traditionally been apolitical, seeing the transformation of individual lives as an end unto itself and being little concerned with social arrangements. This is, of course, itself a political stance, but one representing a politics of upholding the status quo.

When I review these attempts to reinvent psychotherapy as feminist in my explorations of theory, I find myself continuing to wonder whether a feminist psychotherapy is possible, or whether all efforts at both the theoretical and the practical levels are unavoidably impeded by the patriarchal notions that have been the foundation of psychotherapy in Western society. The subtext of the psychotherapy process as invented by the forefathers is a powerful one. Rereading Freud, for instance, one is struck by the tone of superiority implicit in his work; although he was listening to his patients (and it was and still is rather revolutionary for a man to be listening, seriously, to all these women), he alone could tell them what their dreams and symptoms meant. It is impossible for the feminist observer not to notice the preponderance of women among the patients on whom his analytic theory was based; yet gender as a *social* category is minimized in his work, which emphasizes gender as an intrapsychic phenomenon, situated apart from social and political currents. Freud's is the metamodel of all Western psychotherapies, which are either adaptations to or rebellions against psychoanalysis. Why should feminist therapy consider itself genuinely free from these assumptive models of power relationships in treatment and of how gender relates to power in therapy? To what degree is it more than simply another adaptation or rebellion?

The Need for the Political Perspective

Answering these questions is both simple and immensely complicated. The simple answer is that feminist therapy, in order to be genuinely feminist and not simply dressed in metaphoric Birkenstocks, must continually trace the path back from the personal to the political, basing its interpretations and understandings on feminist political analysis and feminist strategies for action. A feminist therapist must ask herself how and if the course being taken in therapy will advance the goal of subverting patriarchy in the client's life, even in the most minute of ways. While therapy may, and in many cases must, attend for a time to the specific and sometimes emergent individual details of a client's life, therapy fails as feminism when the therapist does not draw, for herself and for her client, the linkages between the client's unique experience and the shared realities of others that are shaped by social and political forces. Although not all oppressed people will choose the same strategy for responding to their oppression, therapy that is feminist must assume that each person will, over time, seek and adopt some such strategy as an integral part of the therapeutic process. Satisfactory outcomes, in feminist therapy, rarely find the client's world intact in its pretherapy form, because the social and political connections drawn by feminist interpretations often lead to changes in more than a person's self-esteem.

The complex answer is that these notions take very diverse forms when put into practice. Having a theoretical underpinning to guide one's decisions allows for greater clarity; it helps the therapist to test her decisions against constructs that are implicit in the theory.

An example from my clinical practice that illustrates both the simplicity and the complexity of maintaining feminist analysis in therapy is the case of Ruth, whose story I have described in detail elsewhere (Brown, 1986). My work with her is also an example of how my understanding of theory has emerged from my practice. Briefly, Ruth is a working-class white Irish Catholic lesbian, born in 1944, who had received her nursing education by enlisting in the U.S. military and who had served a tour of duty in Vietnam. That war-zone experience left her in pain, terror, and increasing isolation for the next fifteen years. When she first came to therapy, Ruth was distressed about her recently ended decade of drinking, about her overpowering nightmares and flashbacks, and about her loneliness and social isolation. All of these were immediate concerns for me, because it was quite likely that Ruth would not keep herself alive much longer if she could not have help in dealing with her distress. She was fragile, suicidal, and feeling hopeless.

At first, therefore, feminist therapy with Ruth looked superficially like any other therapy, with an emphasis on the daily struggle for sobriety and sanity. But the feminist theory underlying my interventions allowed both me and Ruth to appreciate how difficult it is for a *woman* to engage in purposeful self-care, how more stigmatizing it is in our culture for a *woman* to be an alcoholic. Focusing on gender in our process of working on basic needs gave us the first clue to the theoretical underpinnings of Ruth's therapy.

Once Ruth's survival was no longer so much in question, and as we began to explore the meaning of her experiences in Vietnam and afterwards to her wounded sense of self, I began the process of linking her personal experience to political realities. I asked her to consider what it meant that she *needed* the U.S. military in order to complete her training—in other words, to consider what her class background had given her as options in a social context where schooling was not cheap and other sources of funds were not available. I asked her what it meant to be a woman in a war zone; more specifically, I asked her to consider the meaning of the acquaintance rapes she experienced as the price of "protection" and companionship. I encouraged her to look at how she had been silenced and to explore her so-called pathology in terms of the price she had paid for keeping silent about her experience. I asked her to look at the price she was being charged for speaking up and to look at how she made decisions about which price she would now pay.

At each opportunity for interpretation, I had the choice of interpreting the meaning of her distress either in political, feminist terms or in the more familiar intrapsychic frameworks in which I, as a clinical psychologist, had originally been trained. Her therapy would be feminist only if the linkages were made to the social context informing Ruth's life. At every turn in therapy, therefore, I served as a bridge between Ruth's internal realities and what I knew of women's oppression, so that Ruth's emerging image of herself would contain that knowledge.

Today, Ruth remains distressed, but her distress is of a very different sort than when we first met. It no longer disempowers her or serves as a source of isolation. Nor is it, for the most part, about herself or in forms that debilitate or confuse her. Rather, she is distressed—angry and outraged—by war, by violence against women, by inequities in the delivery of health care, by other social and political realities that were formerly obscured from her view by the teachings of patriarchy, and finally by her own wounds from that same system. Her anger fuels her social activism—her writing, speaking, and teaching about the political realities that she has uncovered in her healing process. It moves her into bonds with other women, and with some men, for both mutual healing and empowerment and for subversion of those structures that once wounded her. She is angry about sexism and heterosexism and the ways in which she encounters such forms of oppression daily. Her own quality of daily life is good, because she has learned to subvert patriarchy and not herself. But she is not complacent in her comfort.

In order to function in a frame of feminist revolution and social change, a theory of therapy must hold such distress, such feminist visions of what is wrong with patriarchy, as a positive outcome, the end point of the healing journey through the personal and then out again. To quote Rachel Perkins once more, "There are morals and values ... beyond personal adjustment and well-being; broader social and political context must not be lost" (1991a, p. 336).

Therapy and Money

Money is an important signifier of power. A feminist theory of psychotherapy must address the role and impact of money on the power dynamics of a therapy relationship. The lesbian feminist philosopher Caryatis Cardea (1985) notes that current trends to move all passionate emotional communications into a paid and professionalized setting further oppress and disadvantage working-class, poor, and underclass women who simply do not have the financial resources to pay for therapy. The professionalization of caring and emotional relating may also cause such women to be further shamed and disempowered by a relationship in which their use of language and personal ways of knowing are devalued by the actions of the professional and her middle-class values. Cardea questions what, if anything, therapy has to do with feminism in the life of a woman who must work ten extra hours a week to pay for her one fifty-minute therapy session; why should these hours be invested in psychotherapy, rather than spent in immediate actions toward social change or concrete improvements to quality of life? How, she wonders, does the creation of this new form of privileged speech help to eradicate inequities between women, not to mention overturn barriers against women's full participation in the world?

In these questions of class and money we again find matters of genuine merit and concern for the therapist who wishes to practice in a manner consonant with feminism. Money is not an insignificant distraction for therapists practicing in the United States. Nor is it, as psychodynamic theorists would suggest, simply a symbolic phenomenon to be treated as grist for the therapy mill. Feminist analysis directs our attention to the financial environment of psychotherapy. In the United States, as of 1994 more than a third of the population has no health insurance, and for those who do have insurance, coverage for mental health treatment has become the target of misguided attempts to "manage" costs to the employer who buys the insurance by limiting the number of sessions available. Because of intergroup rivalries and guild issues, many therapists, particularly those not doctorally trained, do not have their services paid for by insurance in any case, and such policies exclude many therapists of color and many feminist therapists. Finally, insurance companies refuse to cover "pre-existing conditions," a term that can almost always be used to describe the problems people bring to therapists. In the context of these concrete social and political realities, money and class issues are very present concerns for therapists seeking to practice from a feminist perspective.

The dilemma of money in the therapeutic relationship has been consistently troubling to feminist therapists, although we have been surprisingly silent on this matter in print. Excepting two book chapters by myself (Brown, 1985, 1990b), one by Ella Lasky (1985), and a discussion of financial matters in an article by Paula Caplan (1992), well-known self-described feminist therapists have paid little attention to the issues inherent in being paid for their services. Most of the heat and light on this topic comes from outside of therapy circles, from poor and working-class women themselves, for whom money is not a topic that can be either ignored or trivialized. Feminist therapists who grew up in middle-class homes where money was men's territory, or who did not see women running businesses or coping with the financial realities of poverty, seem genuinely uncomfortable confronting the reality that our work can be a business, much less coping with questions raised about the position of our work in a feminist revolution of value.

To be feminist, theories of therapy must address questions of class and the value of the work of the therapist. The practice of therapy tends to be a middle-class occupation, although not all those who practice it either emerge from or currently inhabit the middle class. Several feminist therapists of my acquaintance live in poverty or on its edge, and many grew up there. Much of what has been written on the topic of feminist therapy practice, however, assumes middle-class standards of living and financial resources. Class and money matters create ethical dilemmas for a therapist situating herself in a feminist discourse. How can we make our work genuinely accessible to all, regardless of ability to pay, without impoverishing ourselves? The notion of equal access, after all, implies such access to therapy as well. Or should we even consider the question of our own financial well-being in responding to this dilemma? Is a therapist betraying her allegiance to patriarchy when she makes her standard of living an important matter? Is therapy something that *should* be made available to all, or is it actually a luxury commodity? And if so, how and why do we construe a luxury as an aspect of feminist revolution?

Some who have written on this subject have theorized that the most radical feminist step is to require that therapists be well paid as a way of shifting value onto the devalued work of nurturance and care that has been associated with women's lives under patriarchy. Others have spoken in a similarly persuasive manner to the equally radical notion that no therapist should be paid for simply offering a relationship to another person. Still others have attempted to offer solutions by exploring the area between these dichotomous positions, examining how the therapist can make a living while still making therapy affordable, accessible, and liberating.

Therapy and Relationships Among Women

This last question of the ethics of paying to have a relationship leads to another issue that is a common thread in feminist critiques of therapy by such feminist philosophers as Mary Daly (1978), Janice Raymond (1986), and Sara Lucia Hoagland (1988). These authors view therapy as problematic to feminism, suggesting that therapy undermines healthy and more natural bonds and relationships between and among women. Because of the availability of therapists and therapy presuming to understand women's lives and experiences, they say, women have become less likely to share those experiences with one another. Instead of bringing to one another their joys, woes, fears, and shame, women are increasingly seeking solace from paid helpers—that is, from therapists. Friends no longer feel emotional responsibility to one another; instead, the woman in distress is adjured to go and see her therapist to deal with whatever brings her grief. Women do not, in the words of Hoagland, "attend" to one another with care and precision when the option of going to therapy is commonly available. Therapy, regardless of theoretical underpinnings, tends to promote an individualistic philosophy and orientation rather than a collectivist one. This can be unfortunate because the latter might more easily be seen as the basis for a more culturally sensitive, inclusive, and liberating process and transformation emerging from therapy practice.

Some feminist scholarship on the psychology of women would appear to support a vision of women as emotionally competent to attend to each other's needs without the intervention of a therapist. Authors such as Carol Gilligan (1981), Jean Baker Miller (1976), and other feminist psychodynamic theorists have posited a view of women as relational, empathic, and more naturally capable of forming emotional connections with one another than men are. Utopian visions of women's relationships with one another, such as those posited by the radical lesbian social commentator Sonia Johnson (1991) or the lesbian feminist speculative fiction author Sally Gearhart (1979), also draw upon these images of women as inherently and essentially relational. From this perspective, one might well ask, do some feminist philosophers, what therapy has to offer that in any way advances feminist revolution or is better or different from what women give to one another intuitively and instinctively (begging, for a moment, the whole question of feminist therapy for men, children, and families). If therapy simply serves to privatize and professionalize such otherwise normal relationships between women, to lend to the expression of feelings a special and somewhat negative or dangerous character by cloaking emotions in diagnostic jargon, to teach women therapeutic jargon with which to stigmatize one another, and to reduce the likelihood that women will seek each other out in friendship and solidarity, than it is unlikely that it can serve the goals of any feminist enterprise.

I would argue, however, that the ideals envisioned by these feminist critics—of an abundance of possible caring connections among and between women—do not currently exist in most women's lives under white European patriarchy. In a world without feminist therapy, women in Western cultures do not seek one another out for support and connection that are subversive to patriarchy except in unusual circumstances. Even lesbians, who might be presumed to seek out women more easily because they do not have primary intimate ties to men, have been isolated from one another by heterosexism and fears of being penalized for their alliances with one another.

Women's theoretical relationality, while an intriguing notion, may simply be an artifact of their position as the oppressed caste in gender relations (Unger, 1990) or, as Sonia Johnson (1991) has suggested, evidence of their inability to take themselves and their needs seriously. It may even be an idea that has been allowed and advanced by patriarchy as a subtle means of co-opting a feminist agenda, a "fifth column" theory to convince women that they are naturally nurturing and should keep out of men's territories of agency and competence (see Mednick [1989] for a cogent discussion of this viewpoint by a founding mother of feminist psychology).

Instead, with rare historical exceptions (such as the Beguines of the European Middle Ages and the Chinese marriage resisters of the late nineteenth century), women's connections to one another have been consistently damaged and obscured by patriarchy, which, as the late Audre Lorde claimed, seeks to disrupt anything in the lives of oppressed people that will empower them to bring about their own liberation. Even the phenomenon of consciousness-raising groups reflected an intentional process derived from feminist analysis and imposed upon women by political activists, rather than any sort of natural coming-together of women in intuitive solidarity. Part of the need for feminist revolution—and for a therapy rising to meet the challenges of feminist ethics and values—can be found in the profound degree to which many women have been separated from one another by patriarchy, and have lacked the sort of careful attending and support that can be introduced in therapy as something to which women are entitled and which they should expect.

Most powerful for me in understanding how patriarchy divides women from themselves and from one another, and informative to my vision of women's lives even in the midst of apparent privilege, is an event in my own life and my mother's life, the event that set me on the path of becoming a psychotherapist, although I did not know its details until I was nearly adult. For a half year when I was six, my mother lived for the most part in a psychiatric hospital, receiving electroshock therapy for depression that developed after the birth of her third child. At the same time, just across the fence, our next door neighbor was grieving the loss of her baby, who had died from the complications of a birth defect a month after my youngest brother was born. But these women as far as I know never talked about their shared and similar pain and confusion; the most contact our two families had during these months of parallel grief was when my grandmother, who was caring for her depressed daughter, called the man next door, who was a therapist, to help deal with my mother in a moment of crisis. The two women, alike in so many ways, never did connect; if anything, the revelation of my mother's pain to our neighbors seemed to create more of a gulf over time, as if her depression were too great a shame to allow for further relationship.

My mother and our neighbor were not unlike other women in the white, Jewish-American, college-educated middle class of the late 1950s. Patriarchy served to divide them from one another by generating impossible models of perfect womanhood that created the appearance and reality of competition and forbade openness and the disclosure of the need for support. Patriarchal norms, in which these women and others before and since were well-schooled, divided them from themselves. No one ever asked my mother, who grew up poor, Jewish, the daughter of immigrants who sewed clothes and delivered mail, how she was stressed by living in the upper-class white Christian neighborhood to which my father's position had brought her and how that stress contributed to the burden of being at home alone every day with three small and highly energetic children. No one asked how her attempts to assimilate and be "American" cut her off from the support of the women of her family, including her own mother. Those sorts of feminist questions, asked by a therapist, might have spared her the time and stigma of psychiatric hospitalization and the electroshock therapy that robbed her of memory and never did much for her depression, which lingered for years. Her psychiatrist had suggested the shock therapy as a way of reducing the time taken away from her maternal and wifely roles; my mother, wanting to do the right, womanly thing, followed his suggestion. I cannot know with certainty that a feminist therapist would have changed this course of events or gotten my mother and her neighbor to reach across the fence and be sources of support in each other's lives. I can say with certainty that a feminist theory of psychotherapy, with its emphasis on the social meaning of experience and its attention to the solidarity of people in shared circumstances, would have guided a therapist to different interventions and interpreted the meaning of these two women's experiences quite differently. It certainly would not have had as its main goal to "fix" her so that she could return quickly to the role of support person for the patriarchy in which she lived.

Therapy in the Feminist Lens

Therapy, in order to rise to the challenges of feminism, cannot be construed as an end in itself. A feminist theory creates a therapy that serves as a way-station; it can be one place, although not the only place, in which a person learns to value connection, loses the shame of psychic wounds, and becomes accustomed to being the focus of good quality attention. Therapy fails as an instrument of feminist transformation, however, if the client becomes satisfied with having only the somewhat unequal and asymmetrical associations available in a therapeutic context and does not develop a sense of entitlement to close, equal relationships in life outside of therapy. In this regard, the feminist philosophers have perceived an important problem inherent in the existence of therapy within feminism. It requires careful feminist analysis by a therapist to attend to the ways in which everyday connections among and between members of oppressed groups are undermined by patriarchal oppression. There is a danger that feminist therapy can itself become part of that devaluation by offering a contrasting sort of relationship that appears more valuable. In my own practice, I find myself constantly reminding my clients that I cannot be the only or most important person in their lives, because ours is a relationship whose goal is to make itself less important; it is a temporary, focused exchange with a specific outcome in mind, even when that temporary state of affairs lasts for several years. This is a contradiction inherent in feminist therapy, which privileges connections but must struggle with how not to overemphasize the value of the therapy connection itself over other relationships. As my colleague Maria Root notes, this utilitarian view of therapy also punctuates the degree to which therapy reflects white, European cultures that overvalue separation. This contradiction can be especially apparent in collectivist or relational cultures in which severing such an important tie, or denying its close relationship to familial and friendship connections, seems strange and even possibly wounding to the client. The liberating potential of intimacy in therapy can be likened to the discovery of a tasty food. There are many ways to learn about a particular wonderful dish; one may eat it for the first time at a restaurant or at the home of a friend. But neither of these first tastes precludes us from learning how to cook it for ourselves once we know that this is nourishing stuff.

A theory of therapy capable of responding to these critiques of psychotherapy as it has been in the absence of feminist analysis is the beginning of a vision of therapy as an instrument of feminist social change. Such a discourse on therapy is highly subversive to the assumptions about "mental health" and "helping professions" to which most therapists are socialized in the course of their professional education and training. For feminist therapists to have a subversive dialogue with their clients, they must continually engage in a parallel subversion of patriarchal assumptions within themselves. Feminist therapy as a philosophy must always be alert to the possible danger of what is done in therapy to the goals of feminism; it must not complacently assume a good fit with the aims of feminist social change. If feminist therapy is to subvert patriarchy one life at a time, one therapy hour at a time, it can only do so when self-criticism and self-scrutiny, within a feminist political framework, are as much a part of the work as is attention to any other aspect of therapy.

Most therapists are trained to pay very close attention to the meaning of each word and gesture, to monitor their feelings, fantasies, and dreams for possible relevance to their practice. Therapy positioned within a feminist discourse requires a commitment to pay similar close attention to the questions raised by feminist politics and philosophies. This additional analysis becomes a defining characteristic of feminist therapy, differentiating it in meaning and application from whatever is done by a therapist who lacks such a vision. As the chapters to follow demonstrate in greater detail, the model of therapy emerging from this new form of attention is one that transforms standard definitions of the role and potential of psychotherapy and expands the strategies for social and political change to encompass the very dreams and visions of feminism.

CHAPTER 2

Feminism in Feminist Therapy Theory

IF FEMINIST THERAPY is to realize its subversive potential, it must have a bedrock relationship to political feminism. The feminist therapist must, as Deborah Luepnitz has said, "set the fee as a feminist." Every action, no matter how slight, that she takes as a therapist should reflect a deliberate philosophical stance that passes the tests of adverse and multicultural feminist theory. Thus a theory of feminist therapy should emerge from some version of political feminist theory, either explicitly and formally or implicitly and intuitively. In practice, the latter is more common; many feminist therapists are not specifically conversant with feminist political theories but find themselves attracted to and practicing out of feelings reflecting one of several available political analyses of gender and power rather than a fully worked out paradigm. A valuable aspect of learning how to think as a feminist therapist and developing one's own personal feminist epistemology of therapy is that it offers the opportunity to become conscious of one's underlying feminist philosophies. The theory gives a theme to therapeutic practice that allows the feminist therapist to communicate about her feminist feelings in ways that can illuminate her epistemology to others and blend heart with mind and critical analysis.

Ironically, most feminist therapists appear to have a clearer intellectual grasp of the patriarchal psychotherapeutic orientations that have been blended with feminism than of the feminism itself. The result is that the feminism may be bent and twisted in an attempt to achieve some fit with the traditional therapy model. The published literature of feminist therapy contains more citations to the mainstream theorists whose work it criticizes than to feminist scholars and theoreticians. In the 1990s this imbalance is no longer due to a dearth of feminist references, as was the case as recently as ten years ago. This irony is because it is feminism, and not knowledge of object relations or cognitive behaviorism, that identifies the feminist therapist (Enns, 1992).

It is my sense that this state of affairs partially reflects a certain ambivalence within feminist theory about the value of therapy per se and about whether such a private, inner-directed enterprise can have any relationship to political analysis and activity. Moreover, feminist therapy has not for the most part been an academically based discipline. While feminist therapists often have advanced degrees, the theory and practice of feminist therapy has largely developed outside of academia. This separation has had its benefits, in that it has allowed for a freer development; North American feminist therapy practice has been a model of meaningful innovation and willingness to take risks. But there are losses as well. One consequence is that the close interdisciplinary relationships that can develop in a university setting often are not available to feminist therapists attempting to develop theory. Experienced feminist therapists often speak of their sense of emotional and intellectual isolation in their role as innovators. Many feminist therapists are unfamiliar with the formal political theories that are the foundation of their work and with current debates regarding these theories.

Why is it important to understand the various models of feminism and the therapy theories that they reflect? It is, I would argue, because the models and theories by which any psychotherapy is practiced inform reality for the therapist and the client. Those constructs that a particular model names and defines become real, present, and observable in the psychotherapy process of practitioners who use that model. For psychoanalysts, for instance, there *is* an Oedipal phenomenon; it is as real to such a practitioner as the keyboard of the computer on which I write these lines is to me. Taking on such lineaments of reality, these notions about what is important in the development of personality and the process of change begin to become salient in the lives of therapist and client alike. Clients in psychoanalysis are likely to dream dreams whose symbology is best explained by psychoanalytic theory; the clients of Jungian analysts encounter Jungian metaphors in their beds at night, in line with the model into which they are being socialized by their therapists. The theory upon which any philosophy and model of therapy are built is a sort of creation story, defining how clients' inner worlds have come to be and describing the nature of the healing interaction, as well as naming those behaviors that constitute health and those that indicate distress or pathology.

Consequently, it is important that theories of feminist therapy be constructed on models of reality in which women are defined in a central, positive, and nondeficient manner. Such models must, as Hannah Lerman (1986) puts it, be "close to the data of lived experience," with a complex and multicultural view of humanity, free of an androcentric norm. They must be models that do not take for granted traditional notions of appropriate outcomes for therapy or for life itself. The nature of the problem must not be assumed to lie solely or even primarily within the client. Rather, the distress or difficulties experienced by the person need to be seen as evidence of what is wrong, deficient, or missing in the social and cultural context, even as a sign of survival in the face of oppression and as a potentially healthy protest against patriarchal norms. This is not to glorify distress and poor function, which do not make life livable and which motivate our clients to meet with us and change, but to frame distress in such a way as to change its meaning to the therapist and eventually to the client as well. Such a perspective fits more comfortably with some feminist political philosophies than with others; some do not construe women (or men, for that matter) as victims but do place responsibility for the development of problems on the shoulders of oppression.

Feminist therapy theory as described here leads to a radically deconstructivist approach to the understanding of human growth, development, distress, and behavior change, founded in the perception that we live in patriarchal cultures that are damaging to human existence. The practice of such therapy is based on multicultural feminist scholarship on the psychology of women and gender, reflecting a broad range of methodologies that sanction a range of ways of knowing and authorizing knowledge (Ballou, 1990). It is a practice informed by ways of seeing, knowing, feeling, and understanding rooted in the refusal of feminism to accept the dominant culture as a healthy or worthwhile model for human behavior.

Foundations of Political Feminism in Feminist Therapy

Several forms of political feminism have been promulgated—mostly by white women—in late-twentieth-century North America. Political feminism has been by no means a single movement, but rather has tended to express several central themes or trends, with variations—both important and trivial—in how such themes are operationalized. There are limitations to the usefulness of each of these political models, to the degree that they derive their analyses from unicultural perspectives, or fail to address how patriarchy might express itself in a diversity of manners. But what each of these perspectives on feminism has shared with others is a vision of women as treated wrongly by the culture in which they live and a commitment to changing that state of affairs. In addition, most North American feminisms have shared certain core themes which have been important organizing principles for feminist therapists.

THE PERSONAL IS POLITICAL

Individual experience does not occur in a vacuum; it is one person's encounter with the social and cultural context, which acts to inform and transform the inner meaning of that experience. This notion begins to move feminist perspectives away from Western models of individualism, and toward more collective and potentially multicultural manners of conceptualizing. In such a framework, personal experience is the lived version of political reality. The feminist technique from the women's liberation movement of consciousness raising was a methodology for making the personal political by exposing isolated women to one another's experiences and drawing forth the secrets that women had held in the belief, fostered by patriarchy and often encouraged by mainstream psychotherapy theories, that they alone were uniquely flawed in some manner. Thus, feminism has a powerful deprivatizing force in calling for the secret experiences of girls and women within homes and families to be brought to light, exposed as manifestations of a male-dominated society at work, and used to illumine the lives of men from a new vantage point.

The idea that the personal is political is of particularly challenging significance to feminist therapists, who often in individual therapy deal explicitly with clients in a milieu that tends to reprivatize and individualize experience rather than deprivatize and politicize it. The dynamic tension in feminist therapy emerges from the contradictions between honoring each client's unique experiences of reality, all the while adhering to the laws and customs that require (with certain exceptions such as child abuse reporting) absolute confidentiality of the therapy session, while simultaneously attempting to make feminist interpretations and interventions that place the private within the framework of the public and collective. The feminist lens, similar to those viewpoints deriving from ethnic, sexual minority, and disabilities rights activism, draws attention to the connections between that unique experience and the external reality of a patriarchal sociopolitical context.

GENDER AND POWER AS CATEGORIES OF ANALYSIS

A second core precept of political feminism is that gender and power are extremely important factors in understanding and analyzing human interactions, with gender seen as a primary category of analysis along which power dynamics operate. Gender has tended to be defined by white, Western feminist theories as being isomorphic with biological, sex; and until recently, power has been framed in these analyses in dominant cultural terms, such as power over others and control of resources. While different feminist political philosophies vary widely in their understanding of the relationship of gender and power and recently have debated the meanings and definitions ascribed to gender and gendered phenomena, all feminist philosophies identify these factors as important variables. The experiences of women are especially highlighted by this attention to gender, as a corrective against the privileging of men's lives and points of view. In consequence, despite its applications to the lives of men, feminism is often confused with so-called "women's issues." Feminist political philosophies tend to value power relationships in which there is, if not equality at least egalitarianism, in which power differences between and among people are avoided where possible and structures are developed to reduce the imbalances where power differences are unavoidable. When power differences appear inevitable, feminist principles necessitate respect for difference, and the avoidance of exploitation of power—important underlying notions for feminist therapy.

This precept has been a source of both strength and difficulty in feminist therapy practice. Understanding the importance of gender in the development of human behavior, in people's sense of self, and in their interactions with one another has been one of the most salient and powerful contributions made by feminist therapy to psychotherapy practice in general. The punctuation of gender, the discussion of gendered phenomena in boldface type, and the attention to the long-ignored details of women's lives in understanding all human behavior have transformed how many therapists understand their work.

Yet questions remain regarding the degree to which gender is *the* explanatory factor in certain behaviors that some current observers tend to describe as "women's ways" of being, knowing, feeling, and relating (see, for example, Belenky et al. [1986] and Gilligan [1981]). Feminist psychology, and to a lesser degree feminist therapy, are in the midst of a dialogue about whether these "women's ways of being" might not simply be artifacts of women's occupation of particular niches in certain types of hierarchies of power, dominance, and oppression, no more essentially tied to female gender than are interests in stereotypically feminine activities. Additionally, in cultures other than those of white Europe and North America, such ways of being and knowing are normative for both women and men, and derive from more referential, collective manners of understanding self and community (Landrine, 1992). In using gender as a lens, it is unclear whether feminist therapists have adequately attended to the issue of power as it artificially defines gender boundaries in certain segments of the dominant culture.

The question of power has more directly been addressed in the therapy relationship itself, as we saw in the last chapter. Because power is such a tangible dimension in the therapeutic relationship, feminist therapists have spoken at length to the question of how to maintain more egalitarian exchanges between ourselves and our clients. Power inheres to the role of the therapist, who is accorded authority, expertise, and wisdom in both real and symbolic ways by clients and by the larger culture. A continuing dilemma of feminist therapy has been how to minimize the power differential between therapist and client while maintaining the frame and boundaries of therapy. The gaps and confusions in our understanding of power, left as artifacts of socialization in cultures where power is consistently distorted and exploited, have led to some interesting and at times painful stumblings on the path to a feminist relationship in therapy.

THE PRIVILEGING OF WOMEN'S EXPERIENCES

A third shared principle of feminist political theory is that the range of women's experiences are important, and the validity of women's perceptions must be known and valued. This idea contrasts with traditional approaches to therapy, in which the human experience is framed by the dominant culture and men's lives; *human* has been strenuously redefined and is no longer the generic masculine. Depending upon the variety of feminist political philosophy and the underlying assumptions about the nature of gender reflected in that philosophy, this precept can be expressed in quite divergent forms. The common thread of these expressions can be found in the movement of women from the margins to the center, be that by relocating women or by repositioning the location of the center. Feminist therapy has developed a substantial body of clinical and theoretical scholarship on the lives of women and the problems that women commonly bring to therapy, which is utilized as a central database from which to practice.

The challenge for feminist therapy and the entire feminist movement has been to have a definition of *woman* that goes beyond white and middle-class; this problematic, institutionalized, and oppressive aspect of feminist therapy remains far from being adequately addressed. White and middle-class feminists have been as consciously and unconsciously exclusionary of nondominant colleagues as white men have been of white women.

These issues appear to be thematic in most forms of political feminism and emerge continually in discussion of feminist therapy practice. There are, however, a number of quite different ways in which a feminist sensibility can be and has been expressed. These different forms of political feminism tend to inform different feminist therapies as well, because they reflect varied understandings of the meaning of women's place in culture and the nature of the change process necessary to achieve feminist goals. While the descriptions to follow are general and somewhat cursory, they reflect my experiences of each of these traditions, put into practice over the past two decades. There is also a considerable degree of overlap between the various forms of feminism depending upon the issue at hand and how, and by whom, it is being defined.

Reformist Models of Feminism

Reformist political feminism has tended to focus primarily on the ways women have been denied equal rights and equal access. A reformist perspective is not usually critical of the system and institutions of dominant culture per se but rather of discrimination against women within that system. For example, a reformist perspective may not question the value of marriage as an institution but rather the practice of denying women equal rights to credit, property, or use of their own name within marriage. Reformist activism has emphasized obtaining for women equal opportunities to participate in the institutions of the culture in ways identical to those available to men or increasing the number of women visible within those institutions (also known as bean-counting.) This version of feminism has focused on changing laws to guarantee equal rights to women and on identifying those aspects of existing law that could be utilized in favor of women's access; it is a perspective that places faith in, and makes a tool of, the legal and electoral systems. This is the definition of feminism understood by popular culture.

Reformist feminism has also emphasized placing women in positions of power within the structure of the dominant culture, opening up to women career and work fields that had traditionally been male-dominated, and identifying and modifying those barriers to women's advancement in the worlds of commerce and politics that denied women economic and mainstream political power. There has been a parallel, although not as active, emphasis on encouraging men's participation in careers, such as childcare and nursing, in which men have traditionally been underrepresented. Reformist feminism tended at first to see women and men as essentially similar in all matters except reproductive biology and external genitalia, although more recently it has adopted a perspective on gender in which women and men are seen as basically different although equal. Both views, however, have been in the service of a norm that says "anything women want to do, they can learn to do," and "people should be treated the same regardless of gender."

For reformist feminists, gender is the only important category of analysis. Thus this version of feminism tends to be explicitly or implicitly exclusionary of people for whom race, class, ability, sexual orientation, or culture are the more salient factors in their positioning on the matrix of power and dominance. Reformist feminist canons often seek to elevate women who privilege their gender oppression over other forms of oppression (for example, Shirley Chisholm, the first African-American woman presidential candidate, was quoted as attesting that she had been more discriminated against for gender than for race).

As an enduring theoretical base for feminist therapy, a reformist feminist therapy appears to be problematic because of its subtle tendencies to shape women to fit within the structures of the status quo, with little questioning of the values of those structures. In this respect it does not meet the criterion of subverting patriarchy. Reformist perspectives, with the theme of "why can't a woman be more like a man," can be seen in some of the very early material published by feminist therapists. There we find a heavy emphasis on teaching women the behaviors they will need to function successfully in the world of men: assertion training, overcoming "fear of success," "fair fighting" in heterosexual couple relationships, and the like. Reformist feminist therapies unconsciously took on a view of women as deficient when compared to men and aimed to help women correct those perceived deficiencies, reflecting what Sandra and Daryl Bem (1970) called "the power of a non-conscious ideology."

The concept of fear of success is one of the most striking examples of this subtle image of woman-as-deficient, defining success in dominant cultural terms only (for example, being at the top of one's medical school class) and reading women's non-conscious fears and feelings about certain occupational roles as a fear of success rather than as valid concerns about violence against women or the lives lived by women who succeed on dominant cultural terms. When research showed that "mentally healthy male" and "mentally healthy human" were considered to be one and the same, reformist feminist therapists of that early period often simply attempted to help women become more "human"—less womanly and more androgynous—ignoring the androcentrism of the concept of human as it was then understood by mental health professionals, feminist therapists not excluded.

Similarly, the structures into which women were attempting to fit, such as the workplace, were not subjected to critique by early reform-oriented feminist therapists; instead the focus was on helping women do better in such institutions. Since all behavior was defined as a learned phenomenon, social learning theory and the behavioral and cognitive-behavioral schools of psychotherapy were seen as admirable models for teaching women new ways of behaving. Because these types of therapy were developing concurrently with second-wave feminism, they seemed to offer appealing alternatives to the misogyny and hegemony of psychoanalytic thought. The aura of science surrounding this approach had not yet encountered feminist criticisms of scientific methodologies. Androgyny, or the blending of masculine and feminine characteristics, was identified as an important goal, because it was seen as "freeing" women from the bonds of femininity; at that early stage, feminists in the mental health professions had not stopped to ask whether women wanted to be so freed or whether women's liberation lay less in changing women and more in modifying the meanings that the culture gave to certain behaviors.

This reformist vision in early feminist therapy work is not surprising, given the times in which it arose. It was the late 1960s and early 1970s, when the critique of dominant culture had just begun and individual behavior change was still seen as the answer to societal problems. This zeitgeist colored the understanding of most feminist therapists, who were still emerging from their training and were uncertain or unaware of the more radical potentials of feminist analysis. Nor do I see that these early missteps negate the importance of that work and its practitioners. After all, the only maps then available were the ones written by patriarchy; it was only when, by using those maps, feminist therapists found themselves lost that they were able to begin to draw their own charts of psyche and society. As one who did my therapist training during this time and who was consequently pointed toward a reformist practice by my early mentors, I consider it important to understand how strongly this perspective reflected our prior socialization into nonfeminist and antiwoman mindsets. It is only necessary to recall the complete hegemony of patriarchal theories in all their various guises, from the overtly problematic psy-

chodynamic concepts to the seductive humanistic paradigms then fashionable, to appreciate how amazing it was that feminist therapy emerged at
all from a field so thoroughly sown with intellectual and emotional salt by
prior training in the dominant mental health disciplines.

It was quite radical, not to say dangerously revolutionary, in the early
1970s for women in the mental health disciplines even to assert that
women would benefit from having women therapists rather than men
therapists or that women's anger and assertiveness should be seen as
appropriate rather than as evidence of "penis envy," "masculine protest,"
or other forms of pathology. When Phyllis Chesler published *Women and
Madness* and came to my hometown of Cleveland on a promotional tour,
the psychiatric and psychological establishment came out in force to
ridicule her for saying these and similarly inoffensive sorts of things
because they were such profound de-silencings of the female experience,
and so subversive to the unimpeded work of that establishment.

In the face of that sort of hostile reception, not confined to Chesler
alone, the steps toward asking more dangerous questions about the worth
of certain kinds of behavior that the dominant culture valued most highly
was not, for the most part, one that many feminist therapists were in a
position to take, either personally or professionally. We were still too busy
uncovering the contradictions between feminism and patriarchal institutions and recovering from the *ad feminem* attacks leveled by both men and
women in the mental health establishment against feminist practitioners.

The development of feminist theory in North America over the past
two decades and the continued revelation of violence and oppression as
aspects of patriarchy have made asking such dangerous questions not
only possible but necessary. Feminist therapists have now had the chance
to analyze both the successes and the wrong turns of early feminist therapy practice and to combine this knowledge with personal experience as a
heuristic for feminist therapy theory. Having done so, many feminist therapists, including myself, have found it difficult to continue to work within
a reformist mode. The empirical data available point out another curious
phenomenon: Reformist feminist therapy has had the potential to be quite
antiwoman in practice.

The first set of follow-ups to assertiveness training groups, which
almost defined feminist therapy in the United States in the early 1970s, are
instructive in understanding how good feminist intentions can ironically
have a bad outcome. Women who had participated in these groups
reported that while they had learned the correct behaviors, the social context had not learned to value these behaviors in women. The consequences
to our clients for engaging in what feminist therapists were then calling

"appropriate assertion" were often quite negative and sometimes even dangerous to the women involved. No one paid very careful attention to the fact that the emphasis on women's "right" to do certain things emerged originally from the jurisprudence of rights developed by and for white male property owners, in which women were invisible. None of us, in the early 1970s, were examining the relationship between women's so-called lack of assertiveness and the social context of pervasive violence against women or how such nonassertive behaviors might have been wise survival strategies for many women. We now have that sort of data and perspective to incorporate into our criteria for a theoretical basis for feminist therapy.

Radical Models of Feminism

Radical feminism takes an entirely different perspective on the dilemma of women's inequality by analyzing it as one of many forms of oppression within a dominant patriarchal culture. Patriarchal cultures and their various institutions—such as marriage and the family, the justice system, and organized religion—are perceived as being inherently misogynist, actually or potentially dangerous to women and in need of radical transformation. Women's difficulties are seen less as the result of inequality of opportunity than as the end products of a systematic devaluation of women and anything related to women's work and ways of being, a devaluation that would persist even in the face of formally equal social structures. Patriarchy is seen as attempting to control and denigrate women through systematic violence against them, the silencing of their voices, and the degradation of their knowledge and ways of seeing and learning. Thus, radical feminism maintains that the oppression of women as a class will be changed only when there is change within the overall culture, when dominance and submission as the mode of relating are replaced by a cooperative, collaborative form of social discourse.

The placement of women in positions of power and authority and the admission of women into nontraditional fields of endeavor are generally perceived by radical feminists as tokenistic, more likely to co-opt the individual women involved than to lead to change within patriarchy. Instead, emphasis is placed on changing those institutions of patriarchal cultures that promulgate the status quo, such as the family, educational institutions, and the justice system, and on developing an integrated analysis of oppression (Kanuha, 1990b) that ties together racist, classist, heterosexist, and other forms of oppression with gender oppression.

Radical forms of feminism were commonly based on a model of gender that saw women and men as essentially quite different from one another at the level of primary psychological development, and for the most part they have continued to use this perspective, which can be called *essentialist*. This term refers to a view of certain characteristics as being "essential" to membership in a certain class or group—for example, the notions that men are essentially more interested in genital sexuality than are women or that women are essentially nurturant. More recently, postmodern radical feminist critics have analyzed the possible pitfalls in such a position, utilizing a social constructivist explanation of gender-based oppression. Social constructivism holds that all categories and divisions of human behavior such as gender or race are arbitrary, creations of a particular social discourse at a particular time and place, subject to change as the defining variables of the discourse itself are modified. For social constructivist radical feminists, differences between women and men, while meaningful within a particular social and interpersonal context, are simply artifacts of that context, built by the social discourse, as it were, rather than essential to and inherent in being female or male. This version of reality suggests different outcomes of the political transformative process than does an essentialist model, which it sees as reifying gender as defined in dominant culture and opting into a dichotomous mode of categorizing that may be patriarchal in nature and reflective of a Eurocentric world view. Because this particular debate over the meaning of definitions of gender has been so important to theory in feminist therapy, it will be explored in greater detail later in this chapter.

Several variant forms of radical feminism have appeared, each with a specific focus. Lesbian feminism has gone forward with certain aspects of the radical feminist analysis to question why and how heterosexuality in its various forms (marriage, mandatory motherhood, sexual objectification of women, common social patterns between women and men) is an important aspect of women's oppression under patriarchy and how heterosexuality has been made mandatory for women. Lesbian feminism defines heterosexuality as a question and problem, rather than as a given (Wilkinson & Kitzinger, 1993). It is particularly critical of the institutions of heterosexuality and the dominant culture's assumptions of the normative or essential nature of heterosexuality in women. A lesbian feminist perspective takes as a given and a norm women's love for and bonding with one another, whether or not that expresses itself in a sexual form. It attends critically to those aspects of patriarchal cultures that tend to interfere with these bonds, as well as the manifestation of such heteropatriarchy in women's lives. Lesbian feminism is concerned with recovering and

describing the variety of emotional bonds between women and developing strategies for strengthening those bonds as part of the overall process
of undermining patriarchy. The creation of lesbian and woman-only
space, both physically and emotionally, is one such lesbian feminist strategy. Lesbian feminist analysis also draws attention to the harmful effects
of the inclusion of men and male perspectives of authority in women's
lives and realities. Lesbian feminism pays particular attention to sources of
expertise and authority as a result of this concern about the bias introduced by male-dominated perspectives; for example, greater weight may
be given to work developed by lesbians, or by women, than to anything
created by men. Compared with reformist and radical feminism, lesbian
feminism is significantly less focused on how women and men can learn to
live and work together and more on how women may learn to see themselves apart from male definitions.

More recently, feminist theory developed by women of color has
become an important part of the North American feminist discourse.
Woman-of-color feminism, sometimes also called *womanism,* a term proposed by Alice Walker, shares many elements with radical and lesbian
feminism in that it tends to be critical of the dominant culture as a whole
and to define the problem of oppression of women as a pervasive one that
will not be solved by increasing the number of women occupying particular roles. Like lesbian feminism, it assumes the importance of loving bonds
between women, although the emphasis is usually explicitly less on sexual
bonds and more on other loving relationships.

Although some feminist women of color are themselves adherents of a
reformist perspective (recall the Chisholm quote), the specifically woman-
of-color and womanist feminist theorists appear for the most part to be
developing an analysis that is incongruent with a reformist vision of social
change; the status quo is simply too rife with racism. I consequently have
classified this model as a strain of radical feminism. Woman-of-color feminism is critical of a tendency within radical feminism and lesbian feminism to define their analyses from the experiences of white women alone,
which has led to the marginalization and oppression of women of color
within the feminist movement itself. It focuses attention on the impact of
the combined forces of race, ethnicity, and gender on women's and men's
experiences in the broader social context. It uses the experiences of North
American ethnic minority women as the basis for critiquing white feminist
models and strategies and uses, and describing how those white-oriented
models have failed to include the experiences of all women.

Woman-of-color feminists have challenged assumptions held by white
feminist theories that gender is the primary category of analysis and

pointed out that the overinclusive paradigms of white feminism have had the effect of excluding women of color and in the process diminishing white feminism's own explanatory power. These feminists have deconstructed the image of "woman" as white and middle class (since, although race is not isomorphic with class in the United States, it is highly correlated with class) and insisted that the experiences of dominant group women no longer be generalized to the lives of minority group women (Collins, 1990; Moraga & Anzaldua, 1983; Williams, 1991). Woman-of-color feminism and womanism have pointed the way toward understanding gender as interacting with other factors on a social and interpersonal matrix, and have challenged facile categorizations of people as either entirely oppressor or entirely oppressed.

Feminist therapy, to be genuinely radical in its core and practice, must be concerned not only with gender but with questions of race, culture, ethnicity, and the various other variables that inform the meaning of women's lives. It must be based on knowledge and draw on sources of authority that are themselves diverse, reflecting the lived experiences and theoretical perspectives of women in all their diversity.

Where Does a Radical Feminism Lead Feminist Therapy Theory?

Many feminist therapists, in the early stages of feminist therapy, held enthusiastic but naive beliefs regarding the malleability of the social context and its openness to change in response to changed behaviors in individuals. In the succeeding decade, those hopes have been replaced with the more sophisticated analysis of radical feminist theories, which appear to offer the feminist therapist a political model consistent with the concepts and meta-assumptions of feminist therapy. This more seasoned viewpoint challenges some of the assumptions that were initially freely borrowed by feminist therapy practitioners from mainstream therapies. Radical models of feminism generate models for therapy that question why and whether women should aspire to forms of behavior and relating that have been associated with male dominance and also challenge the status quo for healthy masculinity. Such models carefully contextualize behaviors, reflecting a feminist science in which the asker and the questions are scrutinized as closely as the findings of the study. This broader and more radical vision of the context leads to a deeper theoretical understanding of how patriarchal oppression creates an emotional environment in which certain trees flourish and others wither, not because of faults in the plant, but because of the barrenness of the soil.

For example, the application of a radical feminist analysis has led to feminist critiques of the various alternatives to psychodynamic thought that were embraced by reformist feminist therapists practicing in the 1970s, such as humanistic, cognitive behavioral, and family systems models. As radical forms of feminism heightened attention to the meaning of context as it informs behavior, feminist therapists discovered that systemic models of interpersonal relationships, which assumed that all participants had equal power to move the system toward change, were as inadequate to our task of personal and social transformation as the notion that women would feel better if only their behavior were more consonant with an androcentric norm. In each case, the model of "human" as interchangeable with "man" was too pervasive; women's—or any marginalized person's— viewpoints on relationship systems were absent. Many of us also discovered, to our dismay, that the humanistic approaches to therapy that had been attractive to us initially were equally ill-suited to women's realities because they failed to speak powerfully to questions of violence and oppression in women's lives and called prematurely for transcendence of differences, such as race and gender, when survival was not yet assured. The radical individualism inherent in such humanistic theories, which increasingly placed all responsibility for experience upon the individual, was at odds with the growing feminist knowledge base regarding the ways in which culturally induced powerlessness could strip away the ability to act authentically, because the need to survive required deception or distance from oneself. Similarly, radical feminism shaped the questions posed to cognitive behavioral notions of "irrational" thoughts by suggesting that for some people, in some places and at some times, these supposedly universally pathological cognitions might be reasonable, or even life-saving.

As Deborah Luepnitz (1988) has so elegantly phrased it, feminist therapy is "a sensibility, an aesthetic"; it is a philosophy and epistemology of human transformation that prescribes, not the tools for change, but the manner in which any tool shall be grasped and used and the skills with which to evaluate the tools chosen. Feminist therapy as a conceptual framework helps the therapist, in the words of Audre Lorde, not to mistake feminist tools for change for the "master's tools," which Lorde says "will never dismantle the master's house"—that is, the representations within all human beings of oppressive dominant norms from the cultures in which we live. Feminist therapy is not defined by the population with whom it is practiced, nor by the topics addressed. It is not "therapy with women," and it is not limited to so-called "women's issues." It is a theory of therapy developed from a particularistic basis (the diverse and complex experiences of women) with universalistic implications. Feminist therapy theory can be applied in many settings and in response to many problems, with women and men, children and adults, in legal settings and with groups. Nor is it entirely clear that only women can be feminist therapists, although this question continues to be debated hotly; I assume it to be the case, simply because that is true in my experience.

The feminist therapy theory that derives from radical models of feminism utilizes questions about the position and meaning of gender and power in personal experience and within human social discourse to attempt to understand the specific difficulties in living that people bring to therapy. Both gender and power as concepts are examined and explicated through a lens ground in the crucibles of lesbian and woman-of-color feminism as well, a lens that changes one's visions and focuses on questions about the meaning of gender, of kinds of power, and of how assumptions about the meaning and interaction of these social phenomena are reflected in the experiences and distress presented to the feminist therapist. Human experience is understood within this theoretical framework as the interaction between internal, personal phenomenological experience and the external social environment. Internal experience gives meaning to external reality, which in turn shapes and informs the comprehension of internal experience, which then plays again upon external reality, in a constantly interactive process.

Different types of external realities will give quite different meaning to very similar internal experiences. In feminist therapy theory, therefore, it is important to know feminist therapy questions; the dimensions of the context, as perceived from a range of subjectivities with no one viewpoint privileged as necessarily more objective than another. Neither intrapsychic factors nor social contextual variables are the sole focus of inquiry; each by itself and both interactively are considered essential for the therapist and client to understand themselves as individuals, their interaction with each other, and their work within the broader social and political framework. A primary goal of feminist therapy deriving from radical feminist theories is a political one: to deprivatize what has been silenced and kept secret in the lives of people oppressed and marginalized by dominant culture and thus to make personal experience a path toward political understanding.

This model of therapy as a subversive act in which all patriarchal verities are open to question profoundly affects how the success of therapy will be defined by feminist therapists and ultimately by their clients. Success in these terms may be invisible to the eyes of dominant-culture institutions and may even appear to be a failure to achieve, fit, or otherwise shape oneself to the requirements of a narrow dominant norm. A goal of feminist therapy is maladjustment to patriarchy, not only for women but for men, children, families, intimate pairs—indeed anyone with whom feminist therapists practice. Feminist therapy is thus often intensely divergent from mainstream approaches to therapy because its underlying theory assumes multiplicity of good outcomes and vigorously questions the good outcome as defined by a mainstream perspective.

Changing the Canon

In order to make this sort of shift in focus, the canon of knowledge from which the therapist derives her understanding of human behavior must be reshaped. Materials considered irrelevant to dominant therapy theories may become essential; conversely, the authoritative volumes of mainstream psychology may shift to the background. The reconfigured canon for feminist therapy theory deriving from the radical feminisms must particularly represent the work of those women whose marginalized status—in a culture where dominance is defined by whiteness, middle-class position, youth, able-bodiedness, and heterosexuality as well as by maleness—have given them a sharper eye with which to gaze critically on patriarchal forms. Radical models of feminism informing feminist therapy suggest that those with the least to lose are more likely to be willing to tell the truth. Mary Daly (1978) noted how valuable the position of the marginal "other" can be as a source of knowledge, strongly stating that women divested themselves of this position at their peril, risking the loss of wisdom that would follow any attempts to assimilate into masculine culture. Consequently, the knowledge and authority of women from outside the dominant white culture will usually reflect a smaller investment in approval from mainstream institutions than is seen in the work of white and middle-class women, who are often, as I myself have been, seduced by the illusion of inclusion in the dominant culture because of our apparent similarities to the white men who are not only our fathers, brothers, or partners but sometimes also the witting or unwitting instruments of our and other women's oppression.

Such a diverse base of knowledge and authority is not limited to information about the lives of people from outside the dominant group. While such multicultural literacy is of value, it can too easily become an undigested lump that is never integrated into feminist therapy theory. My colleague Oliva Espin (personal communication) refers to this as the "add women of color and stir" approach. Such an add-on model carries the assumption that this information is marginal rather than central to feminist therapeutic epistemologies. Instead, the feminist therapy canon includes and integrates paradigms for understanding human behavior, development, and distress generated from within those nondominant groups. Feminist therapy theory assumes that these nondominant paradigms are potentially useful for understanding human behavior, beyond that of the groups from which they have arisen. But feminist therapy theory diverges from mainstream models in rejecting the myth that one paradigm, derived from one sort of human experience, can explicate all of human behavior. Instead, it is intentionally multiparadigmatic. Reflecting Mary Daly's notion of patriarchal reversals, for example, the notion that all patriarchal values are the reverse of what they truly ought to be, such a multiparadigmatic mode of understanding calls for forgetting all assumptions about what is normal and instead questioning whether certain phenomena could be better comprehended from an outsider pose, whether that which has been defined as the norm is in essence the problem.

Feminist therapy theory also leads to a consideration of epistemologies and the manner in which the sources of our knowledge claims have derived their information and authority. As Mary Ballou has noted in her review of epistemological issues in feminist therapy theory (1990), one of the inherent problems in dominant-cultural theories of therapy is that they tend to be narrow in their epistemology. The science of psychology has been dominated by allegiance to logical positivist empiricism, which assumes that truth is unitary and observable under correct and sufficiently controlled conditions; it denies the effect of the knower upon the known, or the asker upon the question and the answer obtained. Knowledge claims are, consequently, less valued by mainstream psychology when they do not derive from such a conceptual model. While some theories of therapy, such as psychoanalysis and some of the humanistic psychologies, derive from more intuitive and clinical methodologies, they have been equally limited in their scope, having arisen from a white male perspective, that of the founding "father" of each specialty.

While feminist therapists may at times draw upon positivist epistemologies (for instance, it is helpful to know the statistics about childhood sexual abuse or wife battering or racist hate crimes in the general population), one important characteristic of feminist therapy methodology is its openness to a range of epistemologies and its insistence that intuitive methodologies be specific about the limitations of their scope so that overly broad constructions will not be given to uniquely personal material. Feminist therapy credits the knowledge claims that are founded in that range of methodologies; the testimony of one woman about her life is, in consequence, as compelling and of value as is any empirical study, although it may be a different sort of value.

Postmodern Radical Feminist Concerns

As we saw earlier in this chapter, feminist therapy theory rests on a base of an informed and critical vision of gender and its construction and meanings. This basis in scholarship and in the enduring feminist discourse on gender and its meanings is of particular importance to feminist therapy theory because of the place of gender as a central category of analysis in feminist theory. The primary producers and consumers of feminist therapy have been women; as a consequence, questions of who a woman "really" is and how a woman can *be* in the world have been commonly asked by feminist therapists and their clients. The dominant discourse on gender has been almost entirely consumed by the study of Woman; men, as the dominant group running the discussion, have seemed reluctant to let the parameters of their definition be put up for discussion (the notable exceptions being gay and bisexual men, whose sexual orientation defines them as outsiders to male dominance). Because gender and its meanings have been so controversial, so rife with stereotype and myth, and so vulnerable to being framed in the terms of so-called conventional wisdom, an informed and critical view of gender is thus fundamental to feminist therapy theories.

One of the more provocative and satisfying aspects of the postmodern radical feminist discourse has been the uncovering of dominant cultural assumptions regarding gender and gendered phenomena. At its inception this discourse tended toward an error rooted in dominant visions—that is, the initial definition of gender and biological sex as one and the same. This assumption quickly became problematic when feminist psychologists observed that the presumed isomorphism of sex and gender implied that behaviors observed at higher frequencies among one group were thereby assumed by most nonfeminists to be biologically, instinctively mediated and thus immutable. This last set of assumptions was a problem to which the earliest feminist psychologists, such as Naomi Weisstein (1970), had pointed as evidence of sexist bias in existing psychological theories. The equation of biology with sex role also wilted somewhat when exposed to anthropological information about cultures in which there were multiple genders whose primary determining factors were not always biological sex (Williams, 1987).

The postmodern radical feminist discourse on gender and its meanings has continued to be caught in the dynamic tension between a biological explanation of gender and gendered behaviors, described earlier as "essentialism," and a perspective that defines all behaviors as only artificially linked to gender by a prevailing social discourse, a viewpoint called "social constructivist" (Hare-Mustin & Marecek, 1990). This dialogue and dissension reflect different initial biases on the part of scholars and practitioners attempting to understand and make sense of observed phenomena. In reality, neither perspective is a complete source of explanation for gender-related behaviors, but the tension between the two is of particular importance to feminist therapy theory and to its connection to political models of feminism as the latter evolve over time.

Why is that the case? As it happens, much of what has currently been written in feminist therapy, regarding both theory and applications, reflects a bias toward essentialism, the perspective that women and men are different in essential, basic ways that can and should be uncovered, reframed, and celebrated as being equal in value to one another. This "different voice" paradigm for gender, which is best represented in the work of Gilligan and her colleagues, Belenky and her colleagues, and other feminist scholars who have attempted to comprehend women's experiences and feelings from the inside out, is popular with many practicing feminist therapists and with even more clients, both male and female. What they say seems to feel right, and that intuitive sense of rightness is an important source of information in a feminist, multimodal methodology.

Certainly the notion that there are innate human characteristics that are based in the unchangeable fact of biological sex provides a simple explanation of many complex and often scary phenomena. The framing of these essentialist ideas within the different-voice paradigm is what is new and feminist about these observations. While in the past statements such as those made by Gilligan (1981) about women's more relational approach to ethical decision making might have been derided as representing sexist stereotypes about women's "tenderheartedness," such assertions, when framed as evidence of women's uniqueness and value, seem to have the effect of being a corrective. They are stereotype-like statements that feel good and seem to praise or valorize feelings and experiences shared by many women from certain groups in the culture, appearing to turn patriarchal values on their heads.

What is problematic about such essentialist constructions of gender, whatever their seductive appeal, is that they minimize alternative explanations of the source of the behaviors being observed and potentially ignore the undesirable meanings given to such explanations by upholders of the status quo. This critique of essentialism can most frequently be found among feminist social constructivists, who argue that reality exists only as it is constructed by and among human beings, within the social discourse that takes place on a topic, both formally and informally. For example, the psychoanalytic construction of reality, as described earlier, posits the presence of certain intrapsychic structures as real. An overtly racist social discourse constructs a reality in which people of color are less than human. The flap over the meaning of "family" during the 1992 U.S. Presidential race is an excellent example; the Republican party attempted to socially construct "family" in one manner and to control the discourse by excluding minority viewpoints from their platform committee, while the Democratic party attempted to socially construct "family" in a far different way. Neither was correct or incorrect, a social constructivist would argue; instead, they reflected different social discourses which were jockeying for dominance. Interestingly, the Republican party has taken the research of the different-voice writers as evidence for gendered separate spheres, an illustration of how context lends meanings to information.

As social constructivists within feminist psychology such as Rachel Hare-Mustin and Jeanne Marecek (1990), Michelle Fine (1992), and Rhoda Unger (1989, 1990) have variously noted, gender as a stimulus variable and gender as an experience of identity are both fraught with excess meaning regarding power, status in certain kinds of hierarchy, and inter- and intra-personal expectations. Fine has been especially pointed in her teasing out ("unbraiding," to use her term) of issues of race, class, sexual orientation, and disability from the body of phenomena that have been assumed to be gender-linked. Such postmodern feminist theory makes it impossible not to see that gender does not have unitary meaning and that a poor white able-bodied woman will construct gender and its meanings differently for herself than a middle-class Hispanic woman with a disability or a working-class heterosexual African-American man. Unger (1989) has conducted research indicating that if the power positions in a hierarchy are scrambled out of their usual gender linkages in dominant culture (for example, male = dominant, female = submissive), then the nondominant people in an exchange will exhibit behaviors similar to those found in the women in the work of Gilligan and other "woman's voice" scholars.

What does this all mean for feminist therapy theory? I would like to suggest that this essentialist-constructivist tension is an important part of the creation of our theories of feminist therapy that illuminates the applications of radical feminist political insights to psychological questions. We cannot readily incorporate essentialist assumptions, even though they appear to be close to the data of clinical experience, because they often depart from that experience when the women or men in question are not white, or not middle-class, or not heterosexual. They reflect clinical experi-ence as narrowly defined, derived from the lives of the people who have done the most feminist therapy practice: mostly white, mostly currently middle-class, and mostly post–baby boom women. While the personal is theoretical, is is also limited in scope and therefore in epistemological use-fulness.

The theories of feminist therapy proposed in this book thus reflect this dynamic tension and this careful awareness of the ways in which the meanings of gender can be overtaken and used oppressively in dominant culture. On the one hand, it is important to know and understand how women, in all their diversity, have lived their lives and to see those lived experiences as of value, not as lesser lives. It is necessary to look to those lives for sources of information about new ways of making sense of what happens in therapy for all participants in the exchange. On the other hand, it is critical that feminist therapists not assume the essentially gendered nature of phenomena that seem to be gender-linked but rather explore the potential plasticity and flexibility of these ways of being and examine the potential danger in assuming that such characteristics are core to one's sense of self because of their presumed gender-linkage. This willingness to continually question the meanings given to dimensions that have charac-terized oppressive norms and institutions remains central to a theory of feminist therapy.

CHAPTER 3

Theorizing from Diversity

But I who am bound by my mirror
as well as my bed
see cause in color
as well as sex.

and sit here wondering
which me will survive
all these liberations.

Audre Lorde,
"Who Said It Was Simple"

FEMINIST THERAPY cannot arise from a theory that would require someone to choose which aspect of her identity is the one to be liberated while others lie silenced, unattended to, or rendered marginal. While I refer throughout this book to the necessity of integrating multicultural perspectives into feminist analysis, it is a topic sufficiently important to merit separate consideration in its own chapter.

While any feminist theory should reflect all forms of human diversity, this standard has rarely been met. White writers on feminist therapy have too often given only lip-service to the importance of diverse and complex visions of human behavior. They have tended to develop theories by and about women of European heritage and then simply comment in passing that what they have said probably applies to people from other oppressed groups as well. At most they may give a pro forma acknowledgment to the importance of multicultural analysis, without going into the details of what such analysis means for theory building in feminist therapy.

Class has also been neglected in feminist therapy literature. A generic norm of middle-class status has prevailed, falling in with the common notion of the United States as a "classless society." Celia Kitzinger and Rachel Perkins (1993) comment that few feminist therapists seem to be describing the lives of women who live on the streets, or struggle to make a living in alienating jobs, when speaking and writing about our clients. Patricia Faunce (1990) has been one of very few U.S. feminist therapists to raise questions regarding therapy with women in poverty, specifically whether the usual rules and boundaries of therapy operate to oppress poor women further. The scholarship of feminist psychology has been equally exclusionary; many of the research participants in the studies reported in feminist psychology journals are university students and more likely to come from middle-class rather than working-class or poor backgrounds. Frequently, the assumption is made that paying attention to issues of racial diversity will cover matters related to class as well, as though the two variables were isomorphic. Such an assumption perpetuates dominant cultural stereotypes equating middle-class status with white people and poverty with people of color in the invisible caste system of Western patriarchies, in which people of color are assumed to be poor when not dressed in expensive business suits, and viewed suspiciously as impostors when they are so garbed.

It has been a struggle for white and/or middle-class feminist therapists like me to acknowledge that issues of culture (broadly defined here as those of race, class, ethnicity, linguistic affiliation, age, disability, sexual orientation, spiritual affiliation, and appearance) cannot be of lesser importance in a feminist analysis than gender and that if our theories are to advance social change and undermine patriarchy we must include all categories in our analysis. The artificial separation of analyses of linked oppressions is itself an artifact of patriarchal structures that promote disconnections and silences. As Gerda Lerner (1993) has pointed out, the subjugation of women by men in patriarchy became the historical model for forms of oppression and subjugation based upon race, class, and other forms of status. People of color, working-class people, and so on are thus socially constructed in the same position as women in patriarchal cultures: as the "other," as property, and as lacking voice or agency. Our various forms of oppression are linked at the root, yet they have played out in diverse and multifaceted manners over time that now require independent attention before they are reintegrated in a web of feminist therapy theory. Reconnection of these forms of oppression also works to undermine separations and dichotomies enforced by patriarchal frameworks in which a perceived scarcity of resources leads members of one oppressed group to identify other oppressed groups as their competitors rather than as their allies.

This importance of integrating analyses of oppression other than those located in gender was not central to early second-wave feminists. At the inception of the U.S. women's movement of the 1960s and 1970s, many white middle-class women such as I erroneously assumed that because gender was the most salient variable for us, it would be similarly salient for women of color, for poor women, for disabled women, and so on. Our collusion in white racism, classism, and other forms of oppression was difficult to see; with our new feminist awareness, we were accustomed to defining ourselves as the oppressed, not the oppressors, and to seeing these categories as dichotomous and discontinuous; we were thus reflecting the dualistic cognition of the very patriarchal systems we were striving to change.

One result of this dynamic was that for much of the first twenty years of feminist therapy the contributions of therapists and theorists of color, working-class and poor therapists, and other thinkers from marginalized groups were frequently absent. Lesbians have been the only marginalized group consistently well represented in the feminist therapy literature, probably because so many feminist therapists were lesbian or worked with lesbians in their practice; and even their writings have primarily addressed the lives of white, middle-class lesbians. Such materials that did focus on multiply oppressed people were often designated as of "special interest" only to therapists working with ethnic minority or other "special" populations, a form of conceptual ghettoization no less exclusionary than actual omission. It was not unusual to hear self-defined feminist therapists declare that they did not need to know about the lives of culturally diverse people because all their clients came from the dominant mainstream.

Moreover, very little information was generated about what feminist therapy might look like when done with multiply oppressed people. It was not that such work was not being done but that it was frequently either identified as "not feminist therapy" or faced obstacles in being communicated to broad audiences. An excellent example of this exclusion can be seen in the development of the *Handbook of Feminist Therapy,* one of the important volumes in the feminist therapy literature. This book, published in 1985 from papers generated at a conference for advanced feminist therapists held in 1982, exemplified the obstacles to the inclusion of diverse knowledge in the emerging canon of feminist therapy. All of the women invited to this conference, and thus all the potential authors, were white, and most were at least currently middle-class. The very setting in which the conference was held, a fancy hotel in a fancy ski resort, acted as a defining variable, subtly determining who would be able to afford to appear or who would feel comfortable enough in that setting to want to attend. Conference organizers today would no longer be unaware of such factors, but in 1982 such issues were not yet central and automatically attended to. Thus, in the image of feminist therapy emerging from this book, culturally diverse people, particularly those of color and those not middle-class or able-bodied, were invisible.

It has mostly been since the late 1980s that we have seen active outreach on the part of dominant-culture feminist therapists seeking to remedy the prior state of affairs by defining feminist therapy as embracing work by and with culturally diverse people. Much of this activity has occurred in response to challenges from feminist therapists from marginalized groups who have demanded that feminist therapy theory and practice live up to its own standards of anti-oppressiveness and inclusion (Kanuha, 1990b) This was not an easy struggle, nor is it anywhere close to over.

But one fairly immediate result of this outreach has been an explosion of new ideas and perspectives that immensely strengthen the feminist project of social change by deriving authoritative data and epistemological authority from the experiences of cultures with little or no investment in the upholding of mainstream society, largely because these groups have been so excluded from that setting that the status quo benefits them little. In addition, international feminist therapy perspectives that expand the North American version of reality have become visible to feminist therapists in the United States. From these diverse sources it is possible to fashion a feminist therapy theory that is rich and complex in its possibilities and that allows for more meaningful and powerful analysis of the distress observed by feminist therapists in their work.

Aside from political considerations, one might ask why it is essential from a feminist perspective to integrate multicultural knowledge and epistemologies into our theorizing. This question can be answered in several ways that have to do with the philosophical integrity of a feminist theory, the potential losses inherent in a monocultural theoretical perspective, and the array of possible visions of normative human behavior that can be gained only by peering through multiple lenses. In addition there are the intangible but enlightening impacts on the therapist of committing to a multicultural perspective and on clients of being introduced to a multilayered view of reality. Let us explore each of these answers more fully.

The Philosophical Integrity of
Theory in Feminist Therapy

A feminist theory of therapy must, to maintain integrity, be based on a model of antidomination and diversity. This is, the theory must be constructed of elements that challenge hierarchies of domination and encourage the upsetting of such hierarchies within persons, relationships, and societies. Knowledge based solely on data from dominant groups and research that asks questions assuming the correctness of a dominant norm do not constitute this sort of challenge. Even the most thoroughly worked out feminist theory of white women's growth and development thus fails to meet all the criteria of a feminist theory because the dominant racial norm continues unchallenged and embedded within it. Feminist theory cannot afford to be any less critical of its own scholarship than of that developed by white men.

This vision of philosophical integrity Val Kanuha (1990b) has titled "an integrated analysis of oppression," by which she means an analysis that transcends patriarchal divisions between oppressed groups but at the same time honors the different experiences of oppression of the various groups. Such an integrated feminist theory would portray the complex manners in which people can both oppress and be oppressed and analyze the interactive natures of dominance and oppression within one individual as well as in a particular social or cultural context. By so doing, it would generate a fuller comprehension of domination and submission as power dynamics informing both the etiology of distress and the necessary components of a healing process.

The importance of this type of analysis can be seen with a client whose identity is shaped by both dominant and oppressed group memberships. If only the dominance or only the oppression is addressed, any theory of the person's development, any understanding of the distress or model for intervening in that distress, would be incomplete. Yet such an incomplete image emerges if gender is the sole dimension on which dominance and oppression are measured. Take the example of a white, never-married, forty-year-old, able-bodied, heterosexual woman of working-class origin, who has been able, through talent, hard work, and careful financial management, to achieve a professional training that has placed her in an upper-middle-class income bracket. This woman, whom we'll call Steffi, came into therapy with me feeling confused, depressed, and anxious most of the time. She ate chocolate compulsively, exercised so hard that she suffered from tendonitis and stress fractures, and worked twelve- and fourteen-hour days at her job. She described herself as unable to understand why she was so unhappy and why she felt so out of place among her co-workers and other members of her profession.

If gender were the only factor examined here, a feminist therapist could not help Steffi untangle the combination of oppressed- and dominant-group memberships contributing to her conflict and confusion. As a white person with a professional degree and an upper-middle-class income, Steffi saw herself as a member of the "in" group. Yet her sense of self, hovering not far below this conscious identification with the dominant, was as a child who had gone hungry and worn dresses made from flour sacks, who now always wondered whether her designer suits fit right or looked as wrong as had the flour sacks of her younger years. Her income felt "unreal" to her, to use her terminology, because she did nothing tangible to create it; as a consequence, she now spent almost every penny that she made and then blamed herself for poor management of her funds. She felt disconnected from and disloyal to her family of origin, who in turn communicated to her that going to college and professional school had made her no longer "one of us." As a woman who had focused on her career, she had rarely had the time to pursue intimate relationships; even early in therapy, she could identify the ways in which she was often penalized for being a successful woman in a traditionally male profession, by not being perceived as sexual or attractive by her male peers. Yet she attributed her single state to unattractiveness and pursued her compulsive exercise with the goal of crafting the perfect, thus attractive, body. Her capacity to see her own power and beauty was obscured by her pain.

Multicultural feminist analysis of Steffi's situation allowed us to attend to the contradictions in and meanings of her dominant-group status (white, professionally educated, high income) and her nondominant status (growing up poor, never married, and female), as they interacted, both in her internal world and her external contexts. An integrated analysis of both external and internalized oppression and domination was far more clarifying for this woman in her therapy process than would have been a sole focus on gender as an explanatory factor. While gender is and was an important variable in explaining Steffi's distress, taken alone it misses other aspects of her distress and struggle. As her therapy progressed, in fact, her "hidden" class status as a working-class person "disguised as an MBA" emerged as the most salient issue in her work, the theme around which issues of gender, single status, and attractiveness were wound. While gender was an important locus of experience and oppression for her, it was not the place from which her story arose.

This integrated, multicultural perspective moves our understanding of oppression and domination beyond dichotomies toward a more accurate and nuanced representation of how these dynamics are experienced in life by people who rarely, if ever, belong entirely to groups that occupy the role of most powerful or oppressor. Even when the person in question appears to have *only* dominant group memberships, a multicultural analysis leads us to inquire as to the various weights given in that person's identity to each component of dominance and thus the differing meanings, for the purpose of diagnosis and therapy, of being white, or male, or heterosexual, or able-bodied in a client's overall personal narrative. The answer in turn may provide therapist and client with strategies for the subversion of patriarchy within that might not be present were gender alone to be analyzed. People do not enter therapy because they are completely satisfied with their lives; locating the ambivalence about aspects of one's dominance may provide necessary clues to the nature of distress, clues that may be more evident when the story is examined from many different positions on the matrix of power, dominance, and submission.

What Is Lost in a Monocultural Perspective

Even if a feminist therapy theory were not attempting to meet its own ideals, our models would suffer immeasurable losses in explanatory power and transformational usefulness if they were limited to a monocultural perspective. One major loss would be in opportunities for learning about both dominant groups and oppressed groups from sources that are unavailable in dominant culture. This kind of information is commonly trivialized as "folk wisdom" and not admitted as a scholarly or authoritative source in the mental health disciplines, yet it can be central to the paradigm-shaking needed in feminist therapy theorizing.

People from marginalized and oppressed groups often know a great deal about the dominant culture. This sort of biculturalism is a necessary survival skill. The outsiders, the "others," fulfill important roles in the lives of those on the inside—as their spouses, house cleaners and child care providers, cooks and drivers, teachers, support staff, customers—even when dominant-group members have used their power to create enclaves separate from others, such as in all-male or all-white clubs and housing developments with restrictive covenants, and various other apartheid-like systems, nondominant-group-people must often interact with the dominant in order to survive economically and have access to financial resources controlled by the dominant group. When separatism does emerge among nondominant-group members, it is frequently attacked by the dominant group as an expression of "hate" (such as white responses to the Black Power movement, or male responses to feminism and the notion of woman-only spaces) and rarely has the chance to flourish uninterrupted by dominant group intrusions. These interactions with the dominant group are powerfully instructive for nondominant-group people, revealing information that the dominant group has little idea that it is releasing. Sometimes, as bell hooks has noted (1989), the oppositional eye with which the dominant group is observed will note behaviors and ways of being that are invisible to the dominants themselves because they are so thoroughly embedded and taken for granted. Stories told by African-American household workers about the strange habits of white folk; women's observations of men's apparently congenital incapacities to ask directions, apologize when in error, or put the toilet seat down; the notion of "temporarily able-bodied" that expresses the knowledge of people of disability regarding the precariousness of that dominant group membership—all this information about the normative development and functioning of the dominant group constitutes a valuable epistemological resource from a feminist perspective.

In some highly oppressive situations, marginalized and oppressed people must learn about the dominant group for the sake of safety and survival. Such observations are then not only especially acute but particularly subversive, since they support forms of survival forbidden by an oppressor. The dominant group becomes the sea in which the oppressed must learn to swim and therefore must observe the characteristics of tide, waves, and currents. These lessons in survival are often passed down through generations, the observations becoming refined and clarified over time. Beverly Greene's work on the legacy of African-American mothers to their daughters (1990) highlights this sort of lesson-passing process in an oppressed group that in turn more fully illuminates characteristics of the dominant group. Greene notes how African-American children must be taught about white culture and its norms in order to survive and thrive in a white-dominated and defined society without being fatally wounded by that dominant culture. African-American parents teach their children how to read subtle signs of racism, how to prepare for the almost inevitable hassle from police without responding with an anger that could get them killed. Such survival knowledge contains snapshots of white America that cannot be taken with the white lens.

Consequently, theories and observations about the dominant group from the perspective of those on its margins will contain fresh and sometimes startling insights about the dominant group itself and about human behavior in general in the dominance-submission hierarchies that are characteristic of patriarchal relationships. These observations, when taken as important sources of data rather than being dismissed as "anecdotal," "intuitive," or "paranoid," help the feminist therapist undermine the assumption that "if you're white, you're right"; they remove from the center taken-for-granted notions about the value of certain ways of being and knowing by clarifying the interpersonal and intrapersonal consequences of participation in patriarchies as the dominant and oppressor. Rather than identifying only the scars of oppression as "pathology" or distress, such multiculturally based knowledge can also identify with striking accuracy what is wrong and malfunctioning in otherwise accepted dominant behavioral norms and define them as less than optimal, even diagnosable, forms of behavior.

As I write this at 35,000 feet (airplanes being a preferred place for composing revolutionary notions because no one can call me on the phone or seduce me away from my computer with interesting company), I am struck by some of the ironies contained in the juxtaposition of my last paragraph with my current physical surroundings. Because I was respectful and friendly to the harried young woman at the ticket counter this morning (a stance I take consciously no matter how harried I am, because of my awareness, as a feminist, of the oppressed position of workers like her in her industry), she made a decision to give me a free upgrade to first class, commenting to me that most of her frequent fliers (men) are "so rude and in a hurry, they have no idea that if they were as nice to me as you were that they could get something they wanted." Consequently, I sit here surrounded by white men in business suits (who presumably did not get these spacious seats for the price of a supersaver ticket), for whom one of the perks of flying up front is the unlimited free alcohol. With my oppositional eye, I can observe how my seatmates disadvantage themselves by their participation in white male behavioral norms of ordering around the clerk at the counter (so that they must pay for their seats) and drinking large amounts of a substance made more toxic by our altitude (so that they endanger more brain and liver cells).

The vision from the margins also allows for the generation of paradigms for "normal" that are inherently challenging to patriarchal values. For instance, I have mused about what might happen if therapists treating intimate pairs took lesbian couples as normative (Brown, 1989a, 1992c). This is not idle speculation. Rather, it is asking what our models of a well-functioning intimate pair would look like if both partners in the paradigmatic couple were relatively equal in power, well-skilled in the creation and maintenance of emotional intimacy, comfortable with flexible ego boundaries, and trained to see such tasks as cleaning the house as their own responsibility rather than someone else's job that they volunteered to "help out" with. In such a new version, the normative pair would also have had the advantage of observing the problems of the dominant norm at close ranges, since lesbians are almost always raised by heterosexual people and have heterosexual people as family and friends; they may have even made a few stabs at membership in a heterosexual couple themselves.

The modal lesbian couple would therefore have had the opportunity to learn what does not work in the typical heterosexual couple dynamic and to make choices to do otherwise. Observing heterosexual couples from the perspective of a lesbian relationship generates a new view of "normal" in adult intimate pair bonds, because the problems that are taken for granted as the price of heterosexuality suddenly come into sharp focus and can finally become the targets of intervention rather than being invisible to the therapist. As Deborah Luepnitz (1988) has noted, in the "healthy" paradigmatic families of the family therapy literature, the women are often depressed and sexually dysfunctional, a norm that has been unquestioned in that field for several decades. A thoroughly multicultural feminist analysis would extend the questions of a normative paradigm beyond gender, as well, and construct multiple possible models of the well-functioning couple deriving from many variations on that theme that emerge in various cultural contexts.

Similar questions about what is normal have come from Afrocentric models of healthy family structures (Greene, 1990, 1992). The family in traditional family therapy, for example, is a nuclear family in which there are two parents (of different sexes, of course), in which lines are clearly drawn across gender and generation for the apportionment of tasks and the distribution of power, and in which an important task of the family is to create separation in the children as they grow, so that they leave the family of origin and create their own encapsulated family units. In this framework, a common African-American family pattern in which the primary adults in the household are several generations of adult women, often a grandmother and aunts as well as a mother, with men either temporary or absent, is frequently pathologized and often blamed by dominant culture theorists for many of the social problems in African-American communities.

Yet as the African-American feminist therapist Beverly Greene has noted, such family configurations provide a strength in the face of oppression and a sense of safety and nurturance for their members that is often absent in standard-issue families. As Greene has pointed out, such family structures do a potent job of inoculating their members against the toxins of racism and often offer a constant and relatively unconditional source of love and support, which white culture too often translates as "lack of discipline." Because of the heritage of slavery in which African-American families were destroyed, disrespected, and ignored, present-day African-American culture places a higher value on maintaining family connections than do many Euro-American cultures. The discipline required to raise and nurture a family in the social and political context of both present-day and historical racism, and to maintain connections even in the face of powerful assaults on the value of relatedness, emerges in forms not necessarily visible through dominant-cultural lenses. This example illustrates the manner in which multicultural views of the family raise questions about healthy family function that are impossible from a monocultural stand-point. Such images are lost when monocultural knowledge claims form the sole or primary basis for theorizing.

Monoculturally based theories also have a disturbing tendency to drift away from what Lerman (1986) has called the "data of experience." The epistemologies of monocultural theories tend to privilege data that is theo-retical and distanced from its sources or denies validity to the experiences of the oppressed. Sometimes data that arises from "unofficial" sources is lost, and the theories developed are inaccurate because their assumptions are incomplete. Excellent examples of inaccuracy resulting from monocul-tural exclusionary bias can be found in the oral heritage literature in which the lives of marginalized women are recorded in their own voices. This material does not usually find its way into the training experiences of ther-apists. Kennedy and Davis (1993), in their study of a working-class lesbian bar community, noted that their informants' stories about the place of sex-uality in their lives and those of other lesbians in the 1940s, 1950s, and 1960s almost entirely undermine the assertions regarding butch-femme roles and the nature of lesbian couple relationships that were made by middle-class lesbian writers early in the feminist movement about the silencing of lesbians' sexual discourse. Kennedy and Davis commented specifically on how classism functioned here to exclude knowledge, with the result that much writing and theorizing on lesbian sexuality is inher-ently inaccurate. Multicultural foundations for knowledge include a num-ber of valued data sources; first-person accounts, myth and folklore, and observations of the group from other-than-psychological frameworks all contribute to a multicultural way of knowing. These sources of data draw theory closer to lived experiences and bring theorizing in feminist therapy closer to the ideals guiding its development.

The Riches of a Multicultural Vision

This alienated knowing of the marginalized other is only one sort of important learning available to feminist therapy theory from a multicul-tural knowledge base. There are also important insights available about marginalized group members themselves which emerge from within rather than being imposed from without by a critical dominant eye. This diverse vision of human experience, when regarded as central to our ways of knowing, permits feminist therapists to conceptualize their clients and their work with them in ways that respect this variety of lived realities. If a theory of human behavior and transformation is to advance social change, such an inclusive and completely informed image of humanity is necessary for envisioning the range of possible outcomes of the transformative process.

A good example of this enrichment of the discourse comes from attempts to study the mental health consequences of violence against women at home and in the workplace. In a recent report by a task force of the American Psychological Association convened to study male violence against women (Goodman, Koss, & Russo, 1993), the report's authors frequently referred to the difficulties inherent in generalizing findings from the available data because the formal data base contained so little information regarding the problems of male violence against North American ethnic minority women, immigrant women, lesbians, women with physical and mental disabilities, and aging women, from both within and outside of their own reference groups. In those instances where information was available about these "nongeneric" women, however, the data generated served the functions of clarifying feminist analysis, extending the meaning of the phenomena being studied and consequently increasing the ultimate usefulness and value of the material under consideration.

One prominent effect of the inclusion of a multicultural data base was that it provided a picture of the impact and meaning of a particular experience when filtered through the lens of marginalized group status. For example, the harmful potential of sexual harassment in the workplace can be seen more sharply when we observe its consequences on women whose status and role are already more precarious because they are not white, or heterosexual, or able-bodied. The manner in which a multiply stigmatized status can be used as an aspect of sexual harassment, for instance, helps to clarify that such behavior is about power and dominance, with sexuality serving as a convenient locus of oppression. The experiences of women who are accused of being lesbian when they resist sexual advances and then are punished for being perceived as lesbian in a homophobic work setting (the U.S. military providing the most ready example of this phenomenon) demonstrate the manner in which workplace violence against women is, although sexually framed, a matter of imposing patriarchal standards of gender dominance. Viewing the phenomenon multiculturally sharpens the focus on the underlying issue of power.

A second effect of the inclusion of data on violence against women from nondominant groups was that it illuminated some aspects of the experience of being a woman target of male violence that might not otherwise have been as clear or visible. These data particularly highlighted the potential economic impacts, as well as the potential for secondary victimization through the effects on the target women's social networks, which were often more carefully studied in the case of nondominant group women. Finally, by allowing for the specific inclusion of information on the experiences of a more diverse population, it created the potential for designing and delivering services better adapted to the needs of women whose experiences include living outside the North American mainstream as well as being targets of male violence at home or on the job.

The knowledge arising from the experiences of feminist therapists from groups on the margins is also an important part of the multicultural vision in feminist therapy theory. Our best sources are the writings of feminist therapists of color. Whether working with other women of color (Boyd, 1990; Espin, 1987) or with white women, as teachers and trainers or in any of the other roles in which feminist therapists find ourselves, feminist therapists of color are in a unique position where varieties of status, power, privilege, and oppression overlap and blend. What the feminist therapist of color hears in her work is different from what the white feminist therapist hears, no matter who she is working with. Other women of color may be more honest about certain realities, white women may reveal, either intentionally or otherwise, more about the meaning that race holds for them both in their interactions with people of color and among themselves; male clients, both white and of color, will also respond in ways that cannot be present when the therapist is white because of the differences in what a white woman and a woman of color symbolize. The data of experience deriving from the lives and knowledge of feminist therapists of color add great richness when they are identified as being of central importance.

The Multicultural Feminist Therapist

When a feminist therapist assumes a multicultural and antidominant perspective for her theory and practice, rather than one that attends only to gender, profound transformations occur in her work. My own experience with this dynamic has been very persuasive to me. When I first began to become conscious of the monoculturalism of my work as a feminist therapist during the early 1980s, my initial responses were a combination of defensiveness and curiosity. I was not seeing any women of color in my practice at that time, and I did not question why that was the case. I was not paying attention to class issues; I assumed that as a Jew and a lesbian I was sufficiently conversant with matters of oppression and exclusion to extrapolate if the need arose for me to do so. I assumed that as long as I paid attention to gender, I was grasping the real and most essential roots of oppression in anyone's lives. I was moderately comfortable making generalizations about women as if they were a homogeneous group. In that regard, I do not think that I was very different from many other feminist therapists who came into the field in the 1970s and early 1980s.

Yet I was also guided, as I think many therapists are, by an ethic of competency, of wanting to do as well as I could so as to do the most good with the people I worked with. Thus I understood intellectually that were I to have a client from a cultural group different from the ones I knew well, I would have to seek information and consultation. Then in early 1983, a woman who had been sexually abused by a previous therapist was referred to me by her attorney. The catch was, she was American Indian; the therapist had been an employee of the Indian Health Service. She would be suing the federal government, his ultimate employer.

At this juncture, I knew that I had better get some consultation about working with American Indian clients. So I went out and bought books, paid for the time and wisdom of a Native American therapist who was knowledgeable about her community, and began to discover how the simple facts of my client's case held layers of meaning that I could never have foreseen. Grasping at a more than intellectual level the symbolic meaning of the federal government and the IHS in the lives of American Indian people and its actual and daily place in their lives was as or more important to my capacity to relate to this client than was any of my knowledge about therapy abuse, adult survivors, or single parents. Although I had always been willing to entertain the theoretical notion that different things held different meanings depending on the context, I had never been confronted as I was at that moment with so clear a demonstration of what happened when you operationalized that theory. For this woman to be seeking justice from the agents of genocide against her people (the U.S. government) was something beyond the usual therapy abuse case.

Around this time, I also began to notice that almost all the graduate students who requested me as a supervisor were women of color. I had never been particularly conscious of the fact, but now I began to ask myself what it meant, and even more, what the implications were that I, a white supervisor, was working with student therapists who were women of color and who were, in turn, usually treating clients of color. I knew that the presence of a supervisor changed the therapeutic dyad, but I started to conjecture about what was happening when a white woman was listening in on an intimate conversation between two people of color. I also noticed that I, a white lesbian Jew, was supervising heterosexual women of color who had been raised Christian, even if they were no longer practicing the dominant religion. So I began to think that maybe this was more complex than it had appeared even at first; I started to look at how I was responding to being in a position of power (as both supervisor and white person) in relation to people who had a number of dominant group memberships in relation to me. I became aware of the complexity of the matrix of oppression and domination, and the factors that could render small the meanings of certain dominant group memberships when a special situation, such as that of supervisor and student, was superimposed on the preexisting social and political picture.

Thus, my first step was to move from a narrow focus on gender to a theoretical acceptance of the importance of multiculturalism and then to personal and experiential encounters with the meanings of culture in my work. The immediate effect was to increase my cultural literacy. I took workshops on working with diverse populations, got further consultations from therapists who had expertise, and read everything I could get my hands on. I thought at greater length and in greater depth about factors influencing both the lives of the students and clients I worked with and my own life, factors that went beyond gender. I began to become aware of how sharing XX chromosome status could mean very little else by way of similarity. My understanding of the concept of "woman" became more varied and multifaceted. It in turn influenced my thinking and theorizing about feminist therapy, as I began to integrate notions of cultural difference into my work in a more intentional and thoughtful manner.

In 1986, at a feminist therapy conference, I listened to a presentation by a colleague, Anne Ganley, about her work in antiracism. She described how she had trod a path very similar to my own and then moved yet another step, to the realization that simply having information about the lives of different people was not sufficient for a feminist perspective. Knowing more about people of color, for instance, did nothing to undermine patriarchy. In fact, it potentially upheld it by constructing me, a white woman, as even more of an expert than I already was perceived to be by simple virtue of my race; now, I was a white woman who knew about American Indians, for example.

My consultant on that matter, Vickie Sears, had commented to me how many of the white women she had trained went on to perceive themselves, and be sought out by other colleagues, as experts on this topic. Her comments made new sense to me in the light of Anne Ganley's presentation. As an American Indian woman, Vickie was devalued as a source of information if the same data appeared to be available from a white source. Simple cultural literacy could be the little knowledge making me dangerous to the people from and about whom that knowledge was gleaned, if my possession of that knowledge transformed me, in the eyes of the dominant culture, into someone more expert on the lives of the oppressed than they were themselves. If I did not reject the privileges accorded to me by virtue of my race and class, I would both have these privileges, and act them out, dominating others in the process.

What Ganley described as the essential next step for herself was to become antiracist. She proposed that for white women, the choice to be complicit with white dominance was always present; they were continually benefitting from the privileges accorded them by their skin, whether they sought them out or not. Thus, if they wished to operate from a feminist principle of subversion of a patriarchal structure of dominance, they had to choose to be antiracist; in this struggle for social change, there could be no stance of neutrality. "Nonracism" was nonexistent, since the term suggests a stance of neutrality and disconnection from the social and political context that is incompatible with feminist methodology and epistemology.

This presentation opened up entire new vistas for me, both because I found Ganley's arguments convincing and inspiring and because, as I began to examine the implications of taking an antiracist stance for my work and life, I began to find how many new corridors of self-examination were opened for me. I began to see the work of feminist therapy in new ways as well; if everything I did was with a goal of undermining patriarchy, how could I be an ally to people whom I implicitly oppressed within patriarchy?

The question of alliance is an especially important and thorny one for feminist therapists, because their work almost inevitably replicates the dominance-submission hierarchy of patriarchal cultures through the power of their role. Understanding how I as a white woman could be an ally to women of color, how I as an upper-middle-class woman could be an ally to poor and working-class women, has clarified for me some of the pitfalls buried in my attempts to be, as a therapist, the ally of someone who has been wounded and is in distress. As a result of making this connection, my work in theorizing the relationship of therapist to client in feminist therapy, which I will discuss at length in the following chapter, has been more closely informed by an antidomination, culturally diverse knowledge base than previously. In turn my thinking has become more firmly linked to a feminist, political analysis and has moved away from an intrapsychic and/or individualistic perspective within that discourse.

In the past seven years, as I have gone beyond antiracism to a more global perspective of antidomination, in which I consider all the aspects of my dominant status in analyzing my behaviors and values (Brown, 1993), I have been able to observe the effects on my work from taking this antidomination perspective, which I see as inextricable from a multicultural basis for feminist therapy theory. These changes seem to have happened largely because the kind of experiences from which theory arises have become richer and more complex; what I can observe in myself and my clients is no longer so thoroughly distorted by the ways in which I participate in domination from my various privileged positions in the social and political matrix. I also find it easier to avoid theorizing a psychology of victimization, even though violence and oppression have been an aspect of many of the lives that inform my thinking. Instead, my vision has expanded to emphasize the strengths, power, and resilience that people derive from their multiplicity of social and interpersonal locations.

This perspective also helps to make me more acutely aware of my own capacity to function as a dominant-group member and an oppressor of my internalized domination (Pheterson, 1986), both in my role as a therapist and in the other layers of my relationships with clients, students, and colleagues. Since the place of power in the therapeutic relationship is of such central importance in a feminist theory of therapy, this heightened awareness of any therapist's capacity to oppress and do harm leads to more careful attention to the meanings with which my actions may be laden.

The Effects of a Multicultural
Perspective on the Client

The therapist's embrace of diverse and antidominant values will have effects on clients as well. Not all these effects will be intuitively obvious or intended. Clients need not themselves occupy nondominant status in order for these analyses to be meaningful; the stereotyped notion that one needs knowledge of cultural diversity only if one is working with a culturally diverse population reflects a narrow vision that simply affirms the patriarchal disconnections between all forms of oppression and domination. Every client benefits from theory arising from this broader and more fully realized base. Feminist therapists are beginning to see how the members of dominant groups embody reactions against the knowledge of their dominance, disowning their connection to the oppressed, and how untangling those webs of oppression and domination requires a well-thought-through political analysis of the client's distress, based on an intimate understanding of the meaning and nature of dominance and diversity.

An example of how such awareness is necessary in work with dominant-group clients can be seen in the case of a man I'll call Mark. Mark came into therapy with me complaining of a vague sense of dissatisfaction and malaise in his life. On the face of it, he was quite different from anyone else I saw in my practice. Like the friend who had referred him to me, he was a very successful attorney in a large law firm who had recently achieved the coveted status of partner. He was single, heterosexual, youthful, able-bodied, and quite well off. His politics were progressive and made him feel a little guilty about driving up to pro-choice fundraising events in his new BMW, "but not so guilty that I'm going to sell the car," as he told me in one of our first meetings. His life had almost always gone very well; he was unhappy with how unhappy he was, confused and perplexed by his failure to achieve a sense of satisfaction with what he had accomplished, and bemused to find himself in my therapy office.

As he pointed out several times over the first few sessions, had I not come highly recommended by his friend (who had, ironically, met me when he had cross-examined me as the opposing attorney in a bitter sexual-harassment lawsuit), he would not have chosen *me* (female, lesbian, dumpy and unfashionable), much less therapy in general. As he noted early on, it was not that he had anything against lesbians; some of his best friends were lesbians. But he didn't grasp how one of those people, skillful therapist or not, could help him. Yet he kept coming, even when I suggested that he might be happier with a referral to a therapist with more congenial characteristics.

These comments, coming as frequently as they did, intrigued me. Why was Mark having to make a point of my intrinsic valuelessness to him? While I found his remarks in equal parts irking and amusing, I also found telling how they focused on certain places on the dominance matrix. I began to ask myself about the relationship between his nameless unhappiness and his apparent need to underline his maleness, heterosexuality, and conventional attractiveness. While he reported that none of these factors had ever been in doubt (going so far as to bring in his pictures from junior high graduation so that I could see that he had been "a cute kid even at that geeky age"), it appeared that at some level he was aware of, and fearful about, the fate of those who did not share his privileges. This awareness seemed to go beyond the factual knowledge of societal wrongdoing that he had gleaned in the course of his forays into progressive social causes.

This conceptualization suggested to me that an exploration of the meanings of his dominant status, as well as the meanings he ascribed to members of oppressed groups, might open windows onto his vague malaise. It also suggested that my differences from him on the social matrix, juxtaposed with my apparent sense of well-being and my position of power as a therapist, were confusing to him because they undermined certain non-conscious assumptions and fears that lay at the base of his distress. I consequently invited him to explore for himself the meanings of his comments to me. Why, I wondered out loud to him, was it so important that he keep saying, in his own disguised way, "Look at how male, heterosexual, and cute I am"?

After we spent a number of sessions dealing with his feelings of guilt and apologies over what he feared was an injury to my sensibilities (which in turn provided information helpful to my own diagnostic conceptualizing about him), Mark and I settled into what became a productive exploration of his deeply felt but equally deeply disowned terror about the possible fragility of his dominant-group memberships. As we explored his fears that he might not be sufficiently masculine, heterosexual, powerful, and attractive, we uncovered his guilt and shame at the oppressive attitudes he had witnessed in his comfortable upper-middle-class family of origin, and the growing dis-ease he had experienced throughout his life that he, too, might be found wanting in some manner and therefore thrust into a position of powerlessness and harm. The only strategies he could see to secure his safety entailed the frantic embrace of the emblems of his dominance. His residual guilt at what he and others like him did to people with less privilege pushed him toward progressive politics, but they in turn twanged the strings of his inner fears, which he then attempted to push farther into the background. By the time he appeared in my office in his early thirties, he was in a state of profound distress, working furiously to ward off the thoughts that "any day now this will all fall apart and I will be nothing and no one."

This conceptualizing of Mark's distress arose from a diverse and antidominant feminist vision that challenged the assumption, embedded in mainstream cultures, that the malaise of a dominant man could have nothing to do with the oppression of other people. The oppression of others, the power of the dominant group to oppress others, and Mark's initial inability to see any strategy except to be "more dominant than thou" were facts that had to be observed before we could make sense of the unhappiness in this paragon of societal success. Therapy with Mark settled into a process in which he learned to explore and analyze the oppressive attitudes that he had internalized and that were oppressing him as well, something he had never been able to imagine possible. We considered how he might experiment with changing his strategies for coping with the notion that his value rested only in his dominant-group membership; he might, for instance, learn the people he had been afraid of somehow becoming achieved well-being and personal power. We found that his political activities had represented attempts to observe the "others" of his childhood safely; he began to consider how he might ally himself in solidarity with those oppressed groups, working in coalition as a way of more overtly risking closeness with those he had non-consciously feared and devalued. He could observe the ways used by people he might have oppressed to successfully resist him and his group, and begin to resist that dominance in himself. He could notice how care for the well-being of the group could be as much a source of enduring well-being as individualistic joy in one's own accomplishments, with the added bonus of the personal connections derived from group membership. His uneasiness began to diminish and was followed by a period of profound grief, a mourning for possibilities lost in his years of driving away any hint of vulnerability.

Mark emerged from this grieving calmer, free of his vague unhappiness, and uncertain of what he was going to do next. He decided that he did not need to stay in therapy but that he did need the support of other white, heterosexual men like himself. His encounter with me, an "other," had been the place in which he could see how his continued pursuit of privilege was at the root of his unhappiness; now he wanted to learn how to live in his skin and find daily ways to reject the notion that white and might equalled right. He found the local chapter of an antisexist men's group and, six months after our first appointment, was out the door. He dropped me a note several years later to let me know that he had begun working with other members of his men's group to raise funds for programs to prevent male violence, using his connections to his own class and profession to move the project along. He told me that he was still happier than he had been before therapy, although there were moments of sheer terror at his decision to stop running away from his humanity. Feminist therapy had been a liberating experience for Mark to no lesser a degree than it would have been for someone more obviously oppressed.

Obtaining Quality Knowledge About Human Diversity

With all this said about political and philosophical necessity and the benefits of basing feminist therapy theory on diverse and antidominant underpinnings, the question arises of how much is actually known regarding diverse human experiences. This can be a difficult question to answer, because the apparent sources of knowledge are often contaminated. Elizabeth Protacio-Marcelino (1990), a Filipina feminist psychologist, has noted that the bulk of the literature on Philippine psychology represents the observations of white male American psychologists using a Eurocentric perspective to study the norms of a varied, complex, Asian culture with a diversity of historical roots—a form of cultural imperialism. She cites a number of examples of the biases and distortions of Philippine lives contained in the standard references. For example, she recounts how North American researchers described the so-called "Filipino personality" as passive and passive-aggressive. This contrasts with the findings of Philippine psychology, which notes that there is no common cultural personality; instead, there are a variety of interpersonal stances taken in response to the dominance matrix and levels of intimacy present in any given circumstance. The behaviors observed by the North American researchers were simply those exhibited, in Philippine culture, in the presence of a nonintimate dominant.

These examples serve as a caution to the feminist therapy theorist and practitioner to consider the biases of the source more carefully than ever when searching for data on nondominant groups. Especially when the writer is a member of the dominant group, it is essential to ask some key questions: What are the writer's assumptions about norms, values, and appropriate behaviors? Are there experimenter effects? Is the researcher measuring a way of being that is usual and normative within a culture or a response to the researcher's own dominant status? Is the meaning ascribed to the behaviors centered in the culture, or does it evolve from a biased perspective? It is equally important to ask whether the observed behavior is an artifact of oppression that has over time been enshrined within a culture and to avoid basing feminist therapy theory on such possibly problematic materials.

Dominant group feminist writers have on occasion, committed errors not unlike those pointed out by Protacio-Marcelino. It is relatively more simple to call attention to oppressive practices in another's culture than to contextualize those behaviors and realize that they are *equally* problematic, but not necessarily more so. The writings of Islamic feminists, for example, challenge dominant group feminists' notions that the veil, or chador, is any more oppressive than the Western requirement that women expose their bodies.

Nor is data developed from within a culture necessarily liberating and useful to feminist therapy theory. As the African-American psychologist James Jones has noted, U.S. psychologists of color have often been so well socialized into the values of their discipline that they may lose, at least temporarily, their ability to see their own culture in a centered manner. Self-hatred, or even simply attempts to assimilate, may distort the perspectives offered by nondominant-group writers. The work of these writers must be scrutinized just as closely as that of dominant group writers to determine whether it is potentially subversive to patriarchal structures of dominance.

Much of the literature developed by feminist therapists from nondominant groups meets this criterion admirably. It avoids the endorsement of oppressive attitudes and values within a nondominant culture, illuminates the norms and aspects of that culture, and refuses to label the oppressive practices of the nondominant group worse than those of the dominant. The work of Christine Ho (1990) and Valli Kanuha (1990b) on violence in communities of color, Oliva Espin's (1987, 1993) extensive body of work on the lives of Latina lesbians, Nancy Boyd-Franklin's (1987, 1989) groundbreaking writing on family therapy with African-Americans, or the work of Espin, Esther Rothblum, and Ellen Cole (1992) on refugee women's experiences—all exemplify the sorts of data sources that can inform a diverse and antidominant feminist therapy theory. We are also beginning to see the result of collaborations between white feminist psychologists and feminist psychologists of color in the development of theory and research (Unger & Sanchez-Hucles, 1993).

Feminist therapy theory also can derive from sources not usually considered by therapy theorists. First-person and semi autobiographical accounts of lives on the margin can provide rich, detailed information about lives in a cultural context, without the lens of distress or the biases of mental health. Self-help books written by and for oppressed people offer another window; volumes like *The Black Women's Health Book* (White, 1990), *In the Company of My Sisters: Black Women and Self-Esteem* (Boyd, 1993), and *Sisters of the Yam* (hooks, 1993) provide access to implicit theories and knowledge within and between members of a marginalized group. Subversive knowledge from within dominant groups in which disloyalty to the caste provides an inside view of life at the center can also be powerfully informative to theorizing in feminist therapy. For instance, the writings of the anti-sexist activist John Stoltenberg illuminate the power of white male ideology to keep men in the United States in line and collaborating in oppression.

Diverse and antidominant perspectives will be both assumed and pointed out throughout this book. These perspectives are not yet so well integrated into the epistemologies of feminist therapy theory that it is unnecessary to underscore their importance or call attention to the manner in which this additional level of analysis enriches all aspects of feminist therapy. But the theory has reached the point where I will no longer accidentally theorize a therapy that would produce the dilemma of which Audre Lorde spoke in the poem that introduces this chapter.

CHAPTER 4

The Relationship in Feminist Therapy

NORTH AMERICAN dominant cultures treat emotional intimacy and the tasks of relationship development and maintenance in a profoundly ambivalent, often dismissive and destructive manner. The stuff of which such connections are made—time, respect for difference and uniqueness, attention, nurturance—are not highly valued by the patriarchal culture. One of the important contributions of a feminist deconstruction of value has been a valuing and privileging of the capacity to relate well and intimately to others, and the construction of this capacity as a source of strength, a style of competence, a type of agency, and a desirable and necessary outcome of adult development. While all forms of psychotherapy focus on the therapist-client relationship to some degree, the models of relating that emerge from feminist attempts at radical rearrangements of social relationships, taken together with the different meanings that feminist thought ascribes to the very processes of caring and relating, lead to a transformed discourse in a feminist theory of the therapeutic relationship.

Therapy is a relationship that is unique, powerful, and at times, seen from the outside with a sober eye, a bit strange. Imagine: You walk into a room, sit down with a person you have never known before, or knew not at all a few months ago, and tell that person your innermost pain and shame. Your pain is the reason for your meeting; otherwise, you two might never have crossed paths. This person, the therapist, becomes one of the most important people in your life. You miss her, long for her, think of her, have conversations with her in your head, write to her in your journal. You know little or nothing of her or who she is, although you search for clues endlessly and treasure each bit of real information that she has offered to you. You worry about whether she likes you, cares for you, misses you when she is on vacation, and about whether you make her too important, give her too much control. You feel angry that when you get better, you are supposed to leave, and you feel confused by this part of the relationship.

Or, as the therapist, you sit in a room where strangers come and tell you profoundly private details of their lives. You listen and try not to show how you feel or how you interpret the meanings of behaviors. You are intimate with these strangers in an odd sort of way, and yet you know and see them only in this very truncated and constricted time and place. They pay you for your time, although there is often no concrete product visible at the end of any given therapy hour. Even the hour is not an hour, lasting perhaps fifty minutes. Although you may know these people for years, your encounter is designed to end, to allow this person for whom you have come to care dearly to depart your life and no longer have need of you, even though at times you feel this as a painful disconnection and loss. How can feminists come to understand this odd relationship of frank inequalities and limited mutuality as a locus for revolutionary social change?

Therapy, this relationship that is not one, is a phenomenon of the modern age, of a time in which natural helping connections between and among people are disappearing or being threatened by the social structures of an increasingly alienated capitalist culture. Yet simultaneously, the permission to define oneself as hurting, needing, or confused and to seek help has increased in many areas of the popular culture as a "recovery" movement sweeps through the talk shows of middle America. While this expression of need is still generally defined by dominant culture as a form of weakness and pathology, therapy has increasingly become an aspect of the lives of people who a decade ago would never have imagined participation in such a process. The stereotypical "YAVIS" therapy patient—middle-class, young, and verbal—is being joined by blue-collar workingmen struggling to cope with the legacy of parental alcoholism and women in their fifties who have just begun to recall the incest of their childhood. This change in the population seeking therapy heightens the importance of understanding how social and contextual factors influence the relationship between therapist and client. While the security of clients' social situations once could be taken for granted, this is no longer the case.

The social realities affecting the dynamics of therapy have become extremely variable and unpredictable. Knowing the factors affecting the relationship in therapy is crucial, for the relationship is central. Study after study of the effectiveness of psychotherapy has yielded the same finding: when all is said and done and all variations in technique are laid aside, what counts, what makes therapy work, is the nature of the relationship between therapist and client. Thus, if feminist therapy is to lead to a subversion of patriarchal culture, it must itself contain such subversiveness toward patriarchy in the therapeutic relationship itself.

Starting with Phyllis Chesler and her analysis of the therapist as patriarch in traditional psychotherapies, feminist therapists have spoken extensively, explicitly, and forcefully about concerns regarding the relationship between therapist and client. Their observations have a particular flavor special to feminist analysis, because they have observed the relationship not only from the perspective of the therapist, which is often done in mainstream theories of psychotherapy, but also from the perspective of clients in their own voices, which have less frequently been heard in this discourse. They have identified the importance of attending both to the symbolic relationship—that which is usually referred to in the psychotherapy literature as transference and countertransference—and to the real, in-the-world-now encounter. Feminist therapy has been uniquely attuned to the manner in which the internal, symbolic components of the interaction are shaped and colored by the signifiers of gender, race, class, and culture that obtain and give actions meaning in the social world. From the start, feminist therapists have struggled to make sense of a relationship whose parameters as commonly defined appear to be poorly fitted to the goals of feminist social change.

If subversiveness is to be central to their therapeutic relationships, feminist therapists must question most of the assumptions they learned in graduate school. What are these problematic assumptions? Most of them have to do with the power relationships and hierarchical structures embedded in the models of therapy theorized by all dominant schools of psychotherapy. Even the client-centered model, which Carl Rogers intended as a strategy to increase the importance of the client's position in the transaction, still gives the authority to assign meaning to the therapist, whose task it is to "accurately symbolize" the client's utterances. Psychotherapy as currently practiced in most parts of North America is a form of relating created by white men. The "fathers" of almost every school of thought have indeed been patriarchs.

The images that these men have generated, and their theories regarding what should constitute the relationship in therapy, powerfully reflect certain experiences valued by dominant culture. In these valued relationships, one person—in this case the therapist—is designated expert and accorded greater value, power, and authority. A hierarchy of power and value is embedded in these models; much of the writing on therapy practice discusses the need for the therapist to manage and contain the client and the therapeutic process. Such a model is clearly not in line with feminist notions of equality. Yet feminist therapists, most of whom learn their professions in dominant-culture graduate, medical, and professional schools, are trained to these standards and carry them around, however uncomfortably, as a paradigm for correct psychotherapeutic practice.

These paradigms constitute the norm for the "frame" in psychotherapy, a term referring to the rules and roles governing the transaction, including such issues as the time of the therapy session, the importance of beginning and ending on time, whether first names or honorifics will be used, payment of fees, touch, therapist self-disclosure, and therapist availability between sessions, to name several topics that emerge frequently in the psychotherapy literature. As the feminist therapist Liz Margolies noted in her article on the frame in feminist therapy (1990), one of the problems for feminist therapists is that for the most part there has been no well-delineated, affirmative feminist image of the psychotherapy relationship—no feminist frame, as it were. Instead, feminist therapists have relied upon piecemeal rebellions against the ways of the fathers, rebellions that were not always well grounded in either feminist theory or clinical reality. Theorizing the nature of the relationship in feminist therapy is thus crucial to envisioning a frame.

Early Strategies: A Historical Note

Rebellion against a patriarchal frame has not been the psychotherapeutic equivalent of feminist revolution. In explicating feminist theories of the therapy relationship, it is instructive to recall what has already been tried unsuccessfully. For a short while in the beginning of feminist therapy practice, the dream was that women sitting together with women and telling one another their truths, as in a consciousness-raising group of two, would provide all of the necessary curative factors that any woman might need (Mander & Rush, 1974). But there seemed to be something about the notion of therapy that carried too much power and weight for the participants to perceive one another as equals, sisters, or peers. No one seemed to feel like "just two women." Early work then focused on strategies for addressing the power imbalance.

Some feminists in the mental health fields made attempts to get around the problem by calling therapy something else: "counseling," "facilitation," or "consultation," to name a few choices. These attempts at renaming what was done by the mental health worker and the client presumed that if the work was called by a different name it would somehow leave behind the inherent assumptions about power and authority that were embedded in the traditional frame of psychotherapy and in the minds and hearts of the "facilitator" and the client as well.

These efforts to transform the nature of the power exchange in therapy via the simple act of renaming had little success. When only the names for the roles changed, the participants tended to move insidiously into familiar positions of powerful expert and powerless help-seeker, with the power dynamics firmly in place even if their presence was denied. On more than one occasion, the pretense at equality on the part of the "consultant" led to outright abuses of clients, who were exploited to meet personal social, sexual, or financial demands of this "non-therapist" to whom they had brought their innermost fears and pains. Less scrupulous therapists used the expressed absence of a power imbalance to assert that rules protecting clients from exploitation were no longer necessary among "equals." Dressed in new clothes, the relationships in these circumstances nonetheless failed to attend consciously and intentionally to the nature of the exchange.

In many of these early, well-meant but often naive attempts, the client's perception that what was happening was simply therapy under another name was silenced. Ironically, some of these rebellions against patriarchy resulted in profound violations of feminist norms regarding knowledge claims and the empowerment of the oppressed. In the process of rebellion, an attachment to the dominant remains necessary. Consequently, the dominant theme of the therapist as most powerful person in the relationship continued to be central in the emotional subtext of these rebellion-informed experiments.

Although feminist theory in general has valued the power of naming as a means of creating new visions of reality, this strategy alone has generally proved insufficient to transform the nature of the exchange between participants in therapy or to create a workable foundation for a theory of the feminist therapy relationship. Aside from the problems inherent in a strategy of rebellion—such as the potential for reaction, which is even more harmful than the system originally rebelled against, and the risks that needless pain will be inflicted in the name of quick change—there appear to be other influences on feminist therapists that impeded initial efforts at greater therapist-client equality.

Feminist therapists live and have been raised in (or in close proximity to) a dominant culture in which there is a paucity of models of a healing encounter in which some kind of imbalance of power does not obtain. The patriarchal healer who often serves as the non-conscious paradigm of how to function as a therapist has not been scared away by words alone. When the attempt to solve the problem of power imbalance has primarily been pursued via the naming strategy, many other fundamental sources of power have been unattended to. Theorizing a feminist relationship in therapy requires going below the surface.

In addition to the dilemmas in theorizing the therapy relationship presented to feminists by the heritage of mainstream therapies, there are dilemmas presented by feminism itself. Feminist analyses regarding power, the impact of social roles in relationships, and the tyranny of "normalcy" and "adjustment" challenge a number of comfortable dominant-culture-based assumptions. Feminism asks how is it that therapists come to see themselves as expert, why they should or should not have particular types of relationships with their clients outside of the therapy session or should or should not disclose certain types of personal information, or why they should even see what they do as being different in kind and meaning from the exchanges of friendship.

Such challenges deriving from the feminist discourse disrupt the frame of therapy, shake up its contents, and underscore the differences between the culture of psychotherapy as it has been practiced in its century of existence and the culture of radical feminism central to theorizing feminist therapy. They lead back to questions addressed in chapter 2 about the potential incompatibility of feminist theory and psychotherapy practice. Feminist therapists have also had to confront the questions raised by such critics of psychotherapy as Szasz (1970, 1978) and Masson (1993), whose image of all "helping" professions as inherently oppressive and destructive to human dignity dovetails in an uncomfortably neat way with feminist criticism. In developing a theory of the relationship between therapist and client in feminist therapy, it is thus necesary to keep such troublesome questions in mind as important to our vision of that relationship as a feminist, subversive, and empowering experience.

Feminist Visions of the Symbolic Relationship

In theorizing a feminist relationship of therapist and client, it has been important to examine critically the mainstream concepts that have tended to define the nature of the non-conscious and symbolic aspects of the exchange. Although these aspects were at first difficult to embrace within a model of psychotherapy as social change, feminist therapist writings in the past decade have increasingly acknowledged the existence of that symbolic connection, existing within inner space and representing the interface of immediate experience with the past. The question then becomes, How can this experience be defined in a manner that will be subversive to patriarchy? In the mainstream therapy literature, the symbolic relationship of therapist and client is commonly described as "transference" and "countertransference." I have argued (Brown, 1984) against the use of these and other terms of mainstream therapy theory (for example, diagnostic labels) to describe what happens in feminist therapy, because I believe that they not only fail to convey the feminist meanings ascribed to a symbolic relationship but also carry the risk of transforming the therapist's perceptions to concepts less firmly rooted in feminism. (This is not to say that one cannot continue to describe what happens in nonfeminist therapy settings in such terms, however, since in those contexts the assumptions of patriarchal models for symbolic relationships will most likely be present and operative.)

For feminist therapy theory, the symbolic relationship is more than and different from transference as typically described. The therapist is not simply defined as a neutral screen upon which internal reality is projected by a client; thus, the client's end of the symbolic exchange is not simply a distortion of the therapist based upon the client's prior experiences. Nor are all passionate responses of therapist to client and client to therapist defined as necessarily derived from disrupted or disturbed elements in each person's past. Instead, the symbolic relationship in feminist therapy consists of lively and interactive responses to the changing meanings of the various factors that carry symbolic significance to either participant in the therapeutic encounter. While individual past experiences lend significance to the relationship in feminist therapy, the present and its signifiers are considered equally important in shaping and forming the symbolic layers of the interaction. In addition, the participants' collective pasts and their positions as members of communities that may have met, touched, and even clashed apart from their individual experiences will inform how they symbolically experience one another. For example, to an African-American client, the meaning of a Caucasian therapist will be freighted with the heritage of white racism. As the social and political context in which the therapeutic relationship occurs transforms in response to daily events, so too does any symbolic interaction in that therapy.

Because feminist therapy *is* feminist, understanding the meaning of gender in the therapy relationship is essential to an understanding of the symbolic relationship, joined in significance in the analysis that I am proposing by a number of other value-laden human characteristics, such as race, class, culture, sexual orientation, age, and disability. All of these function both interactively with gender and autonomously as their own powerful sources of meaning, as emotionally important social constructs and aspects of personal identity. The theoretical questions raised by these factors in the therapy relationship concern the overlapping and recursive ways in which these various factors and their signifiers can lend special meaning to each person in the interaction, with profound effects on how power is experienced and shared in the therapeutic context.

In order to do justice to their meanings in the therapy relationship, the feminist therapist must have carefully analyzed how she herself understands each of these factors. This can be a more challenging task than it would seem at first glance. Dominant culture describes gender, race, and other phenomena as essential and unchanging, and thus presumably easy to make sense of, but feminist political theory has persistently pointed to the degree to which all such factors are socially constructed and consequently hold meanings that require inquiry and disruption—"unpacking," as the feminist social psychologist Michele Fine (1992) calls it, the assumptions about each of these categories in general and the therapist's own use of these definitions in specific.

Thus, feminist therapists must question what they mean by "male" and "female," what beliefs and stereotypes they hold about what is "normal," "natural," and "to be expected." They must inquire how, from whom, and in what context they learned certain supposedly eternal verities; to what degree was this context heavily invested in maintaining a sexist, racist, classist, heterosexist status quo? For example, what I, as a white woman in a white racist society, have learned about race and people of color is likely to be powerfully and often non-consciously interwoven with the requirement to maintain white dominance; the sources upon which my knowledge claims are based are themselves biased and incomplete, and cannot be left to stand alone as my sole resources for understanding the meaning of my whiteness. As a feminist therapist, I must examine the heritage of my personal symbology in order to comprehend the potential of my relationships with clients to subvert a dominant status quo or to adjust to it.

Feminist therapists must also inquire into the requirements—imposed by Western intellectual models and oppressive norms—that people's identities be fixed, dichotomous, and nonambiguous. What meanings are ascribed to people whose race, class, sexual orientation, or other status is unclear, mixed, or changeable, and why and how is it difficult to empower such people to their own construction of self and identity? Excellent exam-

ples of these exercises in disempowerment can be found in the lives of
racially mixed (Root, 1992a) and bisexual (Weise, 1992) people. Members
of each of these groups are pushed to define themselves as other than
complex, to deny certain aspects of identity in order to fit into neat, simplistic categories. Racially mixed people, for instance, may be required to
declare themselves as "white" or "of color," when their genuine experience is that they are both and neither as commonly defined. Feminist therapists must ask themselves such questions if they are to begin to uncode
both their own responses and those of their clients in their symbolic relationships with one another. They must be able to imagine what they might
symbolize to each client and how that will affect the exchange and balance
of powers in the relationship; they must be equally conscious of the meanings their clients have to them. Finally, they must continually attend to the
events of daily life that will shape these mutual meanings.

At the outset of a therapeutic relationship, the feminist therapist begins
the process of asking herself and her client the myriad ways in which these
factors have been constructed in each of their lives and how they will gain
meaning between them. These questions are not only essential to the
nature of the relationship in feminist therapy; they are also basic to a feminist theoretical understanding of growth and development, distress and
healing, and the diagnostic understanding of these phenomena. For the
moment, I will confine my discussion to the question of how these factors
influence the nature of the therapy relationship and contribute to or
detract from egalitarianism and asymmetry, two important competing
tensions in the construction of a feminist therapy relationship.

To quote from Anna Julia Cooper, an early twentieth-century African-
American suffragist, "When and where I enter, then and there the whole
race enters with me." Her statement expresses pithily the factors to which
the feminist therapist must attend in analyzing and comprehending the
effects of gender, race, class, sexual orientation, and so on upon her therapeutic relationships. When and where she enters this exchange with
another, both physically and temporally as well as emotionally and spiri-
tually, she brings to it her heritage, the meaning that this heritage has for
herself, and the meaning that the other person's life carries to her at this
unique moment in the world. She has to know who she is when she
"enters" so to speak, the life of the person who becomes her client, and to
imagine how they will become part of one another's future.

Thus the feminist therapist must be continually exploring the meaning
of her various allegiances, however uncertain she may be of them. She
must therefore be conscious and aware of how those connections are signi-
fied by her clothing, her bearing, her use of language, the way in which

she decorates her office, the holidays she takes off from her practice, her use of body language. For myself, what does it mean that my clients encounter a youngish woman with white skin, whose face, coloring, and vocal cadences suggest my Jewishness, whose short haircut and flowing skirts convey an ambiguous message about my sexuality, while the cut of those skirts and their fabric speak to my upper-middle-class status? What does it mean that before they walk through the doors of my office, they know of my disability, because I have had to ask them to avoid wearing the scented products that will trigger my otherwise invisible chronic illness and render me unable to work? Or that the moment they lay eyes on me, they will see that I am far from fashionably thin? What does it convey that I am "Dr. Brown," a psychologist with various supposedly impressive mainstream credentials like a license and a board certification, yet that I most comfortably operate on a first-name basis, except when I am in my role as the courtroom expert? Later on in our work, what will it mean that I take off certain Jewish holy days but work on Columbus Day in solidarity with Native Americans for whom the beginning of the invasion is not a cause for celebration?

For each person with whom I relate, these factors, which are immediately visible and audible or shortly become so, hold a different weight and meaning. My gender and race may be most salient, for good or ill, to some people; my actual or perceived sexual orientation or culture of origin most telling in determining my meaning to others. The very fact that I can hear means something to a deaf client that it does not mean to those who share my sensory abilities. I can neither know nor assume what those meanings will be, nor can I soothe myself with the fiction that once such meaning has been made apparent it will remain fixed and invariant during the course of therapy. I cannot even predict which of my own personal signifiers will be visible to a particular client.

I can only know that these signifiers are more than simply symbolic representations of internal realities for my clients or distortions stemming from distress or difficulties in function. They reflect real-life encounters between my clients and the groups to which I belong or am perceived to be a part of. My client's response to me and what I represent, and my response to that response, will shape the nature and quality of our relating in unique ways. Moreover, that relationship will be affected most intimately by the ongoing sociocultural reality in the world in which our therapeutic relationship is situated. The African-American feminist therapist and her white client will experience one another differently the day after an urban ghetto blows up in rage than they did the day before, because the meaning of race in their relationship will have been given a new importance and different, possibly unwanted, meanings.

Similarly, my clients hold meaning for me, both concrete and symbolic; I must ask myself the same questions regarding my responses to the people with whom I work. What prior biases and stereotypes, either positive or negative, inform my relationship with each of them? To what degree will I be present or absent, attentive or confused, as a result of my internal resonance to some aspect of this client's heritage? And as my initial meaning to my clients will change over time, so will theirs to me.

A striking example of this potential for change in the signifiers informing the symbolic relationship happened in the year during which this was written. It involved my significance as a lesbian to Denise, a fundamentalist Christian woman who is my client, and hers to me as a Christian. For a number of years, these differences had been acknowledged and occasionally found funny, but mostly they had been in the background, because the matter more importantly at hand was her recovery from childhood abuse and my skill at working with people in that process. Then Oregon Measure 9, a virulently anti-gay- and lesbian-rights bill, which emerged from the Christian right, came onto the scene just south of my Seattle therapy office. My client and I found ourselves with a dilemma; in church every Wednesday and Sunday, she was hearing fundraising appeals to support the measure and protect society from the homosexual menace, while I was sending money down to Oregon to defeat the bill. And she was coming to me for therapy, as ever, twice weekly. Our respective identities became painfully salient; what was I doing empowering the healing of someone who might be my oppressor, and what was she doing opening herself to one of the demonized homosexuals for help and support? And what did it mean, in this new light, that her abusers had been Christians and elders of a fundamentalist church? Her own signifiers took on new meaning for her as well as for me.

As we struggled together throughout the summer and past election day to stay focused on her therapy and yet cognizant of how the world around us was changing the meaning of our encounter, we discovered that, for the moment, our differences had, for Denise, become a new window through which to know herself and her identity. She made important decisions about how she wanted to be a Christian in the world and began to honor herself and her own reading of scripture as a source of guidance rather than the readings suggested by her pastor. She also began to talk more freely about how she was, from time to time, uncomfortable with the subtle reminders of my lesbianism, a discomfort she had been ignoring because she believed it necessary for her to sustain her therapy with me. I, in turn, was affirmed in my trust in the process of feminist therapy and in my belief that people empowered to value themselves will find it difficult to participate in the oppression of others. When Measure 9 went down to defeat, Denise expressed her pleasure at the outcome, as well as her sadness at her heightened awareness of our differences and the loss, as it were, of her denial of what they might mean in the larger social and political context.

All these factors that can affect the symbolic level of the therapeutic exchange are equally salient when the therapy relationship is between therapist and group, or therapist and family, or therapist and intimate pair. Feminist therapists have suggested from the first that groups may be a more fertile ground for the creation of feminist therapeutic relationships, because the power of the therapist is more clearly diluted and the power of peers as agents of change and healing is accentuated. Yet in a group of women, all the various factors we have discussed above will operate as well; the early, naive, white feminist vision of all women as the same does not adequately describe how a middle-class woman in a group otherwise made up of women with a working-class heritage, no matter what their current class statuses may be, will be perceived as symbolically representing a kind of power and an experience of oppression. Differences between women must be addressed and made explicit if a group is to function as a healing experience for all.

Moreover, as the feminist therapist Rachel Siegel (1990) has noted, such differences between and among women (or men, for that matter) must be framed in a manner that does not promote a competition for the place of "most oppressed" nor denigrate one person's experience in order to validate that of another. The feminist model of power as multidimensional and of oppression as multifaceted and complex is an essential analytic tool in such a circumstance. When a heterosexual couple seeks therapy, feminist analysis illuminates a wide range of power dynamics engendered by the combinations and permutations of situational and socially derived roles and signifiers.

This vision of the symbolic relationship in therapy moves beyond that of transference and countertransference by placing the relationship in a broader sociopolitical context. The client's response to the therapist is not only about how the therapist symbolizes a parent or other caregiver; it is also about the various social meanings developed by this client regarding the therapist's actual or assumed group memberships. Feminist therapy theory argues that to strip the symbolic relationship of these sociocultural factors is to decontextualize this non-conscious component of psychotherapy in a manner that denies its relevance to the events of the world outside the therapy office. Broadly construing the symbolic relationship is also an initial step toward situating the important aspects of human growth and development as happening not simply in a familial context but within the larger social world in which sexism, racism, classism, and heterosexism, among other oppressive dominant norms, inform and interact with any family system.

The Meaning of an Egalitarian Relationship in Feminist Therapy

For therapy to be feminist, however, we cannot stop by revising the nature of the symbolic relationship. Instead, we must also examine the actual power arrangements present here and now in the relationship. In attempting to accomplish this goal, writers in the field of feminist therapy have typically described feminist therapy as an "egalitarian relationship." This term as used in the past two decades has vastly misled both feminist therapists and others as to the actual nature of the structure of the relationship in feminist therapy, but it is the adjective that best describes the ideal to which this feminist relationship aspires. "Egalitarian" has most often been construed by those new to or unfamiliar with feminist therapy as suggesting that feminist therapy theory denies the presence of a power imbalance in therapy. This simplistic equating of "egalitarian" with "equal" has never been correct, although the confusion of meanings has been persistent. Yet feminist therapists recognized early on that pure equality was not possible. The simple facts of who decided when to meet for therapy and on whose turf and terms the transaction proceeded (always the therapist's decisions and settings) betrayed the asymmetry lying close to the surface of the exchange.

Understanding egalitarianism as a fundamental construct for a feminist theory of relationships in therapy thus requires precision of definition. I define an egalitarian relationship as one structured to move toward equality of power, in which artificial and unnecessary barriers to equality of power are removed. In this relationship, there is an equality of *value* and of respect for each person's worth between the participants, but there continues to be some necessary asymmetry in certain aspects of the exchange, in part designed to empower the less powerful person but primarily required to define and delineate the responsibilities of the more powerful one.

In an egalitarian relationship in therapy, a primary goal is for the client to come to value her own needs and knowledge as central and authoritative. The therapist is present not to supplant this knowing with her own notions but rather to resonate with, mirror, and engage the client in this process and to assist the client in learning how such self-knowledge and self-value are obscured by patriarchal processes and institutions. This egalitarian image sees the therapist, by virtue of her role, as temporarily possessing more of certain kinds of power within that role. To satisfy a feminist analysis of power, it is necessary to theorize methodologies by which this power is shared with and transmitted to the client in every aspect of the psychotherapeutic transaction.

When equality of power between therapist and client is temporarily absent for the purposes of healing, its lack is brought to conscious awareness by the therapist's analysis of the complex and subtle power dynamics present in the exchange. This work requires close attention by the therapist in order to maintain the delicate balance and not accidentally garner power that is typically ascribed to the therapist in dominant modalities but is avoided in a feminist methodology. The strategies for achieving this balance vary in their specifics across person and situation. Rather than giving concrete examples of how to share power, our discussion will thus turn to theoretical models for understanding the various meanings of this construct, so central to feminist analysis, models that allow a therapist and client to develop together a sharing of power that reflects their unique relationship and their particular positioning within social and political realities. We begin by examining the powers of the therapist in the egalitarian therapy relationship. To do so we must enter a dimension in which we conceive of an infinite amount of power to go around, rather than a closed-system paradigm in which one person in an exchange may have X percent of the power, with only $100 - X$ percent available to the other and less still if there are more people involved. Power must also be defined and constructed in many dimensions; there is more than one sort of power present in any human interaction, and certainly more than one sort of power operant in the exchange that is psychotherapy.

The Power of the Therapist

Essential to a feminist therapist's understanding of how to create and maintain egalitarian relationships is a thorough, thoughtful, and complex understanding and acceptance of her power. It is useful to examine how power reveals itself and makes itself felt, in order to define those forms of power that may exist and operate independent of one's power in the world as defined in dominant terms. The feminist therapist must attend to the manner in which the politics of the context can transform that relational power to enhance or diminish her effectiveness with clients. It is essential to acknowledge and name the ways in which the therapist is powerful, both personally and politically, in her role as therapist and in relationship to any particular client. As the feminist therapists Adrienne Smith and Ruth Siegel (1985) have commented, one aspect of feminist therapy in practice is to remind people of power that they already have but are unable or as yet unwilling to see, feel, hear, and name. This is as much the case for the feminist therapist herself, in developing an epistemology of the therapy relationship, as it is for her clients.

Discussions of the therapist's power have tended to dichotomize the issue into real power—that is, the socially constructed power of the role and its various concrete manifestations, such as charging money or setting the frame and boundaries—and symbolic power, as manifested in the sorts of symbolic relationships discussed above. How any individual experiences these two phenomena bears little relationship to so-called "objective" realities; while the therapist herself may experience little real power, she may have great symbolic power, depending upon the client and the context in which the relationship emerges. The most basic confusions about egalitarianism in feminist therapy have reflected this "real" versus "symbolic" issue. The earliest feminist attempts at untying this knot, which centered mostly on manifestations of so-called real power, tended to deny or downplay the presence of any symbolic power, demonstrated the pitfalls of simply changing behaviors when the unique contribution and meaning of each layer of the exchange to the power dynamic was ignored.

Some of this problem seemed to reflect a pervasive discomfort with seeing oneself as having power, even though its construct was much discussed and analyzed in feminist theories. When I consult with other feminist therapists, throughout North America and Europe, I have been struck repeatedly by our collective difficulties in owning power of any sort. Few feminist therapists seem willing to be caught in the act of being powerful. It seems as if our encounters with power in its official guises have been so damaging to us, or to those people and cultures important to us, that we shrink from any association with it. Power is presumed to equal oppressiveness. Yet power ignored becomes power out of control; when it is disowned, when we declare it to be outside of ourselves, it runs amok, and once denied is more powerfully oppressive. The power we have does not disappear when we distance ourselves from it. Instead, it is free to settle into familiar, usually patriarchal, forms, no less present simply because we deny or minimize its existence.

Ironically, the greatest abuses of power in which I have seen self-named feminist therapists engage occurred in circumstances where the therapist in question actively disowned any connotation of power or authority in her behaviors (that is, saw herself as having no "real" power) and clung stubbornly to an image of herself as either utterly powerless personally or lacking any special power by virtue of role. Such a stance, which distorts feminist notions of egalitarianism by claiming a false equality, tends to disempower and frustrate clients, because it denies the meaning of their internal experience of the therapist as powerful in their lives, the symbolic power manifested in the relationship. This denial of the client's reality is an imbalance of power far more potent than any overt claims to power by a therapist might ever be. Its parallel can be found in the naive denials in the early feminist therapy literature that the therapist's race has meaning as regards power and in assertions that feminism would somehow sweep away racism and that a woman of color would be safe and at home in the hands of a feminist therapist, an assertion that is similarly disempowering (Boyd, 1990; Kanuha, 1990b).

Some of this confusion and distortion reflects mainstream constructions of power, those in which most feminist therapists have been raised. Typically in dominant cultures, power is defined as control over resources or over the authority of the discourse: who owns, who's in charge, who's the expert. Within the context of such a definition, many feminist therapists experience themselves as relatively powerless and become confused about their power in a therapeutic context. Few are among the power elite who run the countries in which they live, and even those who are financially comfortable are usually in a continually precarious position where only arriving daily at the office will keep the bills paid and there is always the spectre of illness or disability disrupting their cash flow and moving them into poverty.

Many feminist therapists have had direct experiences of oppression and marginalization because of gender, race, class, sexual orientation, religion, age, or disability—experiences that can be profoundly disempowering and that can have effects more meaningful to our self-definition than does our role as therapist. Because feminist therapy continues to be marginal to most of the mental health disciplines, few feminist therapists perceive themselves as experts or authorities in the eyes of their mainstream therapy colleagues. While they may know that their insights and information, particularly as they apply to issues of gender, are unique and of value, they know that such recognition is not often granted to them by the mainstream of their professions, which often continue to deny that feminist therapy has anything to do with, for instance, clinical psychology or biological psychiatry.

Moreover, the occupation of psychotherapy itself can lead its practitioners to enormous feelings of both power and powerlessness. In many types of psychotherapy practice, outcome is less than guaranteed, and change may at first appear to be slight, slow to emerge, and difficult to sustain for many clients. The social and political milieu does not always support, and may impede, change. Even though the therapy professions tend to attract people with a high tolerance for ambiguity, no one's ability to detach from outcome can persist forever in the face of a process that can be painful and demanding to witness and participate in. The world, meanwhile, is creating new clients for us every minute as another child is molested, another woman raped or beaten, another act of racist violence committed against a person of color, another law passed threatening the civil rights of sexual minorities, another war of "ethnic cleansing" pursued. While a cynical observer might suggest that this external reality is empowering to therapists of any ilk because it potentially fills our practices and pocketbooks, feminist principles make it difficult if not impossible to act and feel that such events have no meaning other than to keep the engines of the therapy machine going. As feminists we have strong commitments to the end of this state of affairs. (I often say that I would love for the world to put me out of business forever.)

Finally, feminist therapists, by allying themselves with revolutionary social change, can sometimes become the direct targets of outright violence by those whose control and privilege are threatened when their clients are able to free themselves. Feminist therapists have been shot at by batterers, threatened with jail for refusing to turn records over that would harm clients, and denied opportunities for work, advancement and promotion for being "too political."

Feminist therapists thus often do not see themselves as powerful. Because of these factors that can obscure the vision of their power, it is essential that feminist therapists, in understanding the nature of the relationship in therapy, acknowledge and own the extraordinary degree of power that they do possess *in the context of that particular relationship,* a role-and-relationship-mediated power that exists separate and apart from any so-called "real" power that they experience themselves as having or that is ascribed to them by others apart from their work. Denial of this power can be dangerous, both to the theoretical construct of egalitarianism and to the welfare of their clients and themselves.

Nurturance as Power

Any attempt to comprehend the nature of the relationship in feminist therapy must include a recognition of the powers of presence and nurturance as sources of impact, influence, and ultimately of authority. To deny that these are forms of power and competence is to fail to capture the essence of feminist deconstruction of the social narrative of power, which notes how these skills have been devalued as part of an overall scheme in which behaviors associated with women are perceived as forms of weakness.

The power to create and sustain relationships, often felt as present in the client's phenomenological reality, derives from both the actual and the symbolic aspects of the role of therapist. It is similar to transference as defined in psychodynamic theories, yet from a feminist perspective it is different, because this power is shaped and formed by external contextual factors as well as by generic, intrapsychic phenomena of the sort posited in psychodynamic models of transference (Brown, 1984). It is the power found in the capacity to offer nurturance and care, the power to be present with and encompass emotions and experiences that are terrifying to others, the power that comes from simply sitting and listening unflinchingly to racking sobs or pounding rage. It is the power of standing witness to the pain and courage of people telling their truths, often for the first time, of honoring their lives with attention and validation. It is the power invested in the meaning of the roles of healer and teacher in our clients' minds as well as our own. In non-Western cultures, such powers of nurturance and presence are more frequently acknowledged and honored than in Eurocentric societies, in which they are typically devalued. They are powers of the healer, intangible, often subtle, the power to help someone feel powerful, to be willing to see, hear, feel, and know that which is still, or at first, silent, invisible, hidden, nameless.

Janet Surrey, a feminist therapist, and Carter Heyward, a lesbian-feminist theologian, have written of the importance to feminist therapy of "mutuality" in the psychotherapeutic relationship (1990). They are referring to the genuine human encounter that occurs between therapist and client and to the ways in which each person affects the other in a manner that then circles back to its beginning in a continuous flow within the exchange; this is an egalitarian image in which client and therapist each has impact on the other. It does not obscure the power of the therapist but rather defines that power in relational language. Surrey and Heyward draw our attention to the therapist's power of "compassion," the ability to be "passionate-with," to engage intensely with another person emotionally so as to empower the other's emotional knowing. They identify the importance of such engagement, from a feminist perspective, to the creation of feminist therapy. The power of relational mutuality, of our passion for one another and for justice, is an example of the profound impact that simply passionately attending and being present with profound intentionality can have upon another human being. This exemplifies the power available to the therapist. For the client who has been silenced, or whose truths have been distorted by individual experience or cultural oppression, the mutuality of the exchange, in which the therapist serves as an attentive witness to those truths, provides the most powerfully transformative experience imaginable. Mutuality does not necessarily imply sameness; in some instances, the willingness to hold and acknowledge difference, to refuse to cover over disconnection but to name its presence in the relationship, can become the empowering act of mutuality as practiced by a feminist therapist.

These powers of the therapist are real to our clients, present and impossible to put away; they are even stronger, in fact, when the relationship is framed—as is explicitly the case in a feminist psychotherapy—to subvert the effects of patriarchy in the lives of the participants and their communities by embodying respect for the powers of the weak. This greater potential power of the feminist therapist derives, ironically, from her capacity to choose rejection of more typical therapist powers to diagnose, define, and determine the reality of the client, when this in turn respects the client's power and choices, or to take that power back when the therapist's use of it empowers the client further and undermines patriarchal uses of those official functions of the therapist role. It is in being willing and able to decide to give away those "real" powers and honor the power and value of the client that the feminist therapist's symbolic power is often ironically enhanced.

An example of this use of power can be found in my work with a client I will call Trish. When she became intensely suicidal and uncertain of her desire to stay alive, I decided, after careful consideration of the meanings of my decision, not to evoke my power to have her committed to an inpatient unit, even though it would have made me more comfortable and made it easier for me to work with her. Instead, I honored her strong preference to work more intensively with me, meeting daily and having regular between-session phone contact. I told her repeatedly that I trusted her to know what she needed in order to make a decision to stay alive and that I would respect her and attempt to empower her in that knowledge, because I believed that it would ultimately accomplish the goal of turning her toward life; she, in turn, told me that to hospitalize her would be to strip her of her power and dignity—what little she felt was left—and might kill her. She was right about what she needed to stay alive; my acknowledgment of her wisdom, and my choice to empower her to as great a degree as possible has subsequently led her to trust me more and to give more weight to what I now say when I comment on her actions—

sometimes more than I am comfortable with. I have become more powerful in my relationship with Trish precisely because I chose not to use the official power of my position but to hold firmly to the power of presence, witness, and alliance.

Real Power in the Therapist Role

The therapist also has the power to engage in certain defining behaviors that are real and concrete. She sets the fee; decides the time, place, and circumstances of the meeting; and determines what she will share about herself and what not to disclose. Even when she allows some leeway in negotiating these and similar points, this allowance proceeds from the implicit understanding that it is within the therapist's power to give, and to take away, such compromises. These are asymmetries which may be necessary for the therapist, who may need to feel some sense of power in defining the terms and conditions of her employment, but they are not asymmetries inherently necessary to the healing aspects of the therapeutic exchange.

But even when we consciously choose to eschew these official powers of the mental health professional, their odor clings to us. Understanding one's power as a feminist therapist requires attention to this, and an analysis of how to respond to this reality. A feminist therapist continues to carry the power that her role derives from the position of therapy within the dominant culture, as well its unique placement in any specific cultural context in which she practices. This may vary widely within the life and work of any given therapist, and between therapists, as the power ascribed to the role of therapist changes within different settings.

For example, the therapist practicing in North American white lesbian communities has more power by virtue of her role than many therapists in mainstream culture, because of the high value accorded therapy in this cultural group, of whom almost three-quarters see a therapist during their lifetimes (Brown, 1989b). The therapist working with North American women of color may have less power as a person in a context where therapy is perceived (often accurately) as white people's foolishness (Boyd, 1990; Fine, 1992). Or her power may be perceived as a negative force where therapy has been a dangerous tool of oppression and the denial of familial rights and relationships, as has also often been true for people on the cultural margin. The therapist working with some cultural groups may need to grasp the power of her role more firmly in order to respect the desire of that client for an expert authority; this may be a case in which the only way to empower a person is to first firmly accept the hierarchies they carry with them, rather than disrespect them from the outset. The therapist who works in an institutional setting conveys a different message than does a private practitioner working in her home regarding her power in her relationships with clients; there may be implicit or explicit subtexts regarding the power of the institution to distort or transform the interaction, which in turn lend different meaning to the therapist herself when she is seen as, or presents herself as the representative of the institution.

There are also times when legitimate exercise of therapist power can become problematic. I, for example, like most psychotherapists, set aside certain days and times during the week when I do not see clients. For one woman, Suzanne, these limits were disempowering, since the day and time she preferred for therapy fell during my hours of unavailability. She challenged me to explain how I could theoretically support the notion of an egalitarian relationship while being unwilling to modify my schedule and eventually left therapy with me, because my ability to say no and my power to determine when I would and would not work were such painful reminders of her unequal power in our relationship. Her distress pushed me to ponder how and when it was legitimate for me to exercise this power, to ask myself what good it was to tell clients that they had the power to disagree with me or tell me what they did not like when, on some matters, I would not change. My analysis of this situation, which took place over many months in consultation with several feminist therapy colleagues, helped me to remember that power, interpersonally and relationally, does come with inherent limits and that my power to decide when to offer myself to clients was matched by their power to decide to engage me or not and thus to pay or withhold my livelihood. I gave Suzanne the information about when I would work; I supported her in her choice to leave me when I would not bend my rules and did not tell her that she was resisting me, avoiding the work of therapy, or manifesting her own pathology—all parting shots that therapists can and do take as a means of exercising power.

For a feminist therapist, the temptation at such times is to fail to respect her own limits and boundaries and to give in, in a naive attempt to achieve equality and reassure a client. But a dilemma remains; I continue to ask myself what it implies that I could, and after due consideration did, say no to this not unreasonable request, simply because I did not want to work on a particular afternoon that I had set aside for other things. I continue to wonder whether this experience exemplifies the incompatibility of therapy and feminist politics by underscoring the ways in which therapists can always assume certain important kinds of interpersonal power. Because I did not control all the therapy resources, and could make referrals to therapists who could meet Suzanne's needs, this dilemma was solved. Understanding the power of the therapist in the psychotherapeutic relationship from a feminist perspective requires this sort of continual close inquiry into the cultural and political context in which each therapy relationship is situated, into the meanings lent to therapy and the therapist by that context, and into the significance of the therapist to all players.

The Power of the Client

The development of a feminist model of the therapy relationship requires an understanding of the power of the client and how that power differs from the power of the therapist. In a feminist epistemology of power, power exists at many different levels and in a diversity of forms. As chapter 8 discusses at greater length, that acknowledgment of the client's power does not relieve the therapist of certain responsibilities to the client, the therapy relationship itself, or the community of therapists, nor does it negate or obscure the power of the therapist herself. Acknowledgment of the client's power is, however, an essential aspect of the creation of a genuinely feminist relational matrix in the therapeutic exchange.

The powers of the client, like those of the therapist, reflect role, person, and context. Identifying these powers requires subtlety, because the phenomenology of the client is most commonly the experience of powerlessness. In the context of therapy, certain types of power otherwise available to the client are often ceded to the therapist or weakened by the nature of the symbolic dynamics in the therapy relationship. Clients in therapy, feminist or otherwise, usually feel younger, weaker, and in greater need within this relationship than they do in other relationships with adults. All these experiences may decrease the client's power interpersonally. Even the client who is powerful and knowledgeable, peer or more to the therapist in their roles outside that relationship, is likely to experience this sense of greater need once in the therapeutic exchange because of the factors that commonly motivate people to enter therapy. That is, people do not come to see therapists because they feel good and their lives are going well. The subjective experience of pain which propels a person into the therapy relationship creates a temporary yet extraordinarily real and meaningful dependency upon the therapist and enhances feelings of powerlessness.

A step toward construing the client as powerful is to acknowledge that entering into such a relationship of dependency is itself a statement of a certain type of power hidden in patriarchal realities. Some of the power of the client, which feminist therapists can identify and name, emerges from the very experiences that appear to enhance powerlessness. My analysis here reflects Mary Daly's (1978) concept of "patriarchal reversals," the theory that whatever patriarchy stigmatizes as weak or deficient is likely to be a source of strength, courage, and power when viewed through a feminist lens. If one looks subversively upon patriarchal definitions of weakness or powerlessness, it is almost as if signs and banners are being waved desperately to direct one's gaze away from potential sources of power. Dependency, a phenomenon that evokes tremendous ambivalence and fearfulness in the writings and practice of mainstream therapists and that we normally experience as a form of powerlessness, is an excellent example of such a patriarchally reversed phenomenon.

The lesbian-feminist therapist Dorsey Green (1990), who has written extensively about questions of dependency and autonomy in intimate relationships, has commented that overt dependency is stigmatized within patriarchal forms because of its hidden importance in the lives of the officially powerful classes, who are often extremely dependent on others for functions that most adults perform for themselves, such as being driven from place to place, having their home cleaned, or having their food cooked. While the ostensible reasons for such dependency have to do with the desire not to "waste time" on such self-nurturing tasks, as well as the prestige and status the dominant culture attaches to the ability to purchase such care, the application of a feminist vision would suggest that there are other reasons. Seeing through a feminist lens, Green argues that the ability to purchase care allows some people to *appear* impervious to what are otherwise shameful dependency needs, while being able to indulge such needs to a far greater degree than possible for most adults. This hiddenness and outright denial of dependency in dominant culture serves to enhance the shameful nature of dependency and to create the illusion that to be powerful is to transcend dependency.

A feminist analysis of the client's power thus constructs the client's ability and willingness to become temporarily yet voluntarily dependent as a statement of resistance to these patriarchal norms, even when clients experience themselves as being in such pain that they have no choice but to enter this dependent relationship. Such ability to resist, to risk a dependent stance in a relationship even though the client may experience it initially as a form of weakness or deficit, is one unique dimension of power inherent in the role of the client. What differentiates feminist therapy at this point from any mainstream theories of psychotherapy is the recognition of this dependency as a hidden form of power and resistance to patriarchal norms. Framing and reflecting it back to the client as such is one step in facilitating the client's knowing embrace of power on this and other dimensions.

An example of this power in dependency comes from my work with Yvonne, a working class white heterosexual woman who was struggling to cope with her profound stress from work. Her work as an aircraft mechanic was objectively stressful and difficult, although so well-paying that it was hard for her to leave it. But her difficulty in saying no, setting limits, and being seen as other than supercompetent was an added aspect of her stress, and the part she wanted to change. When she first came to see me, she noted that she didn't trust people easily, and she was going to have some difficulty trusting me. I told her that was fine, and we commenced therapy.

In time Yvonne did come to trust me, very profoundly. So when we began to discuss the use of trance and visualization work as a strategy for reducing stress and empowering her to set limits, she told me that it was only because she could feel safe now depending on me that she thought she could do this sort of work. She discovered that the use of trance was profoundly empowering; for the first time, she felt a shift in how she coped with stressors that went deeper than her behavioral strategies for change. In her dependency in our relationship, she had been able to derive power that had not been present when she could not yet lean.

Clients also have enormous power in their impact on the therapist's life. The client is, ultimately, a consumer of the therapist's services. In many cases, the client has the power to hire or fire her, in some instances to determine the quality of her financial life. But more important is the client's power to be a source of unique knowledge and wisdom for the therapist, both regarding herself and regarding the therapy process when she construes authority as lodged in the client.

Feminist therapy theory defines clients as the experts about the meaning of their lives and their pain, the goals of their therapy, and the success of their treatment. This view of clients as experts on matters that in dominant models are always the purview of the therapist is another radical departure from mainstream constructions of the client, because it rejects the notion that the therapist has the ability to know these things unilaterally. In a feminist analysis there is no pretense to mythological therapeutic objectivity or the possession of greater wisdom, although this last can be very difficult for a therapist, no matter how strong her feminist analysis, to let go of. Rather, the client is explicitly, carefully, and persistently given back the power to define self, and the meaning of self, in the manner most attuned to the person's present identity and cultural context and heritage.

"Self" and the values and behaviors that accrue to that construction may thus be construed in manners unknown to the therapist but entirely congruent with the client's reality. The therapist in feminist therapy must see her wisdom in a new way, as the ability and willingness to continually empower another with knowledge and wisdom.

It has been my experience that most clients enter therapy unaware of this power of self-definition and expertise. Instead, stripped of self-knowledge by patriarchal dominant cultures and often by a lifetime of exposure to the insidious traumata of oppression, many clients initially perceive themselves to be ignorant and believe that truth and knowledge rest within the person of the therapist. The most common response to my initial questions of "What do you want?" and "How will you know if this is working for you?" is "I don't know," often followed by "I don't know *how* to know what I want." At times I will hear from clients of the dangers to them, past and present, of being conscious of such knowledge and their fears that my stance of willingness to empower them is simply that—a stance and pretense that they will be punished for believing and acting upon. It is essential for the development of a feminist relationship that the therapist not collude in this patriarchal conspiracy to induce feelings of ignorance but instead be committed to acknowledging and calling forth the hidden expert power within the client, while respecting how frightening and tentative this role of expert may be for the client.

This commitment takes form as a cooperative partnership of differing forms of expertise, one manner in which an egalitarian ideal can be made real. The therapist is defined as having expertise regarding the processes of change and empowerment, expertise that is specialized yet can be made generally available and is neither mystical nor inaccessible. This paradigm for expertise as a healer is a departure from most other models, because it defines the skills that constitute this expertise as open to acquisition by the client as well, rather than as mysteries to which only the initiated can be exposed.

Additionally, feminist therapy theory defines the healer as limited in her ability to heal by whatever unwillingness she may have to engage the client as an equal partner. Psychotherapy as commonly practiced has tended to obscure itself with jargon (see Szasz [1978] for a lengthier discussion of this problem) and what Hannah Lerman describes as particularistic terminology, which lend excess expert power to the therapist at the expense of the client. The terms therapists use to describe the experiences of the therapeutic relationship can be so highly specialized and obscure in their meaning that they suggest that clients must always rely upon the therapist to translate their own internal realities. If the therapist rattles on about "withholding internal part objects," clients will shortly get the message that whatever it takes to understand their problems is a sacred mystery understood only by the initiated. Even if the use of apparently accessible terms—calling a client's interpretation of reality an "irrational idea," for example—assumes the therapist's authority to define rationality and its obverse and locates rationality outside of the client. Constructing a feminist relationship in therapy in which the client can be an authoritative knower requires not only describing the therapist's expertise in language accessible to clients from a variety of life experiences but locating knowledge and reason equally in the client and in the therapist.

Empowering the Client

As therapy progresses, the therapist and client are provided with many opportunities in which the client's power can be either acknowledged or ignored. At each juncture, a feminist analysis leads us to ask how the therapist might craft her response to the client in a manner that underscores that intrapersonal power. An example of such a teaching moment in the therapeutic relationship occurs repeatedly at points where the client reviews the personal narrative, the story which each of us tells ourself about our life and its meaning.

Many people enter therapy with a narrative marked by distortions and at times outright lies, which have been corporated in the story line as a result of various encounters with patriarchal oppression. Racism, sexism, heterosexism, classism, violence, scarcity—these and other forms of oppression can deform the personal narrative in such a manner that when clients arrive at the beginning of therapy, they have been turned into agents of patriarchal oppression of themselves. They have learned to tell themselves a powerful story of their lack of self-worth, their badness, their helplessness, their utter lack of choice. As I sometimes say to my clients, it is as if we have learned to read ourselves a bedtime story each night that says, "You are worthless, your life has no meaning, and there is nothing you can do about it, the end," a bedtime story which we feel required to read and from which we may never deviate.

In uncovering this personal narrative and identifying it for the client as a strategy for intrapersonal power, a feminist therapist can empower the client to begin to change the story. While all approaches to therapy involve this process of rewriting personal stories to some degree, feminist analysis utilizes interpretations of experience that place the client's experiences within a social and political context and focus on how these experiences have been deformed by patriarchal imperatives. This contextual interpretation acts as one of the powerful deprivatizing aspects of a feminist psychotherapy.

An example of this approach can be seen in therapy with Steve, a white, heterosexual man from a working-class Protestant family, who made his living with his hands. Steve came for therapy because of vague feelings of sadness and anxiety that had haunted him all of his life and with a concept of himself as a "wimpy," low-energy person. He had difficulties in getting emotionally close to and open with people, although he desired to. In retelling his story, we began to explore what it had meant to be a quiet, shy, and gentle little boy in a cultural setting where these qualities were stigmatized and devalued as "sissified" and "effeminate." We explored together what it means to be a man who, in the words of the antipornography activist John Stoltenberg, "refuses to be a *man*", in the stereotypic sense, and how Steve had internalized this meaning as an aspect of personal devaluation. Introducing Steve to the work of Stoltenberg and others in the antisexist men's movement allowed him to see how he was not alone or negatively unique, and that gave him safe access to possible alternative interpretations of his life experiences. While the wounds of patriarchy to women are more obvious, the stories of patriarchal power and control damage men as well. In Steve's therapy, the development of his image of himself as a man of worth and value *because* of his difference from the norm, rather than in spite of it, constituted the core of the transformation of his narrative. While we never talked directly about how this process undermined patriarchy, we did talk about how Steve's increasing embrace and value of himself was a source of discomfort to some other men, although (to his pleasure) it was a cause of delight to the women he began to encounter as his self-deprecation fell away and he felt more comfortable making social excursions.

As their stories begin to be transformed by experiments with slightly different story lines, clients become acutely aware of their power to influence self and to break the bonds to patriarchy, emotional handcuffs in the form of assumptions and interpretations that favored patriarchal values about the worth of human beings and the meaning of their experiences. Assisting clients to discover that they can make up their own stories, realizing that all of the stories are manufactured by someone, with none more "true" than the next unless the client decides that it is, and supporting clients to come to believe those narratives more strongly than any other adds to their sense of personal power. They begin to see themselves as the source of good in their lives as they rewrite their stories and thus start to understand how powerful they can be, and have already been in their own lives.

The Client as Actor in the Life of the Therapist

In theorizing the client's power, it is also important that therapists acknowledge both to themselves and to their clients the power that clients exert in their lives. The influence and impact go in both directions, and clients are important shapers of the therapist's life and narratives, although they may be unaware of this power and perceive themselves as only the recipients of what therapists do. Therapists working from dominant perspective have not ignored the impact of the client, but their work has been framed in a manner that infers only pathology flowing from client to therapist. Typically, therapists have concentrated on the difficult and problematic aspects of this influence. Most such back-handed affirmations of clients' impacts portray therapists in the role of victim to the client, complaining about "resistance" or "manipulation," terms that I would argue are inimical to a feminist construction of the relationship in therapy.

These put-downs masquerading as diagnostic inferences and interpretive comments, which are all too common, reflect the requirement that the client submit all power and will to the therapist. Clients who do not or cannot self-abnegate in this way are perceived as difficult, bad, uncooperative and ungrateful, "manipulating" to get what they want, "resisting" giving what is required of them. In hearing their behavior described in such terms, clients receive the meta-message that they are taking power illegitimately, power that the therapist does not wish to share or prefers not to see them have, be that the power to move her, the power to help her forget how to care for herself in this relationship and make her do something she wishes she hadn't, the power to become hostile, the power to offer the client an indulgence she knows will not help, or the power to violate some boundary.

In fact, some of the people that therapists work with can be difficult to be around. People who have experienced abuse, oppression, or discrimination often respond to these experiences by being angry, rigid, or controlling. As therapy clients, such people can be irritating and troublesome, disrupting weekend afternoons with calls for help, making suicide threats before, during, and after vacations, being jealous of the therapist's partner, children, and sometimes even pets.

So there is a dilemma for the feminist therapist; she is constantly made to wonder if she wants to affirm *this* particular example of the client's power or simply wishes that it would go away. For all therapists communicating to clients how the latter affects them is a delicate balancing act, requiring therapists to honor the reality of the psychotherapy relationship as an entity in their own lives from which they can never get distance. For feminist therapists, it means remembering how this work is only one action in a feminist revolution that is their very raison d'etre. In practice, it means being honest about the tranformative effect of the work in their lives, the ways in which they are moved to rage, pain, excitement, joy by the people they work with, the manner in which their own wounds are mirrored or reopened, the dreams they dream of their clients' traumas, the exasperation and fatigue they may feel when it seems as if they are struggling against the oppressors internalized within this other person, who seem to be holding onto the client against all of their cunning. This last is a good way to reframe the client's obnoxiousness and get some empathy; remembering that it represents the wounds of patriarchy helps to recreate compassion.

Without the framework of an egalitarian relationship that assumes this interplay and interdependency and celebrates the client's awareness and ownership of power, it can seem impossible to speak of all these things without somehow asking the unaskable in a therapy relationship: that the client reverse roles and offer the therapist the kind of presence, attention, and nurturance that therapists give in psychotherapy. The concept of egalitarianism provides a theoretical frame upon which to develop the concrete strategies for sharing with clients the knowledge that they are powerful in therapy interpersonally. In proposing such an exchange as necessary and integral to an egalitarian psychotherapy relationship, feminist therapists are entering the realms best described by science fiction, places where no one has gone before. Healing relationships within patriarchy, where hierarchy and power imbalance are embedded and requisite, do not admit to these forms of relating in which there is a mutuality yet a continuing and necessary asymmetry, where not everything is shared by the therapist and such feedback does not happen all the time, as it might in a friendship.

Communicating the power of the client as a human being to affect the therapist at their shared human level requires an exquisite awareness of and attention to the particular developmental needs of each client, taking into consideration that person's capacity to hear about these effects and the ways in which that message can best be framed to make it useful for the client. Therapists need to think about who is listening, about that person's capacity to accept being a powerful actor and readiness to embrace a radically different version of a personal story of a life lacking power and meaning. They must give similar focused attention to their own needs and motivations in delivering certain communications to their clients: They must ask who is telling, and why.

Such a process of acknowledging the client's power lies at the heart of the egalitarian relationship in feminist therapy. Such relationships happen when the therapist knows and embraces the reality of her own power and uses it responsibly, as an agent for justice and change, and when, simultaneously, the power of the client is made manifest and strengthened. Whether it is power within the self, power in the therapy relationship, or power to transform the broader social context, the client's power is a factor to which feminist therapists attend, celebrating it and calling attention to it. There are many ways to accomplish this goal; feminist therapists must repeatedly ask themselves how they are succeeding. It is a highly subversive activity, for it means uncovering and affirming the powers of those who have been denied power, the power to know and name the previously alienated self.

In my own life and work, one concrete way in which I have acknowledged the power of the people with whom I work has been to ask my clients if I may use examples from our work together in my writing. By requesting this favor, I can convey the importance of a particular person, and my relationship with her or him, to my understanding of feminist therapy theory and practice; I am thus demonstrating the importance of the client to an aspect of myself that I clearly value greatly, my writings and the development of theory and practice. People learn how they have affected my thinking, my work not only with them but with other clients, and the ways in which I train therapists. The challenge has been not to use this technique in an exploitative manner in which I might knowingly or inadvertently avoid doing work in therapy; there is a risk of creating such an excess of good feelings and mutual appreciation that my client and I would collude in avoiding taking next steps that are not as ready to be put down on paper. At such moments I have to consider carefully who will be empowered by such a request and who made so overly grateful that she will be further disempowered by losing her sense of her right to challenge me when I go wrong, misuse my power, or simply miss the point. This dilemma for me as a therapist who writes about therapy exemplifies in a very concrete form the dilemma for feminist therapy in general; that is, we must find ways to acknowledge our clients' power that do not burden, confuse, or frighten the recipients of these messages.

This illustration underscores the nature of the dilemma; not all clients will want to know how they affect the therapist. Not every impact will be one which the client will wish to have had, even if it appears to be of value to the therapist. I recall one woman's rage at me for revealing to her my sadness at abuse she had suffered; she did not want my sorrow at that moment, because she could not yet tolerate knowing of her own grief, which I was prematurely evoking. Respecting clients for who they are, and learning from them what they want to know about their effect on the therapist, rather than attempting to intuit their desires, are uniquely feminist ways of understanding what is important in the therapy process. That is, a feminist analysis calls upon the therapist both to respect where and how the client is as yet uncomfortable with power and to seek continually for healing and empowering means by which to convey that powerfulness, so that the client sees herself or himself reflected in a mirror in which that power is visible. In the case just described, I was able to let this woman know of her power by responding to her anger with respect and acknowledgment that I had been insensitive to her timing, reaffirming that she was an authority about her needs. This response in turn opened the door to her healing process, and later she was able to ask that I tell her, now that she was ready, of my sadness for the battered child she had been.

The egalitarian relationship is thus one in which power as a factor and force in the process of psychotherapy is made explicit. The power of the client is emphasized, enhanced, and framed to become more tangible. The power of the therapist as a change agent is respected, but the client's ability to internalize that power and eventually leave in possession of that power is never allowed to slip entirely into the background. In a relationship so constructed, patriarchy is indeed subverted one life and one hour at a time, because each therapy session becomes a paradigm for feminist modes of relating in which therapist and client resist the presence of hierarchy and oppression between them.

This clarity also aids in explicating the feminist frame discussed earlier, which is flexible in response to the social realities of each therapy relationship, while remaining clear as to the power and responsibility of the therapist to act in the client's best interest. If, for example, we are attempting to make the relationship between therapist and client more symmetrical and power-equal, then we will search for concrete strategies that de-emphasize the therapist's power without denying its presence. For example, the therapist can avoid using honorifics. She can, as discussed in greater detail in the following chapter, involve clients in the development of diagnosis and case conceptualization by actively soliciting clients' views and feelings about the nature of their problems. But the therapist should avoid rebellious strategies that only superficially appear to equalize power. One such failed strategy, tried out in the early days of feminist therapy, was for therapists to become friends with clients. This turned out only to enhance the power and importance of the therapist, who now filled yet another role in the client's life, a role that could and should have been filled by another person who was more the client's peer from the start. The more roles filled by the therapist—healer, friend, co-worker, and so on—the more power she may have available to exploit. As I will discuss in a later chapter on the ethics and boundaries of feminist therapy, the edges of the therapeutic relationship are drawn by a complex understanding of what will empower clients at both real and symbolic levels and will tell the truth about the power of the therapist and its influences on the client, rather than pretend that certain forms of power do not exist in feminist practice.

Understanding the relationship between client and therapist in such a manner is, in consequence, an essential step toward a vision of how feminist therapy will unfold. The conscious attention to power and its various meanings, the continuing inquiry into the ways in which various social signifiers affect the interaction in both concrete and symbolic ways, and the privileging of relationality, all in the service of a more egalitarian connection, are characteristics that must inform every aspect of feminist therapeutic practice. When the relationship is woven of such elements, then the fabric of the therapy is more likely to remain feminist, because the central aspects of the interaction will be those most tied to feminist understandings and analysis. This aspect of the methodology of feminist therapy is crucial; without it, the most basic form and substance of the therapeutic exchange will cease to be feminist, no matter what content is examined in therapy or what the therapist's own feminist politics may be in other contexts. This way of knowing about what makes a relationship feminist in psychotherapy helps to define the distinction between a feminist psychotherapy and other forms and approaches.

CHAPTER 5

Naming the Pain:
Diagnosis and Distress

WHEN PEOPLE arrive at any therapist's door, they come bearing a load of distress that threatens to overpower their best skills and coping strategies, if it has not done so already. People do not, after all, usually spend time and money on therapy when they are feeling well and happy, or even when they are simply functional. The popular stereotype of the "normal neurotic" buying friendship and attention from a therapist has little to do with reality. People come into therapy because they no longer sleep or cannot remember when they ever slept well; because terror strikes in their hearts when they leave home or enter a crowded room; beause their dreams are filled with images that frighten or confuse them; because they cannot stop crying or are too numb to feel. They come because a quarter of their hour is absent; because they experience a profound distance from themselves, their feelings, their capacity for action. They come because a relationship is strangling on itself; because a family is fraying at the seams; because illness has robbed them of what once gave pleasure and value to life. For some, the pain feels almost physical, palpable, sometimes so much so that death feels more attractive than an endless future with such distress. Once in a while, people come to therapy because they cause pain to others and have become so numbed to the capacity to know about and empathize with the pain that they are unable to change and put an end to their own oppressive actions without help. But rarely does someone who is feeling fine most of the time walk through my office door, or that of any therapist.

Traditionally, the mental health professions have responded to the distress experienced by therapy clients by defining these experiences as pathological and developing a complex system of diagnostic labels, a taxonomy of the various types of distress. This taxonomy, diagnosis, has become a way in which therapists can make their clients into the "other," the "not me," not truly human but rather a label or a case. Feminist therapy has never comfortably embraced this conceptual strategy for comprehending distress. Of all of the relics of mainstream psychotherapy, diagnosis is the one that has seemed most distant from feminist realities and most grounded in the problematic parameters of dominant culture. Diagnosis contradicts a political analysis, because it locates the problems in the individual, thereby privatizing both the distress and its implied solutions, and defines the distress as illness, moving the locus of analysis from context to person.

To the early feminist therapists, diagnosis was no more than negative labeling; it pathologized people's survival strategies and gave spurious authority to oppressive understandings of the actions of people from marginalized groups. From a feminist perspective, psychodiagnosis exists as a strategy for differentiating the forms of distress that are acceptable culturally (that is, things not diagnostically labeled) from those that are considered excessive and irrational, and thus as perpetuating a dominant normative vision that is antithetical to pluralist feminist methodologies.

Yet how is one to understand and name the subjective experiences of distress that are undeniably present not only in the lives of therapy clients but in many other human lives? It is not enough to lump all distress together under "feeling bad"; not all subjective distress has the same form or meaning. Some distress is either objectively or subjectively disabling; some is not disabling but does profoundly interfere with people's capacity to take action on their own behalf. Nor is it either clinically or politically useful to glamorize distress, as did R. D. Laing and other psychiatric radicals, as "madness" to be savored and entered fully into. But it has not been simple to arrive at a feminist solution.

For most of the two decades of the existence of feminist therapy, feminist therapists have seemed content to treat diagnosis as so irrelevant to their work as to require no attention. They did not need diagnosis; they knew that the problem was not pathology but patriarchy. Since they could not, as one colleague of mine pointed out, formally diagnose "internalized oppression," then they would not diagnose at all. It is possible to scan the first decade and a half of feminist therapy literature and find little about diagnosis beyond the critiques just outlined.

This rejectionist stance has had the unfortunate effect of diminishing feminist input into the formal diagnostic process of dominant mental health disciplines and leaving feminist understanding of distress poorly formulated, ill-prepared to answer the question of how to know when the distress was an aspect of an illness process and when it was a survival strategy whose half-life had expired. The dearth of genuinely feminist alternatives for describing distress in an organized fashion has undermined the power of feminist criticism of dominant diagnostic systems over the longer term. While the issues of gender and power first identified by feminist analysis have become increasingly salient to mainstream practitioners on many other psychotherapeutic dimensions, those essential feminist variables are almost absent in discourse on diagnosis. When I survey feminist writings on diagnosis, however, an implied model for understanding distress emerges. It is that model toward which this chapter focuses its arguments regarding how distress can be theorized in a feminist frame.

Needed: Feminist Diagnosis

If a feminist theory of distress is not to replicate the errors of patriarchal systems, an analysis of the problems in mainstream psychodiagnosis must go beyond the standard and somewhat superficial critiques. Psychodiagnosis as commonly practiced is for the most part theoretically incompatible with feminist therapy, because the assumptive models, methodologies, and authoritative data sources upon which standard diagnostic techniques are founded are profoundly tainted by patriarchal and monocultural assumptions about normalcy and the pathological nature of distress. As diagnosis is currently practiced, it maintains power imbalances between clients and therapists, encourages monocultural and androcentric models of mental health and functioning, and reifies artificial distinctions between problems that are "real pathology" (read: deserving payment for their treatment and inherent to the individual) and those that are merely "situational" (read: response to life events, thus not to be treated with the same degree of seriousness).

The diagnostic systems developed from such methodologically narrow and biased models, reified in the *Diagnostic and Statistical Manual of Mental Disorders (DSM)* and *International Classification of Diseases (ICD)*, are paradigmatic of oppressive dominant cultural norms as expressed through the mental health professions. Sexism, racism, heterosexism, ableism, classism, and ageism can all be found embedded in current diagnostic usages

(Becker & Lamb, 1994; Caplan, 1991; Kaplan, 1983). Diagnosis reflects the worldview and phenomenology of the dominant class; like history, it is written by "the winners." Diagnosis, the power to call behavior pathological as opposed to normative, or to define it as illness rather than criminality, carries extraordinary weight in dominant culture. The diagnosis given can determine such factors as imprisonment versus treatment, the duration and setting of therapy, the availability of payment by third parties (for example, treatment for "normal" distressed responses, called "V-codes" in the *DSM,* is usually not eligible for reimbursement by insurance companies), the willingness of a given therapist to work with a person, whether or not drugs will be offered or required, who will be allowed to intervene, and whether the person so diagnosed will be admitted to various valued social roles such as parent, teacher, or physician later in life. Learning to diagnose mental illness has come to be framed as an exact, arcane science open only to specially trained professionals who can tell the difference between one mental illness and another, or between a "real" problem and "malingering."

All of these are good reasons for feminist therapists to be wary of diagnosis. They are not, however, a brief for neglecting this matter. Instead, the realities of dominant cultural diagnostic paradigms are the best argument for a feminist theory of diagnostic thinking in which both distress and its absence are conceptualized in a new way. Feminist analysis must take social meanings of diagnosis into account at every turn, going beyond an analysis and critique of mainstream diagnostic categories to an examination of the potential for oppression in the application of nosology. Mainstream diagnoses, even the "good" ones, distort the therapist's vision so that distressed behaviors are judged and categorized through a patriarchal eye. It is not that all diagnoses are prima facie bad. Rather, it is that accepting any diagnosis without carefully questioning its origins and embedded assumptions may lead a therapist in directions that support rather than subvert patriarchy. Diagnosis is not simply labeling; a diagnosis positions a person in the social hierarchy in a particular and often immovable manner that may subject that person to exclusionary dominant attitudes toward the normative behaviors of a marginalized and oppressed social group.

As Rosenhan noted almost two decades ago, once a diagnosis has been awarded to a person, it is difficult to separate the two, even when the evidence makes clear that the diagnosis was incorrect, as was the case with Rosenhan's research participants, who feigned the schizophrenia with which they were diagnosed and whose clinicians clung to those diagnoses even when confronted with the truth of the experiment. Diagnoses con-

tained in the official manuals are images of dominant definitions of normalcy and deviance, containing assumptive models that ignore human
diversity and cultural variability. Even when a person appears to fit well
into a particular diagnostic category, a seductive image that can lure a
therapist into the unthinking use of various diagnostic terms because they
"feel right," feminist ways of knowing make it imperative to stop, think,
and question whose truths are contained in each standard term. Whenever
I note my own careless participation in this process, I am provided with
evidence of the power of diagnostic terminology and how easy it is to
exchange critical thinking for a quick and apparently simple way of conceptualizing a complex human being.

But diagnosis per se is not the problem, nor should one attempt to excise
it like a growth from the body. Feminist therapists need, instead, to
endeavor to *think diagnostically*. Diagnostic thinking, which may include
but—importantly for feminist therapy theory—is not limited to formal psychodiagnosis, provides a cornerstone of the epistemology and methodology of the feminist therapist. I use this term to refer to a system of intentional creation of hypotheses, working models of clients and their
phenomenologies. Thinking diagnostically requires the clinician and client
to work jointly to develop organized hypotheses about the nature, origins,
and meanings of the client's distress. These hypotheses serve to maintain a
course in therapy and to situate the therapy within a feminist analysis.
They allow for greater resonance between client and therapist and help to
differentiate between the client's core and the outgrowths of distress. Diagnostic thinking in feminist therapy leads to ways of naming distress; it may
even, in some circumstances, result in the application of a dominant diagnostic term. But this hypothesis-building process is done with the flaws
and biases of mainstream nosology kept firmly in mind by the therapist.

Why should feminist therapy concern itself with theorizing a model for
diagnosing? Isn't it enough simply to meet one's clients phenomenologically and respectfully? I don't think so. Diagnosis as an exercise in the
development of a theory of the person in therapy can be a powerful light
illuminating one's understanding of how this client, in this unique combination of circumstances, has come to this experience of distress and confusion. It is not enough, for the purposes of diagnostic understanding, to say
that this person is, for example, an incest survivor. One incest survivor is
not another incest survivor. The nature and meaning of this person's experience is mediated by contextual variables, such as gender, race, class, culture, and sexual orientation, as well as by individual variables: at what
ages the incest happened, how often, in what manner, with what accompanying experiences, harmful or strengthening, and by whom perpe-

trated. In feminist diagnostic thinking, these variables are all considered in relation to the political understanding of the meaning of incest to patriarchy as a strategy for control and dominance. This entire complex process of making sense of experience is diagnostic.

When diagnosis is regarded as unimportant or not a part of feminist therapy, there are unexpected and unwanted results. One unintended consequence has been the infiltration of feminist therapy practice by the very mainstream diagnostic labels it rejected. Feminist therapists write and speak about working with "borderlines" or "major depression" without examining either what these terms mean or what their use does to the development of the therapeutic relationship. Nor has there been a careful examination of the implications of the casual use of mainstream terminology in the absence of feminist analysis of the patriarchal assumptions and methodologies on which it is based.

Another unintended consequence is that in practice, feminist therapists have often accepted other sorts of labeling systems that had intuitive appeal, but were equally patriarchal or undermining of feminist social change goals. Later in this chapter I will explore at greater length the importance of questioning such grass-roots, implicit diagnostic models as strenuously as one challenges the nosology of the *DSM* and *ICD*.

Diagnostic thinking is not necessarily an exercise in creating new, feminist names for things that now have patriarchal titles, although for ease in communication some feminist therapists have attempted to reify their observations with particular terms such as "abuse disorders" (Brown, 1992a; Walker, 1989b). Rather, what I am exploring here is generating hypotheses about how to best encounter clients, maintain boundaries, and make choices of interventions. Diagnostic thinking gives us a framework for answering the question, What does it mean for the course of therapy if the client has had X experience in Y context and is from Z culture, is reporting Q symptoms and relates to me in A and B manners? Thus, in feminist diagnostic thinking, large, overarching categories of classification become less important than precise and complex delineations of each experience within a given social context.

On the Importance of Knowing Your "Enemies"

Let us then carefully examine the specific problems in mainstream psychodiagnosis as a model for understanding and classifying distress—problems that are many and not trivial even to the nonfeminist practitioner and theorist. The "science" of diagnosis as practiced today reflects a neo-

Kraepelinian (after Emil Kraepelin, the great nineteenth-century German classifier of psychopathology) obsession with the classification and numbering at a minutely distinct level of any sort of distress that might lead a person to seek the help of a mental health professional. In the words of Dr. Robert Spitzer (personal communication, spring, 1990), a well-known leader of the modern psychiatric diagnostic community, the viewpoint of the neo-Kraepelinians is, "If we treat it, it must be diagnosable, since anything that is not diagnosable would not require treatment from a professional."

In this somewhat tautological framework, the diagnostic process is aimed at identifying "pathologies," forms of "mental illness" to be treated and rooted out. This image of distress as a pathogen alien to the basic nature of the person and either unattached to social and political realities or representing an "excessive response" to external events when those are factored into the equation, harmonizes with a tendency in Western culture to tolerate behavioral deviations only when they have been medicalized and constructed as evidence of weakness or deficit. Deviant behavior not so diagnosed tends to be regarded as criminal; several current "mental illnesses," most notably alcoholism, were once socially constructed as forms of criminality. Homosexuality followed a similar route and now struggles to accomplish a final transformation from illness to minority group status.

An example of how such bias informs traditional diagnosis is described by feminist psychologist and cognitive behaviorist Iris Fodor (1992), who has traced the evolution of a diagnosis from "anxiety neurosis" to "panic disorder" across time from *DSM-II* to *DSM-IIIR*. The first term carries an underlying assumption of a disrupted psychodynamic process, reflecting the primacy of psychoanalytic paradigms for distress during the 1960s when the *DSM-II* was in use. The latter term is actively construed as a biological illness with unfortunate emotional overtones, in line with the increased emphasis on biological models that emerged during the 1980s as a primary basis for understanding and treating human distress. As the knowledge claims supporting mainstream diagnostic systems become increasingly biomedical in nature, so, too, do the diagnoses themselves.

While this change of emphasis is purported to represent advances in science, such claims to improved authority must be taken with a grain of salt. Feminist clinical psychologist Esther Rothblum and her colleagues (Rothblum, Solomon, & Albee, 1986) have noted that the politics of research funding determines to a great degree what kind of questions will be asked, and, consequently, what types of answers will be available. Biological models for understanding depression, anxiety, psychosis, and violence are afforded stronger support by the extant empirical data base, because research assuming the primacy of biology has been more likely to receive funding, both from the governments of the socially conservative 1980s and the managed-care 1990s, which sought to minimize and disclaim the influence of social factors and oppression on people's well-being, and from the drug companies, whose products are more salable in a context where distress is attributed to neurotransmitter deficiencies. Research that attempts to support a more psychosocial model is less likely to receive funding, less likely to occur, and less likely to become part of the published canon.

Interestingly, in none of the formulations of panic disorder (or any other diagnosis, for that matter) are attempts made to answer why women are extremely overrepresented among people diagnosed with this disorder. While gender prevalence is commented upon in the *DSM*, analysis of gender and its meaning is absent in every mention of this supposedly neutral bit of information.

Diagnosis is a very *inexact* science, despite all the trappings of formal criteria provided by the *DSM*. The emperor's new clothes are quite threadbare, if not nonexistent, although the beauty and sumptuousness of the garments of *DSM* diagnosis, otherwise known as the reliability and validity of the diagnostic categories, are persuasively touted to the degree that even many feminist therapists assume the value of this supposedly scientific data base. Even by mainstream standards, the norms of logical positivist empiricism and scientific method have been repeatedly violated by those developing the supposedly reliable and valid materials found in the *DSM* and *ICD* (for a complete discussion of the violations of empirical methodology in *DSM-IIIR*, see Brown [1992a]). But these lapses are not well known outside of a small group of professionals who have special interests in the science and politics of diagnosis, and they are rarely made available to the general mental health profession in an easily accessible form. The consequences of this fuzziness masquerading as science and precision can be quite profound when added to the asymmetry of power and authority in a psychotherapeutic relationship.

The Power of Naming, or, If You Call It a Skunk, You Will Assume That It Smells

What happens to the person who experiences a complex range of distress, including disturbances of interpersonal relationships, of self-care, of identity, and of consciousness? The decision of a therapist to name that client's distress "borderline personality disorder" as opposed to "complex post traumatic stress disorder" (Herman, 1992, 1993) will determine everything from how the therapist perceives the client, to the warmth and care that the client receives from this and other therapists, to the degree to which the client comes to feel shamed by the distress.

The first diagnostic term, borderline personality, as commonly used, construes this client as having a characterological pathology—to be deeply flawed as a human being at the very core. The name identifies the client to other therapists as a difficult case, a person toward whom one may express negative feelings and resentments and about whom one may legitimately complain. All these responses to "borderline" clients are extremely common and affect the quality of care received by those so diagnosed. Morever, there is the not inconsiderable problem of misdiagnosis with this term; many people with other disorders (multiple personality disorder being the most common) are diagnosed "borderline" because, at times of crisis when they first enter the mental health care system, they "look borderline." In other words, if you see a white stripe down its back, be prepared for a bad odor, whether it turns out to be a skunk or a paint-spattered squirrel (Becker & Lamb, 1994).

The second diagnosis, complex PTSD, has quite different meanings. It implies initially adaptive strategic responses in the service of survival by a person faced with repetitive interpersonal trauma, strategies that are now problematic because they no longer function for self-protection. This construction of the client's distress and reality is more likely to evoke in the therapist feelings of warmth and compassion and an enhanced willingness to identify with the client and see that person as capable of change. There is also less risk of misdiagnosis; the problem has been placed conceptually within the framework of post-traumatic phenomena. But this last diagnostic category, unlike borderline personality disorder, is not an accepted diagnosis and was left out of the final drafts of the *DSM-IV*, despite striking research evidence for its presence in a variety of field trials (van der Kolk & Roth, 1992).

Or perhaps the problem is that the person can neither sleep nor eat, cries frequently, feels guilt and self-criticism, lacks energy and motivation. Most therapists of any orientation would call this cluster of symptoms "depression." How the therapist construes the etiology of the depression, however, can make all the difference in how the client understands the meaning of the experience and in the treatment. Current mainstream models lean heavily toward biological explanations and medication-based treatments (American Psychiatric Association, 1993). Clients receiving this explanation may feel that they are no more than passive recipients of drugs; they may never be asked to examine how their lives may have been a factor in their sadness and lethargy. A feminist perspective (Jack, 1991), while not ignoring the biological components of depression (McGrath, Keita, Strickland, & Russo, 1990), would also ask how this depression might be the result of silencing the self, how it might be a desperate "going on strike" or even the long-term neurochemical results of trauma-mediated changes to the brain (van der Kolk, 1987). Or, attending differently to biology than mainstream psychiatry does, the feminist therapist might inquire how this depression could reflect genuine fatigue from overwork, or an overload of body systems due to stress or toxic exposures. Here the problem is less that of potential misdiagnosis but rather one of misapplied interventions arising from narrow explanatory models that are prevalent in dominant diagnostic thinking.

Given the hegemony of the *DSM* system and the reified nature of diagnoses, it is essential for feminist therapists to recall that the particular label and underlying explanatory model chosen by the therapist usually reflects less a scientific understanding of distress than the therapist's own specific theoretical orientation and biases. The name chosen reflects the therapist's degree of willingness to identify with the client and the therapist's hopefulness or cynicism about the client's potential for change. Diagnosis as commonly practiced thus functions as a dividing line between "we," the therapists (that is, the mentally healthy ones), and "they," the clients, the ones with the mental illness.

Diagnosis and the Larger Zeitgeist

In addition to those intrinsic to American psychiatry, other forms of bias and politics also inform and distort the contents of the diagnostic manuals. The politics of the greater culture, and the degree to which certain behaviors are tolerated and sympathized with or demonized and stigmatized, often determine what goes into and what is kept out of formal diagnosis. The fates of two recently proposed diagnostic categories are instructive. In the late 1980s, conflicts arose within the professional community over a series of diagnoses being proposed for inclusion in the *DSM-IIIR*. One of these diagnoses, initially called "paraphilic rapism" and later "paraphilic coercive disorder," represented a transformation of criminality into mental illness by proposing a diagnostic category for repetitive sex offenders, constructing rape as a form of paraphilia, or perverse sexuality. This category was not accepted into the *DSM-IIIR*, largely because of the protests of law enforcement agencies, who saw in this reframing of rape as a mental illness the ultimate diminished-capacity plea for any person so accused. Aside from the legal establishment, however, few people questioned the desirability of defining male sexual violence against women as a form of mental illness deserving sympathy and treatment.

Simultaneously, a category first titled "masochistic personality disorder" and eventually named "self-defeating personality disorder" was proposed. Its intent was to describe those individuals who appeared to undermine themselves and their treatment. This category was strenuously opposed by feminists within the mental health disciplines (including this author) for many reasons. First, masochism had long been associated with femininity in the psychoanalytic literature, and there was a bias toward diagnosing women with this label. Other important problems in this proposed diagnosis were its tendency to stigmatize women survivors of violence and its categorization of such response patterns as a personality disorder, a severe form of characterological pathology assumed to be chronic and difficult to treat successfully.

As the protests grew and critics of this proposed disorder were given access to the decision-making process by which the diagnosis had been developed, several interesting facts emerged. The diagnostic category had been developed during a fishing trip by three psychiatrists who were bemoaning the intractability of certain of their patients. They decided that perhaps a new diagnostic category was called for and set out to develop one. After these three proposed their set of criteria, a group of patients who appeared to meet the criteria were studied for a period of several years in a field trial of the diagnosis.

Of interest to the critics of this new diagnosis was that, while the symptom picture described by the diagnostic criteria was quite similar to that seen in women victims of interpersonal violence such as rape and battering, the group running the field trial had neglected to ascertain whether any of their subjects had histories of such violence. The critics pointed out that defining what were likely to be post-traumatic responses to interpersonal violence as a personality disorder would have the effect of stigmatizing and misdiagnosing a large group of patients, primarily women. When little empirical data to support the presence of such a diagnosis emerged, the group proposing it sent a questionnaire to a group of psychiatrists asking them if they believed in the existence of such a diagnosis. Only the believers were then asked if they thought that the proposed criteria gave an accurate picture of this diagnostic entity; nonbelievers were excluded from further input. This last survey was then put forward as empirical evidence of the existence of self-defeating personality disorder (Brown, 1990c; Walker, 1989a).

The new diagnosis was finally placed in an appendix to the *DSM-IIIR*, for "further study," not because of any evidence supporting the diagnosis but rather in deference to the power and authority within the American Psychiatric Association of those who had championed the diagnosis. Because no authority stronger than the American Psychiatric Association intervened, this diagnosis, clearly based in sexist stereotype and laden with stigmatizing potential, was not dismissed out of hand, as was paraphilic rapism. With the publication of the *DSM-IV*, this category appears to be banished from the lexicon entirely, since even research from a mainstream perspective did not support its existence and inclusion (Skodol, Oldham, Gallaher, & Bezirganian, 1994).

The decision to call a cluster of behaviors a mental illness, as well as to place it in a particular category of mental illness, is responsive to many factors that have nothing to do with science but a great deal to do with the feelings, experiences, and epistemologies of those in positions of power and dominance in mental health disciplines. In the case of self-defeating personality disorder, the feelings of white male heterosexual psychiatrists about difficult female patients, the assumptions they made about the motivations of such patients, and the sexism lying close to the surface of these feelings and interpretations were more informative to the development of this diagnosis than were any data from other sources. While a feminist methodology is open to a variety of sorts of data—including, importantly, clinical experience—in this instance the clinical experiences of white male psychiatrists with their female patients had never been exposed to the scrutiny and feminist analysis of the therapeutic relationship, described in the previous chapter, that might have illuminated other reasons for difficulties in therapy aside from characterological psychopathology in the women being treated. A feminist analysis at the very least would have examined questions of violence, and would have explored the manners in which certain behaviors might be reasonable responses to the demands of difficult social settings. Such analysis also would have examined what, besides the client's so-called resistance to treatment, might be leading to the client's apparent sabotage of the therapist's intentions.

Acceptance of this diagnosis was made easier by the larger social context in which the debate occurred. In the 1980s in the United States, social conservativism, misogyny, and backlash against the small gains of the women's movement were the cultural norm. Susan Faludi's study of the popular culture of woman-bashing (1991) described an external social reality in which victim-blame was modeled from the top down (for example, the comment by the president of the United States that homeless people wanted to be so), and where women's every move toward self-determination was met with authoritative statements on the terrible prices to be paid for daring to break away from patriarchally prescribed roles. In this zeitgeist, the diagnosis of self-defeating personality disorder was a perfect fit with emerging cultural attitude toward "losers." The not-very-subtle message of this diagnosis was that if life continues to place obstacles to well-being in your path, you must be doing something to create that reality. Such an assumption supports patriarchy most powerfully.

The Problem of the Normative Assumption

Not all diagnostic categories have been the targets of feminist critiques. Some have been accepted as descriptive; others lauded as reflecting movement toward a more context-based understanding of human distress. But feminist questions about dominant models should not stop with the overtly problematic diagnosis. Even diagnoses that have been embraced by many feminist therapists contain inherent assumptions that are problematic when subjected to more careful scrutiny. The inclusion of the diagnosis of post-traumatic stress disorder in the *DSM-III* in 1980 was hailed by many feminist therapists as recognition of a diagnostic category founded in social realities, less stigmatizing than most because its etiology was presumed to be a traumatic event, not any inherent pathology. Yet the opening lines of the first criterion for the diagnosis, the definition of a trauma, are instructive in what they say and what is assumed and omitted. Trauma, says the *DSM-IIIR*, is an event "outside the range of usual human experience." This assumption of the generic human becomes instantly problematic when base rates of certain events in the lives of certain groups of people are tallied. If one-third of all women are sexually assaulted as children, one-quarter beaten by partners and spouses, and almost one-half sexually harassed in the workplace, are these events less traumatic because they are not "outside the range" (Brown, 1991c, 1992a; Root, 1992a, 1992b)? Or are women not "usual humans"? If both direct and vicarious exposure to racial hatred is a daily experience for some people of color (Essed, 1991; Greene, 1990), then is this commonplace stressor excluded from a definition of trauma for the purposes of this diagnosis? Are people of color in white societies not "usual humans"? Who defines the normative "human" for the purposes of determining which experiences fall "outside the range" of that normative life?

These are not trivial questions; without that initial diagnostic criterion of exposure to a stressor as defined in the *DSM-IIIR,* the diagnosis of PTSD technically cannot be made. The same set of symptoms can be and usually is described in other, more pejorative ways; in practice, self-defeating personality disorder is often considered by clinicians instead, despite the warning in the *DSM* not to use that label yet. (One can even purchase a popular psychological test, the Millon Clinical Multiaxial Inventory, that will render this diagnosis.) Misdiagnosis and ineffective or even harmful treatment are the result. While the *DSM-IV* contains revisions that define trauma more in terms of the person's subjective experiences, the presence of powerful normative bias in even this most context-sensitive diagnostic label is instructive regarding the meta-assumptions of an objective human norm that inform formal nosology. Indeed, having tried out the use of the new definition for a traumatic stressor in court upon the arrival of the *DSM-IV*, I have found that the question of what constitutes a threat to personal integrity (one possible characteristic of a traumatic stressor in *DSM-IV*) is still open to patriarchal deconstructions. The failure to protect against harm, which can be frightening to vulnerable people, is not yet sufficiently visible to be considered traumagenic to mainstream interpreters of this wording like the attorney cross-examining me on it.

The application of feminist analysis and epistemology exposes the dominant norms and assumptions powerfully embedded in the diagnostic description, functioning to exclude further and stigmatize people whose "usual human experience" does not fall within a dominant generic definition of humanity. The *DSM-IIIR* definition of trauma also helped to maintain the dominant fallacy that trauma is an unusual event. At an international conference on trauma in 1992, Lars Weissath, one of the "fathers" of the trauma movement, arose during a discussion of changes in this criterion for PTSD to plead that this definition not be changed in any way, because of what this might say about the nature of the world in which too many people now live, where trauma is not "outside the range." (In a recent publication of the PTSD committee for *DSM-IV*, however, a number of mainstream trauma researchers note that women's life experiences of rape and other assault are quite common yet should still qualify their targets for a PTSD diagnosis [Kilpatrick & Resnick, 1993]).

Diagnosis and Power

Another problematic aspect of diagnosis for feminist theory is the manner in which it imbalances power in the therapeutic relationship. In standard diagnostic systems, knowledge and authority are placed entirely in the hands of the professional. The client or patient is defined as unqualified and unable to understand or know the real nature (that is, exact diagnosis) of the problem and is often allowed little input into the diagnostic decision aside from a recitation of symptoms, which are construed as "subjective" (hence, less valuable) data, differentiated from the "objective" observations of the evaluator.

This power to name and define reality serves to deepen and exacerbate the power imbalance and inequities between therapist and client. In unilaterally imposing a diagnosis, the therapist lays a claim to sole knowledge of the true nature of the client's difficulties; this act establishes the authority and expertise of the therapist in no uncertain terms. Moreover, the therapist's decision has profound implications beyond that particular therapist-client relationship, for how the client will be perceived and treated in other, later contexts. Diagnosis as commonly practiced, utilizing some of the special language of the initiated, adds to the apparent mystery of psychotherapy. Doing diagnostic naming without knowing what assumptions are inherent in the language increases the risk and likelihood that a feminist therapist will inadvertently transform her work into something different from the feminist therapy relationship discussed previously.

Some Missteps in the Direction of Alternatives

Knowing the problems of mainstream diagnostic models is a first step toward a feminist model of diagnostic thinking. A second is a willingness to scrutinize with equal care any existing alternative diagnostic systems. The fact that the person proposing a name for a problem is *not* a representative of the American Psychiatric Association does not mean that the name is any more useful clinically or more supportive of feminist goals of social justice and social change. Simply going in a direction opposite from mainstream nosology will not necessarily lead to truly feminist diagnostic thinking.

One false step that has been taken in the name of disrupting diagnostic hegemony has been the privileging of diagnoses developed by grass-roots movements, such as the incest-recovery movement, the adult child movement, or even the women's movement. These social phenomena, which focus on sources of distress, often come up with diagnostic labels as a form of shorthand for self-description, such as "incest survivor" or "ACOA" (adult child of alcoholics). The embrace of such terminology cedes the right of diagnostic naming to the therapist's clients, giving them the power and authority to decide the nature of their own problems. While intuitively this simplistic strategy seems right, in practice it ignores the ways in which the grass roots are affected by the constructions of dominant culture and the oppressive assumptions that are often well hidden in those constructions. Codependency, a very common client-originated diagnosis that arose from a grass-roots movement, provides an excellent example of the problems with this approach to finding an alternative to patriarchal diagnosis.

In the early 1990s, the notion of codependency had a certain attractiveness and currency among some feminist therapists, because superficially it appears capable of standing up to the scrutiny of feminist analysis. It is not in the standard diagnostic manuals, thus it is free of the overt taint of association with dominant norms in the mental health professions. It is a term many clients use to describe themselves, and it arises from a self-help movement. These are all powerful arguments for its embrace by feminist therapists. Yet this term is one that I, and several other feminist theorists (Brown, 1990c; Hagan, 1989; Tavris, 1992; Lerner, 1993; Johnson, 1989) have identified as extremely undermining to women and possibly antifeminist in a variety of ways. When the assumptive models underlying the notion of codependency are carefully examined and deconstructed under the feminist microscope using the same criticisms leveled at the *DSM*, the problems inherent in this term, as well as the dangers of using any diagnostic term without careful feminist analysis, become more apparent. The questions of assumptive models and the norms for "health" embedded in this term are as cogent for this label as they are in the case of self-defeating personality disorder.

The concept of codependency emerged in the alcoholism counseling field during the 1950s and 1960s. Beginning with the term *co-alcoholic*, used to describe the spouse or partner of an alcoholic, the idea reflected the influence of systemic models of analysis on the alcoholism treatment field. Such models construed everyone close to the "identified patient" as equally responsible for the alcoholism, giving rise to a trend in which the behaviors of the nonpatients were made part of the problem. In the historical context in which this analysis developed, for all practical purposes the prototypical co-alcoholic was the Caucasian wife of a Caucasian male alcoholic. (Heterosexual women alcoholics with male partners were largely invisible to the alcoholism treatment field until very recently, and lesbian alcoholics and their partners were simply unimaginable.)

With alcoholism as the central category of analysis as well as the sole explanatory model for any and all problems in the marital systems under scrutiny, the developers of the concept of co-alcoholism did not give thought to the possibility of links between the female gender role and the supposedly co-alcoholic behaviors identified as problematic and in need of treatment. That is, no one asked whether these behaviors were simply well-socialized heterosexual femininity in the context of an alcoholic husband. Nor do they seem to have noted that because women are perceived both by ourselves and by others as having primary responsibility for the emotional well-being of heterosexual relationships (Bernard, 1981), women's sense of guilt and shame at a relational "failure" such as a husband's alcoholism might render them more willing to seek treatment for this presumed deficit than was the alcoholic himself. The fact that women accepted this label was taken as evidence of its accuracy. The co-alcoholic was presumed to have some responsibility for both the alcoholic's drinking and his recovery and sobriety, and her behaviors in response to her spouse and his drinking were described as forms of pathology assumed to predate her relationship with him. This diagnosis is also particularly likely to be unintentionally racist, since many normative social relationships in cultures of color in the United States resemble codependent behaviors. This is especially a risk in the American Indian community, where high alcoholism rates are some of the most visible components of the genocide practiced against American aboriginal people, but where caretaking behaviors are often the remnants of healthy traditions, and not co-alcoholism. Here, the relationships of family and tribal members are complex and interlocking; the imposition of a codependency model of what constitutes healthy relating would shame people for relational dynamics that are necessary for the health of the group and thus the recovery of alcoholic members.

When this concept was taken up and expanded upon in the middle and late 1980s by clinicians working with the children and extended family systems of alcoholic and chemically dependent people, it was again not subjected to a feminist analysis. The concept expanded beyond its original boundaries until the presence of an alcoholic in the relationship ceased to be a criterion for the diagnosis of codependency; anyone who behaved as the experts described was eligible for the diagnosis. As currently used, codependency is a broad term describing a pattern of interpersonal relating in which the person diagnosed codependent needs to be needed and places others at the center of her life, reading their minds, hypervigilantly attending to their wants, and doing whatever is necessary to preserve the well-being of the relationship—presumably at considerable cost to the codependent's own mental health. Codependent persons are also often described as "addicted" to relationships, love, romance, or some combination of these. When women, especially white middle-class women, began to recognize themselves in this diagnosis by the thousands, making best-sellers of such books as Robin Norwood's *Women Who Love Too Much* (1985), no one stopped to ask what was meant by this overrepresentation of women among those self-diagnosing as codependent and thus as chronically addicted and at risk.

Feminist analysis notes that the behaviors defined as codependent by even the most precise and scientific materials on the topic (Cermak, 1986) parallel those first identified by feminist sociologist Helen Mayer Hacker (1976) as present in the relational patterns of all members of subordinate groups. Hacker's commentary on the parallels between all oppressed groups' behaviors in the presence of the dominant, later expanded by feminist psychiatrist and theoretician Jean Baker Miller (1976) as well as by feminist social psychologist Rhoda Unger (1990), argues that when people are placed in submissive or oppressed positions in a social hierarchy, their relationships with members of the dominant class will be characterized by the sort of care-giving, mind-reading, "enabling" behavior considered to be pathognomonic of codependency. As feminist theoretician Kay Leigh Hagan (1989) points out, as long as women are oppressed, they will present evidence of being "codependent."

The concept of codependency functions to stigmatize, with labels like "illness" and "addiction," ways of relating that may be normative for certain groups of people, women and people of color among them, who are oppressed in hierarchies of dominance and submission and to supplant calls for revolutionary social change with prescriptions for lifelong attendance at support-group meetings.

Read with the aid of this multicultural feminist lens, codependency as a concept is as much a pathologizing of common and ordinary nondominant modes of functioning as is the formal diagnosis of histrionic personality disorder. Its supposed "grass roots" are, when given careful scrutiny, deeply misogynist, in that they are grown from the soil of blaming wives for the problems of their alcoholic husbands and fertilized with the manure of the illusion found in classical family systems theory that all people in a relational system are equal in power, regardless of matters such as gender. It is a term, however, potentially more dangerous in some ways than standard diagnoses when used by feminist therapists, in that it grows out of a grass-roots self-help movement many of whose leaders and teachers have themselves been white women; one of the most prominent of these codependency gurus was at one time self-described as a feminist therapist. Consequently, it is a descriptive label that a feminist therapist is more likely to utilize, because the client herself uses it, or because it was developed by people who were not mental health experts in a context superficially appealing to some. In such an instance, the feminist analysis may be undermined or neglected because of the assumptions present in the name given to the problem.

Another diagnostic category proposed by a feminist psychologist is delusional dominating personality disorder (Caplan, 1991). Although attractive at first glance, it too has basic problems. DDPD describes as a form of serious character pathology sexist and misogynist attitudes and behaviors and the tendency to solve conflicts via violence. It thus defines the problematic behaviors from the viewpoint of the oppressed, rather than the oppressors. From a simplistic interpretation of feminism, this makes sense; why not call oppressive behavior a sickness in need of treatment? In line with Perkins' (1991a) critique of the tendency to psychologize that which is political, however, it is necessary to ask what happens if this cluster of behaviors is moved into the psychotherapeutic realm. The implication is that if only there were sufficient feminist treatment, sexism would disappear. Locating the problem internal to the person, as diagnosis does, removes it from the sociopolitical realm. While artifacts of oppressive attitudes do manifest themselves in many persons' internal structures, it may be more subversive of feminism than of patriarchy to identify the problem as primarily psychological and thus located in individuals rather than in the culture of patriarchy.

Toward a Feminist Theory of Distress

A feminist theory of distress makes an important distinction between subjective pain, interactive experiences of problematic behavior, and pathology; the latter is placed primarily *outside* the person, in the social and political matrix. Not all feminist theorists of distress agree entirely with this notion that the pathology lies in oppressive social and political structures. Judith Herman (1993), a feminist psychiatrist, has criticized other feminist therapy theorists such as Ellyn Kaschak (1992) for de-emphasizing the possible pathology of the individual. While I would not disagree with Herman's assertion that there are some forms of biological pathology (or, more accurately, deviations from the human neurochemical norm) that manifest themselves as subjective distress and interpersonal difficulties, I *do* disagree with the notion that these variations in neurochemistry are evidence for some forms of psychopathology that are primarily in and of the individual. After all, by the time the brains of people diagnosed with schizophrenia or bipolar disorder are presented to the scanning instruments of psychiatric researchers, the bodies encasing those brains will have lived through many varied life experiences that might themselves profoundly alter brain neurochemical functioning (van der Kolk, 1992). While the supposed heritability of such "disorders" is much touted in the research literature, the biologically oriented literature still offers few good explanations of those factors that are greatly salient to a feminist analysis:

the overrepresentation of the poor and people of color among those diagnosed schizophrenic and the profound differences between males and
females in age of onset, the course taken by symptoms, and the response
to standard biological treatment modalities, of schizophrenia (Greenwald,
1992). If these factors are taken into account, then the currently fashionable
model of a neurological pathology makes less sense.

On the other hand, the pathology—the wrongness—of oppressive
social structures is less open to dispute and has informed the thinking of
practicing feminist therapists from very early on (Greenspan, 1983). While
there are risks in framing political oppression as *psycho*pathology, it
appears to me to be necessary that a feminist model of distress locate the
problem centrally in the culture of patriarchy, thereby strengthening the
argument, advanced at greater length below, that distress not only is not
pathology but is often a sign that something within a person is struggling
to resist and thereby undermine patriarchy, but doing so with tools that
are not currently adequate to the task at hand.

There is an undeniable utopian metatheme to this placement of the
problem in the oppressive social context. The seductive—or perhaps hope-
ful—assumption is that were the feminist project of radical social transformation ever to be accomplished, most of the unmanageable subjective distress that now creates work for feminist therapists would disappear. One
feminist therapist, theorist, and writer has even published a work of speculative fiction in which this utopian vision has been accomplished
(Starhawk, 1993). One main character, once a feminist therapist, has long
ago been put out of work by the success of her revolution—a reason for
unemployment to be devoutly wished by myself and most of my colleagues. It is some measure of the commitment of feminist therapists to the
overarching feminist project of radical social transformation that we
would choose for a model of distress one whose eventual goal would be to
render our profession obsolete.

Resistance, Resilience, and "Normalcy"

While traditional models of diagnosis focus solely on the nature and
specifics of a person's distress, with various lists of criteria, feminist con-
ceptualizations of distress emerge from a framework in which a person's
strengths, skills, and competencies are first theorized. The notion of defining "normal" behavior is somewhat paradoxical within a feminist context,
because feminist theories are so strongly antinormative, opposed to the
creation of an actual or implied model of the right sort of human being. It

is not necessary to define a norm, however, in order to describe the parameters of well-being, or even simply of the absence of distress. It may even be useful to be able to describe those forms of distress that are welcome evidence of health, rather than the harbingers of pathology.

Consequently, feminist theorizing of distress also pays careful attention to the sources of strength, resilience, and resistance present and available in individuals, their cultures, and the surrounding environments. The questions raised by this focus have to do with a person's capacity to withstand, transform, and subvert oppressive and potentially damaging experiences; thus, the person is theorized as an active, interactive agent, participating in personal, social, and political processes that may have various forms of both distress and well-being as outcomes. This focus also explicitly acknowledges that people have different degrees of privilege and resources that differentially affect their capacity to be active participants. The person who is well sheltered by social and environmental factors, such as material comfort, is likely to be resilient in different ways from a person who has never had such a contextual cushion. For some people, the need to respond to oppression or other travails will have led to the development of response capacities that will give them the advantage at times of unusual challenge. While this attention to resilience is not unique to feminist theorizing, its central place in diagnostic thinking, and in particular the attention given to the ways the disenfrachised and marginalized express resilience, are particularly feminist. Moreover, resilience is conceptualized in feminist theorizing as both individual and cultural resilience, with the notion that people may draw upon not only resources unique to themselves (for example, a biological endowment of a quick mind or a strong body, or an individually well-crafted social support network, some of the factors identified as sources of resilience in the mainstream literature on this topic), but also those available in their culture of origin (for example, a well-developed set of strategies for coping with the experience of exile, or a powerful spiritual practice that offers means for responding effectively to oppression).

Resilience often gives a person the capacity to resist patriarchy by utilizing resources, internal and external, that are less dependent upon patriarchal structures of reward. Such resistance constitutes the person's intentional or unintentional unwillingness to participate in oppressive dominant norms. There are times at which the strategies utilized for resistance are themselves a source of distress. This does not, however, make such strategies pathological. The story is told, perhaps apocryphally, of the Jewish woman who, starving on meager rations in a Nazi concentration camp, nonetheless fasted on Yom Kippur, the Day of Atonement, on which Jews traditionally abstain from food. Because this was a hunger that she had chosen, her fasting constituted an act of resistance in which her Jewishness was expressed and defined by her own actions, rather than by those of her Nazi tormentors. Similarly, some acts of resistance, perhaps less consciously attempted than those ascribed to this nameless woman, may be subjectively distressing in the way that she, on Yom Kippur, was even more hungry and weak than on other days; the subjective distress, no less felt, signals the manner in which a person draws a line and says no to being disempowered and dehumanized. This vision of pain as a possible voice of internal personal power is a unique aspect of the feminist lens on distress and fundamental to the view that the pain is not necessarily the ultimate problem or even symptomatic of a problem in the person experiencing that pain.

A Feminist Biopsychosocial Model

In recent years, mainstream theorists of psychopathology have begun to speak of the importance of a "biopsychosocial model" for understanding the etiologies of distress. This term implies that weight must be given equally to the contributions of biology, psychology, and social interaction in any attempt to comprehend how and why a person experiences certain varieties of distress. In practice, however, this has simply been a new term for the old attempt to balance "nature" explanations—those focusing on inborn temperament or models of biological illness—with "nurture" explanations—those that focus on learned experiences—with a token bow in the direction of epistemological inclusiveness. These models have also called more attention to biology than to the other components; the biology in question is usually the neurochemistry of the human brain, the locus of interest for North American biological psychiatry today.

Feminist therapy takes this interactive model quite seriously, however, in theorizing and naming distress. The contributions of psychological and social factors to the development of distress are somewhat transparent in feminist models. The psychosocial environment is conceptualized as including individual relationships, the common focus of psychological theorizing, as well as the spiritual, political, and cultural forces that shape and hold those relationships. The feminist biopsychosocial model emphasizes the necessity of understanding the multiple roots of people's styles of being in the world. There is frankly a bias toward the social component of the biopsychosocial model of feminist therapy, in its insistence on the preeminence of political analysis. But this self-same emphasis on the contributions of culture to experience directs attention to the biological, as well, framed in a particularly feminist manner. Here, biology is envisioned as something more than neurotransmitters, including all the varied experiences of living in the body itself.

THE BODY IN FEMINIST THERAPY THEORY

In the feminist model, the body is the locus not simply of neurochemical interactions but of lived experience. It is the stimulus for responses from the psychosocial environment. In and on their bodies, people remember and reenact their experiences of pain, grief, joy, and strength.

Feminist psychology has for the most part rejected psychobiological explanations of behavior (see Bem [1993] for a recent thorough review of this literature). Specifically, in theorizing distress and resilience, it does not assume that any behavior observed is "innate" to the body, an expression of a way of being that would be the same in all social contexts. This feminist insistence on the malleability of human behavior and the low level of our hard-wiring has often been interpreted as a rejection of the biological. But this is not the case. Instead, it is an understanding of biology as an interactive, socially and politically mediated phenomenon, rather than some sort of pure and overpowering force that breaks through the veneer of social context. It is the insistence that such categories as gender and race are socially constructed rather than fixed and physical, and that those social constructions of the body are politically meaningful.

If, for instance, a feminist therapist wishes to explore the contribution of the body to a client's distress, feminist theorizing might focus attention on some of the politically and culturally salient aspects of that person's body, as well as the purely biological features of that body. The body's sex, a biological feature, potentially has multiple social and political meanings. There are differences in genetic contributions; each of the many different combinations of X and Y chromosomes carries different risk factors for both physical and mental difficulties. Additionally, not all bodies are neatly isomorphic from chromosomal to structural level; people with XXY, XYY, and XO chromosomal structures, for example, will appear to be members of the better-known XX (female) and XY (male) groups but will vary in some degree from their apparent simulacrums. People with androgen insensitivity—chromosomally XY but structurally "female" in appearance—or those fetally androgenized—carrying XX chromosomes with "male" or ambiguous external genitals—will have a different history written in and on their bodies than will those people for whom all aspects of the biological sexual equation match up. The person whose body has been operated upon so that it matches the internal experience of gender—a convert, as it were, to either male or female status—will have still other meanings ascribed to and felt within the body than will those born into the physical appurtenances that fit with their self-perceived gender identity.

Other facets of the body as it is perceived socially will also be of importance in comprehending a person's experiences of strength, pain, and coping. The color of the skin, the texture of the hair, and height and weight; the ability or inability to see, hear, or speak clearly, to process information in those forms culturally privileged, to move with ease and grace, to practice self-care autonomously—all of these are biological experiences with social, relational, and political implications (Panzarino, 1994). Being "too smart for a girl," having "bad hair," or passing the paper bag test (in pre-Black Power African-American middle- and upper-class social groups, anyone darker than a paper bag was considered less attractive), being born with cerebral palsy or a cleft palate are aspects of the biological that are also not purely of the body because of the social meanings that attach. Being able-bodied once and then disabled also transforms personal and social meaning and can reposition a person within the political matrix.

The particular history of a body as a source of resilience or distress is centrally important. The body constitutes the first stimulus that a person offers to the social context; it provides the concrete reality in which subjective experiences of pain, pleasure, strength, and confusion reside. Attempts to change the body and to find environments that will offer a different series of responses to the body, are part of a broadly envisioned biological contribution to both risk and resilience, as is the body's very movement through the world. What is known in the body may yet be known nowhere else in a client's personal epistemologies, yet may be invaluable in the transformative process (Moss, 1985).

An example of the importance of the body and its life story in a feminist comprehension of distress can be found in Carla's therapy. Carla, a white woman from a working-class Southern family who worked in social services and about whom I first wrote a number of years ago (Brown, 1991d), entered therapy to address her possible infertility. Her difficulty in becoming pregnant and bearing a child—a problem that is often painful for a woman in U.S. cultures where biological child-bearing is privileged—had been made even more fraught with meaning by the experiences previously written on her body. She had been repeatedly sexually abused during childhood and adolescence by family medical care-givers. One of her resistance strategies had been to become adept at disso-ciating herself from experiences of pain and pleasure alike, thus denying the abusers the satisfaction of controlling her responses to their manipula-tions. Being in control of her body was supremely important to Carla.

So, too, was the pursuit of an experience of bodily normalcy; she imag-ined that being pregnant would be a healing experience, one completely untouched by the hands of her abusers. Bearing a child would be an act of pure health, of being able to participate, at long last, in an experience of female biology that held no shame, pain, or secrets. She had never imag-ined that she might be unable to get pregnant.

When she began trying to become pregnant and for many months did not, she became first terrified and then enraged at herself. The possibility of infertility was an almost intolerable reality; she felt outraged, betrayed by her body's failure to cooperate in this "perfectly natural" female experi-ence. Her distress, which emerged in the forms of self-hatred and shame, rang loudly with the importance to Carla of being able to control her body, no matter what. She could barely tolerate the irony that she had been able to control her responses to sexual abuse but could not control her fertility; therefore, in her own eyes, her body had become a failure. Many of the ways in which she expressed her distress centered in and on her body, for it was her body's past experience and current apparent recalcitrance that were the focuses of her distress.

For Carla, the meaning of her body in her life and the centrality of her body's experiences to her personal narrative and sense of self were the fundamental aspects of the biological portion of the biopsychosocial framework of her distress. In her case, it was less important to know what might be happening biologically at the level of her neurotransmitters and more important to know something about the lived biology of her bodily experiences. While there was certainly something happening to her neu-rotransmitters, to judge by the various symptoms she reported, it would have done little good just to address the brain chemistry aspect of her dis-tress if the problem of how she experienced life in her body were left untouched. "Betrayal by the body" has thus been a more meaningful diagnosis, as it were, through which Carla and I have understood and worked to alleviate her distress, than would any formal diagnostic label-ing of what could otherwise easily be called depression and post-trau-matic stress. Naming her experience through her own terms transformed diagnosis into a feminist process in which Carla began to discover her own voice.

AN EXPANDED VIEW OF THE ENVIRONMENT, OR, FAMILIES ARE NOT THE ONLY SOCIAL ECOLOGY

In the feminist biopsychosocial model, political factors are also considered important possible sources of distress. This attention to the impact of political factors in the social environment is both unique and necessary for a feminist theory of distress. While most psychosocially oriented mainstream models of distress theorize the family as the most important locus of psychosocial experience, feminist therapy theory shifts the focus away from the family and places personal relationships within the complex matrix of larger social and political realities before they are analyzed for possible etiological factors. The politics of the family as a whole, not just the individual interpersonal relationships found there, is of concern in a feminist analysis. Cultural and politic phenomena that shape family experience are necessary aspects of a feminist view of psychosocial realities.

In some cases, cultural and political factors can be longstanding, ongoing dynamics. Maria Root (1992b), a feminist clinical psychologist, has written about the ways in which exposure to racism, sexism, heterosexism, and other forms of oppression can constitute an "insidious trauma" that has a long-term effect on the well-being of people in target groups. A person from such a target group coming to a feminist therapist with complaints of depressed mood and impaired self-respect might have that distress theorized as the result of many years of exposure to devaluation, actual or threatened bias-based violence, and the lack of emotional resources available in a community that has had to spend its efforts in a defense against invasion. The therapist would also, however, explore the client's resilience and strategies for resistance. She would ask how this person has been able, in the relationship to self and others, to transcend or fight back against the oppression that has been the constant background noise to life.

The interplay of meaning between family and larger social context can be particularly informative at this juncture, as the therapist and client inquire whether and to what degrees the family colluded with or taught resistance to oppressive dominant norms. The expression of social forces within the microcosm of a family structure can be understood as central to the expression of power dynamics among family members. Rather than simply describing a person's family of origin as "dysfunctional," this political analysis attends to the manners in which any apparent dysfunction might represent an expression of external or internalized oppression.

For example, Renee, a middle-class white heterosexual woman, described being taught by her mother to be a "nice girl"; when she began her therapy work, she was angry at her mother for these lessons and blamed her for the problems that she, Renee, was experiencing with self-esteem and interpersonal assertion. Feminist analysis in therapy gave her a different perspective, enabling her to see her mother and herself in relationship to Renee's father, a strongly authoritarian family patriarch, and to understand her mother's lessons as instruction in survival in relation to this man. While Renee continues to be angry at her mother at times, she can now see her family as an example of patriarchal oppression in mid-twentieth-century North America, rather than as an especially pathological entity. She can also see how both of her parents reflected broader cultural values regarding gender, power, and the nature of heterosexual relating; this perception in turn has given her greater awareness of her own non-conscious participation in patriarchal ideologies and supports her choices to disconnect from those values. And now she can appreciate her mother's attempt to protect her in the ways that were available, healing some of the split between mother and daughter wrought by patriarchy, as well as by their particular patriarch.

Returning to early second-wave feminist analyses of the family in patriarchy, we might also ask whether it is possible to envision as functional and healthy any family in which patriarchal dominant norms of sexism, racism, heterosexism, and so on are the defining variables, no matter how benignly expressed toward individual family members. The upper-middle-class, abled-bodied white woman who cannot understand why she feels so valueless may gain insight into her distress when her "normal" family's profoundly oppressive attitudes toward women are exposed by feminist questions. The political function of families as agents of the dominant culture is consequently a central component of a feminist therapy theory of the role of the family in the development of distress.

All this is not to say that families as a source of distress are unimportant to feminist understandings of psychosocial factors. The documentation by feminists in the mental health disciplines of violence against women and children in families, and the cogent commentary of feminist family therapists regarding the replication of societal patterns of oppression at the level of family structure, are valuable contributions to our comprehensions of distress (Bograd, 1984; Goldner, 1985; Luepnitz, 1988). Rather, the point being made here is that in a feminist epistemology of distress, the family is perceived as simply one unit of social interaction, rather than the sole crucible in which personality is formed or deformed. The family is not constructed as a private entity; it is a political phenomenon, relating to other political phenomena.

This view, in turn, necessitates a movement away from placing blame on individual parents, particularly individual mothers, as sources of distress. Blaming mothers for their children's distress has been one of the most common outcomes of mainstream theories in which the family is viewed absent a political analysis and context; mothers, as the common emotional centers of family life and the designated primary caregivers under patriarchy, cannot be seen through a feminist lens unless the life of the family is purposely deprivatized and conceptualized politically. If the actions of parents—even profoundly abusive or neglectful parents—are placed within a social context and given meaning in feminist analyses by the political realities informing that social environment, then the interpretation of what constitutes psychosocial factors in distress becomes more clearly feminist and disruptive of dominant theorizing.

In addition to exploring for the presence of longstanding social and political phenomena in their clients' psychosocial and emotional environments, feminist therapists acknowledge that an otherwise resilient, well-functioning person can be powerfully affected by phenomena in the here-and-now. Acute, temporally located political events in the world can also be sources of distress as well as of unexpected healing and strength. Excellent examples of this can be found in responses to the resurgence of right-wing movements against civil rights. In 1992 in Oregon and Colorado, sexual minority persons and their allies were faced with concerted efforts to deny their civil rights, in the form of ballot measures that failed in Oregon but passed in Colorado. The effects of these political campaigns were profound on people's mental health, in several directions. Many lesbians and gay men sought therapy during these times, describing themselves as overwhelmed and frightened by the hate directed at their communities, and thus implicitly at them personally, by the advocates for these anti–civil rights ballot initiatives (Maryka Biaggio, personal communication, 1993; Martha Pearse, personal communication, 1993). At the same time, however, many lesbian, gay, and bisexual people also found themselves activated and angry, and in some cases they reported resolving longstanding emotional difficulties and distress when faced with the necessity of responding to the concrete and present threat to their well-being. One woman described her realization that while as a child she had been powerless to fight off the people who hurt her, as an adult she actually had access to the skills and opportunities to "at least try to make a difference."

In my own practice, three hours' drive away from the Oregon border, these issues played out as well. Alix, a white office worker in her fifties, raised in a rural, fundamentalist family, who had long struggled with the heterosexism of others and her own fears of what would happen should her lesbian identity be discovered, came to her sessions during the height of the Measure 9 campaign describing herself as "relapsing" in her fears and having a reactivated sense of self-blame. Therapy times with Alix during the fall of 1992 were often spent examining what her options might be for making different sense of what was happening in Oregon. She began to be able to focus on the many people who had come forward against the anti-gay-and-lesbian initiative, including religious leaders from the group in which she had been raised. She observed that as she did so, she made a profound and, she felt, more enduring shift in her beliefs about the allies available in the world for sexual minority persons.

Alix commented to me at one point that until this anti-gay-and-lesbian initiative had emerged, she had never had the chance to see so many straight people coming forward to support people like herself; she was able to see how without this frightening event, she would not have been afforded the chance to know in a real, rather than theoretical, way that not everyone hated sexual minority people. While Measure 9 frightened her and was a source of distress over the short term, in the end its presence in the world gave her an opportunity to reverse the meanings of that distress, to see it as her revolt against the oppression that had trapped her for most of her life. She made a decision to send some money to the campaign against Measure 9, commenting to me that this was the first time she had ever been able to risk having her name on a mailing list associated with lesbian and gay issues.

From Diagnosis to Conceptualization

Diagnosis is a place to begin. It allows therapist and client together to develop a name for the pain and a manner of comprehending its origins. It creates a name that can be owned by both therapist and client, a name that does not create otherness but serves as a powerful source of self-knowledge. It also, within the feminist framework, focuses the therapeutic relationship on the strengths and skills brought there by the client. From that beginning comes the next step: envisioning the work of therapy and the lineaments of the relationship, in which clients recover and learn the use of their own voices. In the next chapter, we will explore this process in greater detail.

CHAPTER 6

To Speak the Mother Tongue: Models of Case Conceptualization

U NDERSTANDING DISTRESS is only a beginning. For feminists, the process of conceptual analysis goes well beyond knowing how to understand and name distress. Typically, when a therapist meets a client, the therapist begins a formal or informal process of conceptualizing the story told us, called "the case" by mainstream approaches to therapy and making some sort of diagnostic assessment: determining what's wrong, what might be going on, and what direction therapy might take. All these steps are necessary for the therapist to have some initial plan; none of them are inherently problematic for the feminist therapist, although some recent research suggests that the tendency toward quick case conceptualization forecloses the exploration of alternative hypotheses regarding the client's distress far too early in treatment. But feminist case conceptualization cannot stop with the diagnosis of the problem and the application of the apparently correct *DSM* label; it must factor in the many complex variables that I have identified as important to feminist therapy practice.

As the previous chapter pointed out, feminist therapy conceives of diagnosis and the meanings of distress quite differently from mainstream theories of therapy. It thus stands to reason that the process of conceptualizing and planning work with a client will be different as well and must reflect feminist principles of creating a work that will advance feminist social transformation. The manner in which each therapy relationship is theorized will recapitulate the process of theorizing feminist therapy, in that this conceptual framework will offer therapist and client alike the possibilities of engaging in acts of feminist social change via the healing process.

Such a conceptualization takes the direction of an affirmative model of the process of diagnostic thinking, as broadly construed. In this model, the feminist therapist does *not* come up with the diagnostic label and proceed from the assumption that it tells the story of who the client is. Rather, she looks for a way of telling the story of who this person was at the beginning of the journey through life and how this person came to today's place of distress, in a manner that leads to a liberating, empowering, and healing vision of who she or he can be after learning powerful ways to affect the environment and subvert the patriarchy within. This vision requires not simply a description of distress but also an understanding of how power and powerlessness have functioned in the life of the client and the client's important reference groups, together with a sense of how the balance of power in that person's life can be restored, so that inter- and intrapersonal power becomes a reality and patriarchal power structures are further undermined.

Such an affirmative model of conceptualizing the client's position in the world and the goals and work of a particular course of feminist therapy must withstand close feminist scrutiny. It must not be based on normative models of distress, nor use monocultural or androcentric imagery of health. It must consistently place the client's experience of distress within a sociopolitical framework. It must not psychopathologize what is primarily political, but it must identify the political meanings in internal experiences. The overrepresentation of certain patterns of distress in specific groups of people must be explored as evidence of patriarchal processes of oppression. This model must draw upon knowledge claims that are empirical as well as qualitative and intuitive, idiopathic as well as nomothetic. It must be a relational model, in which therapist and client come together to comprehend the meaning of the client's difficulties and develop a shared and useful construction of reality toward personal change. It must be a model of the whole person, in which strengths and sources of resilience are as essential to the diagnostic formulation as pain and deficit. It must also be a powerful model, sufficiently so to reduce the temptation to overutilize dominant models simply for their apparent explanatory capacities and to serve as a consistent guide to decision making at each step in the ambiguous universe of therapy practice.

Learning and Speaking the Mother Tongue

The metaphor I find useful for describing the successful outcome of this feminist conceptual model is that it allows therapist and client to come together to learn the client's emotional "mother tongue," the "native language" in which an undistorted image can be told through the freed voice of the client who is no longer silenced (Jack, 1991). There is not, in this metaphor, the necessity for an actual change of spoken language. It is more about how the client comes to rename experience, retell a narrative, in a way that no longer violates well-being, but rather empowers and liberates.

My use of this terminology as a metaphor for how to identify the process of health and healing comes from the poet Judy Grahn's evocative notion of the "other mother tongue" of lesbian and gay cultures (1984). Grahn suggests that the processes by which lesbians and gay men have come to know and name themselves in the presence of heterosexism and hate have required them to develop descriptive language for feelings, relationships, and ways of being that are not present in dominant usage. The alienating language of heterosexism, although it appears to be the "natural" language of human relationships, pathologizes and distorts same-gender affections. In this new language, words that were formerly insults become praise: "nelly queen" or "stone butch" become descriptions of valued characters in the life of a sexual minority community, rather than terms of derision. Therefore, another mother tongue is needed, a psycholinguistic construct of self-knowledge that transcends the assumptions of dominant cultures and transforms demonized ways of being into evidence of power, strength, and beauty and names and praises forbidden relationships.

The metaphor of the mother tongue also resonates to how concretely the processes of oppression sometimes operate. This is most vivid when we observe how the destruction of language goes hand-in-hand with actual and cultural genocide. In many American Indian communities, elders who are the only living speakers of their nation's mother tongue are attempting to bring it back to cultures where the suppression of the language was an important tool of genocide. The practice of literally and figuratively stealing children from their families and placing them in government-run boarding schools in which speaking the mother tongue was forbidden and severely punished was one way of destroying American Indian cultures and spirituality. The distress and self-destructive behaviors that arose from these forced alienations from self (since, for many

Native Americans, self cannot be separated from family, nation, land, language, and spirituality) and the toll taken on American Indian communities are well-documented in statistics about alcoholism, violence in families, and suicide. The movement for healing, renewal, and recapture of power in American Indian communities has been accompanied by a move to seek out and return to the use of mother tongues, so that their speakers may feel whole again.

At the beginning of the process of therapy with any client, the therapist is not yet speaking the client's mother tongue. To "diagnose" a person at that point would be to speak of the client in another language. Standard diagnosis assumes a clear and deep knowledge of a person based upon the person's distress; a feminist conceptual model assumes that what both therapist and client hear at the beginning is not what will be heard when healing, social transformation, and access to power have occurred. There may not always be large differences, but, we can assume that some transformation of personal voice will occur in feminist therapy simply because of the placement of this exercise in a sociopolitical context.

The steps of conceptual thinking that I will be describing can lead to this voice by uncovering the meanings embedded in the client's life story and experiences of pain, as well as the inferences hidden in each aspect of relationship between the therapist and client. Until that mother tongue is found, the story that a person tells will be distorted to some degree by patriarchal structures. The goal of the feminist process of conceptualization is not simply to describe and categorize distress and impairment but most importantly also to recover and come to value the strengths, skills, and talents hidden in the distortion and to name these strengths as intrinsic, the "mother tongue" of this person. This process can often be problematic. Since we can never know what was the "true" or essential self, both the client and the therapy stumble through many emotional dialects, each seeming to ring a bit more clearly, until they arrive together at a melody that sounds the closest to true, the language in which clients can name themselves in the most powerful and liberating ways.

This image of listening for the native language within to comprehend the nature and sources of alienation and distress and to discover ways to subvert dominant introjects brings out the fact that in the conceptual process in feminist therapy, therapist and client are not seeking the true *pathology* of the person, as is the goal of mainstream diagnosis and case conceptualization. The conceptual process ceases to be a matter of matching a person to lists of criteria for a particular named disease or predicting the difficulties that are likely to arise during the course of therapy. It is, rather, a first step in witnessing to the client's struggles to achieve and maintain integrity. It is an exploration of the manner in which the therapist will be able to sit respectfully with her client in the relationship of feminist therapy in which empowerment and mutuality are not only goals but necessary components of the entire process. This approach to conceptualization is a "hearing into speech" of the client's dilemmas and distress through a mutual exploration of the manner in which this person's experience of the world is expressed, both verbally and otherwise. Symptoms, which frequently cut across both formal diagnoses and feminist diagnostic understandings of distress, become in this conceptual model the "words" with which that experience is communicated. The shape and form of distress tell a story of what has been silenced and how the silencing has deformed and rearranged the relationship to self and the world.

Understanding Symptoms as Communication

The symptom of self-harm is a case in point. Most people who engage in this behavior are women with a history of childhood abuse coupled with neglect; thus this experience is of interest to feminist therapists (Miller, 1994). A client who cuts, burns, or otherwise harms or mutilates herself often evokes feelings of rage, disgust, and fear from the therapist. Therapists commonly respond to such behavior with severe and pejorative diagnoses and impose directives to the client to stop the behavior, even when it is not life-threatening. Often such clients are medicated or forcibly hospitalized, more to assuage the therapist's anxiety over this powerful and provocative behavior than to heal the root causes of the self-harm.

Conceptualizing this symptom from a feminist perspective takes a very different course. It would begin with an examination of the relational experience of the client's self-harm: What does it mean to be in an emotional space where behavior that may be comfortable and natural invites such strong responses from others? What has made it necessary or important for this person to do things on and to her body that are culturally perceived as painful or threatening? How does the client experience the self-harm? What meaning and purpose does it have for her in relationship to herself and in relationship to the world, which includes the therapist? How does this behavior give a person a sense of power or a strategy for coping with powerlessness? The feminist therapist in search of these answers might even turn to the self-published literature of women dealing with what one newsletter calls "self-inflicted violence" as a source for understanding the phenomenology of self-harm; the therapist might—and as a feminist presumably would—note the intentional choice of the term *violence,* which places these experiences of harm in the larger feminist discourse on violence against women and other marginalized people. She would also note that this seizing of the parameters of the discourse by the client overturns patriarchal hierarchies of value within psychotherapy.

In this example, the use of a feminist conceptual process focuses, first from the client's perspective and then from a relational viewpoint, on the function of the behavior and the internal processes that lead up to it. Next, it asks what the behavior means in context: What do women learn about the worth of their bodies in a cultural context where eroticized images of violence against women are commonplace? How have these messages informed the development of this symptom? What is told here about power and powerlessness? Why are the therapist and the mental health system often engaged in interventions in this sort of violence, the violence of the disenfranchised against themselves, while failing to intervene in other sorts of violence, the violence of the powerful that masquerades in forms that are often socially acceptable aspects of racism, sexism, or heterosexism? Failing to ask such questions may lead us to an inability to know that one person's self-harm is a communication about anger, another's about the need to feel safe. Such failure by the therapist can lead to missed opportunities for offering alternative strategies for accomplishing these goals. When the feminist therapist does ask such questions, she gets closer to knowing the client's native language; she begins to listen to the ways in which the client talks to herself and to the therapist, to become familiar with the client's symbolic internal grammar and syntax.

While the answers to these questions may vary from one client to another, analyzing the symptom in this manner transforms it from evidence of severe pathology evoking controlling urges in the therapist into a window onto the phenomenology of the client and her transformation of prior experience into the decision to cut or burn herself today. It also places the symptom within the social and political framework that has informed both its inception and its development and begins the process of raising feminist questions about the meaning of the symptom that may lead to liberating approaches to psychotherapy. The analysis of the problem as one expression of a social and political process manifested in the individual creates the possibility of communication between client and therapist.

Case Conceptualization: Cui Bono?

Another difference in the conceptual process as theorized in feminist therapy lies in the desired beneficiaries of our diagnostic thinking. Although the usual goal of diagnosis has been to facilitate communication among professionals (the notion being that when one therapist says "schizoid" another should thus instantly and easily know what to expect in the client), a feminist theory of diagnosis has as its intent the improvement of the client's self-knowledge and the strengthening of the client's authority to know and name self, freed from the restrictions placed by patriarchal epistemologies that know difference primarily as deviance. Authorizing the client's knowing via the diagnostic and conceptual process is an important feminist goal.

For example, for Lisanne, a Cuban-American working-class lesbian woman with whom I have worked for several years, our explorations determined that, at the outset, she had no emotional vocabulary for dealing with an angry authority figure aside from offering sexual access to herself, a distortion in her internal language bequeathed by a childhood full of horrendous abuse. She had learned to make dangerous grownups be more peaceful and less threatening by "letting" them sexually abuse her. This lifelong behavioral pattern of submission and sexualization had led to previous diagnoses of both dependent and histrionic personality disorders; these are both common mainstream diagnostic labels for women such as Lisanne, whose acquired emotional language is that of sexual availability.

She found these diagnostic names shaming, but they also confirmed her initial sense of herself as sullied and flawed in some essential and unchangeable way. It was by those diagnoses that she "knew" herself when our work together began, and it was in this acquired emotional voice that she spoke, both with me and with other persons of real or perceived power in her life. I had suspicions about these diagnoses and suggested that we might want to center our work together around an exploration of how these names might or might not be accurate.

We learned the errors of this diagnostic formulation and arrived at our new shared understanding of the meanings of her experiences via my continual questioning of the functions of her sudden "attacks" of attraction to me. Instead of treating her emotions as simply a manifestation of histrionic dynamics in the symbolic psychotherapeutic (that is, "transference") relationship, which would have been a common interpretation from a dominant perspective, I suggested that these feelings had a meaning that we could understand if we were able to identify the contexts in which they occurred. By contextualizing the experience, she was able to notice when it happened—at times when she feared my disapproval. She noticed that this was true elsewhere, as well; she began to recognize situations in which she could predict, with some degree of accuracy, that she would begin to have sexual feelings toward someone and started to see her experiences as much less out-of-control. She began to be able to name it for what it was: a request for reassurance that she would be safe and still cared for.

From that insight on Lisanne's part, it was possible for us to move backwards through time to the places where this strategy had been horrifyingly successful; as she explained, it was less painful to "allow" her caretakers to have sex with her than to fight them and have them beat her. These were the two options available to her in her home environments from ages three through nine, and she had taken the one that she could live through more easily. This discovery flipped the meaning of the behavioral pattern on its head; no longer was it a sign of weakness, as Lisanne had always read it (asking, "Why am I always giving in to people and letting them have sex with me when I don't even want to be touched?"). Instead, it represented her resistance, her decision to reduce physical pain when and however she could at times and places where her options were severely limited. It was a means for her to experience some sense of power in her life, however distorted that sense was by the realities of her social and interpersonal powerlessness. It was also a disguised way for her to communicate the need, hitherto felt as too dangerous to acknowledge, to know that she was safe.

This uncovering of her sexualized behaviors as a communication about the anger of powerful others, about her need for reassurance, and as an attempt to cope and feel powerful made it more possible for Lisanne to begin to search for the time when she had, in fact, possessed metaphoric language for responding to anger. She could also look for the ways in which that capacity had become lost to her; she began to explore where, within her acquired emotional language, the accents of her mother tongue might be. Reclaiming the mother tongue meant she could possess the capacity to ask, to set limits, to know that she could name and define her needs and wants without terror or the threat of violence. It was learning to believe that human beings like herself could make such demands of one another safely. She began tentatively to reassert the capacity for disagreement that had been seized by her caregivers as a rationale for beating her two- and three-year-old self. She came to learn that her currently sexual-appearing responses to these beatings were not essential to her, not her diagnosis, but evidence that something had been misplaced in her emotional vocabulary. This, in turn, helped Lisanne to create a sort of psychological Rosetta Stone from which she could translate back from her wounded vocabulary to a more full and empowering internal language. She can now "diagnose" her own behaviors; "I am feeling sexual attraction out of the blue. Therefore, I must feel that this person is angry at me. And I must want reassurance that I am safe. What else could I do? How else can I protect or care for myself? Is it possible that I might be angry, too?" Lisanne now can find other means of experiencing herself as powerful that are more accessible to her, actually feel powerful to her, and have a noticeable and desired effect on her interpersonal environment. While I comprehend her better as a result of our conceptual process, what is more important is that she has begun to hear herself speak in her mother tongue.

Speaking the Language and Knowing the Audience

In addition to facilitating clients' ability to hypothesize compassionately and effectively about their own difficulties, the feminist conceptual process has as a goal the greater attunement of the therapist to her client. Reframing diagnostic and conceptual thinking as described in the previous chapter pushes a therapist to inquire into the client's experience before attempting to assign meaning and value to a symptom or syndrome. This inquiry in turn heightens empathy and concretizes the question that therapists so often ask themselves: "What would I have done, faced with these dilemmas?" This paradigm for conceptualizing thus informs important aspects of the therapeutic relationship by enhancing the sense of mutuality and connection and reducing distance. Symptoms of distress are phenomenologically no longer evidence of pathology on the part of the client; the therapist must then strenuously examine any attempts on her part to construe difference, or to locate problems within the person out of context.

This model of diagnostic and conceptual thinking points a therapist to questions about who the client is beyond the obvious and tangible stuff of their distress and symptoms. It creates a richer knowledge of the client. I call this "knowing who is on the receiving end of your behaviors." Concretely, this thinking translates in my own work into such things as wondering who would hear an offer of a hug—the adult man ten years my senior in a business suit, or the sexually confused adolescent he once was and has grown little beyond, or the child whose beloved older cousin mixed fondness with sexual exploitation? And in what sociopolitical context will this hug occur? Is this the "New Age guy" who is trying to learn how to desexualize physicality, or the recently laid-off corporate executive who could never have imagined being in therapy before this blow fell? How vast is the gulf of power between us? At what non-conscious levels do these differences in power manifest themselves? If I have been tracking symptoms in the manner described above, I will have some tentative answers to these questions; I will be able to make some informed guesses about who is on the receiving end and what is being communicated. I can then act in accordance with who is there, rather than risk introducing dissonance by proferring the hug, a gesture that would be reassuring in one context but terrifying or seductive in others.

The importance of knowing the recipient of the therapist behaviors is highlighted by the power imbalancing that can happen when the therapist fails to take it into account. It is not unusual to find therapists excusing behavior that has confused or frightened clients by saying that their own motives were clear and that the client simply misinterpreted their intentions. This sort of statement betrays a failure to think diagnostically and shifts the burden of responsibility away from the therapist in a manner that does not share power with the client but only blames and shames. Asking who is on the receiving end creates a different level of clarity for the therapist that can, in turn, shed light on clients' responses to people outside of therapy. This sort of insight *can* be empowering to the client; when I can serve as a useful mirror to someone by sharing my observations about how they are receiving me in our interaction, they may for the first time have a compassionate glimpse of a disowned aspect of self.

This use of diagnostic and conceptual hypothesizing that moves beyond naming the pathology is also a useful tool for understanding the precise nature of the asymmetries of a given therapy relationship at any given moment. It guides the feminist therapist to ask who she represents, both in this unique relationship and in the larger context. It offers guidance on how and when a therapist can move in certain directions; for instance, when will self-disclosure by the therapist help by serving to normalize experience and when will it oppress because the client is currently able to hear the information only as a directive about how to be, rather than as a sharing of the therapist's responses to a common dilemma? This diagnostic process leads the therapist to consider the various images of who she and her clients are relationally. What therapists evoke in their clients and vice versa—the varying symbolic representations that they offer to one another—create a framework for the expression of the client's distresses and strengths. Therapists must ask themselves how their presence may seduce clients into speaking not in their mother tongues but rather in one of their repertoire of acquired interpersonal languages. Part of this process of feminist diagnosis and conceptualization is to understand how we as therapists may be what our client is responding to when they evince certain problematic behaviors.

Clients who have been sexually abused or exploited by another therapist are an excellent illustration. It is unusual for such clients to reenter therapy, but when they do, they often do not disclose for many months the story of what happened to them earlier; they feel too much shame and self-blame, and they assume that yet another therapist will join with the previous one in condoning the behavior or blaming it on the client. Few therapists who do not specialize in this problem will routinely ask in the intake process whether a client has ever had such an experience. It is therefore quite possible for a client to work for months with a therapist who is not aware of being sadly but literally "the-rapist," a trauma trigger evoking posttraumatic responses in the client that are specific to therapy, therapists, and the untold secret of abuse. It is equally likely that the therapist will have meanwhile diagnosed these reactions as evidence of quite severe pathology, unaware that they are seen nowhere other than in therapy, the site of the most recent emotional wounding.

As a therapist working with this group of people, and as a consultant to other therapists in this situation, I have been fascinated to watch how this process of incomprehension changes after the story of victimization in therapy is told and after the current therapist's support for the client and repudiation of the therapy abuse enter the therapeutic relationship. This is a striking example of the importance, for feminist therapists, of remaining humble in conceptual formulations and acknowledging that they cannot know at first what they represent to their clients, only that they may evoke painful or problematic modes of expression whose meaning may not be intuitively obvious.

Identifying Acquired Emotional Languages: Some Proposals

Getting to the point where the therapist and client can ask these hypothesis-building questions together begins in feminist therapy, as in any careful approach to treatment, with the history. But a feminist ear, eye, and analysis are brought to the story that emerges, and feminist theory informs the sort of questions asked. It is important, after all, to get not only the official version of this person's life but also the hidden heritage that can be found by going outside the lines of standard diagnostic interviews. Feminist therapists do not stop after tracing the history and emergence of symptoms. They start with the body: What was this person's biological endowment? What resiliencies and vulnerabilities did the person bring into the world? Were the marks of oppression already present, such as low birth weight from maternal malnutrition? Was this a quiet child? An energetic child? How was this child held? Fed? Welcomed?

They then move to experience. Feminist therapists ask themselves and their clients, Who learned what about life, and from whom? Were the sources of authority the allies or the oppressors, individually or collectively, of the learner? Or were these confusing sources—a loving parent who was also depressed, or a teacher who praised skills as unusual for the child's race or culture of origin? How were lessons cemented into place? How and when in life were such lessons challenged, subverted, undermined? What have been the social, political, and cultural environments in which internal, phenomenological reality was viewed? How has the cultural context given particular meaning to certain lessons of life? How has membership in certain groups increased the likelihood that some lessons were learned, some emphasized, and others neglected or lost? How have these experiences lent existential, spiritual, or transcendent knowledge to a person or culture—or stolen it? How are certain experiences and difficulties in current life evidence of missing, distorted, or hidden facets of self-knowledge? What do the losses tell us about how these factors can be found? How has the client learned to resist? What has been the outcome of that resistance? What does it mean if no resistance can be uncovered? What languages has this person developed, inter- and intrapersonally? How far are such voices from the mother tongue? How does this voice convey the capacity to know and name in an empowering and liberating manner?

These are not the questions of the standard mental health history form. Yet they are necessary for feminist conceptualization, because they highlight ways of knowing and understanding the constant flow between the phenomenological and the political that engenders human development. In answering such questions, a feminist diagnostic epistemology can draw in part upon empirically derived knowledge regarding the intellectual and emotional developmental processes of human beings and the effects of experience on the capacity to achieve certain skills and ways of relating. The capacity to understand and encode such abstract but important knowledge as the limits of our own agency, the real as opposed to the imagined powers of others, the plasticity and stability of material reality, and the contribution of randomness or predictability to the occurrence of certain experiences varies as we grow and age. Certain kinds of learning experiences at one point in the journey may also transform or distort how we make sense of external realities at other junctures. In order to survive, a person may need to cherish certain ways of learning and knowing because others are potentially dangerous. For instance, to ensure a sense of personal safety the survivor of trauma may need to forgo the development of abstract thought and capacity for tolerance of ambiguity and instead hold tightly to a highly dichotomized manner of interpreting reality, because the "more developed" modes of operating might reduce vigilance and increase the risk of further harm. In other words, it can be more functional for some people to have a "danger/no danger" way of interpreting external reality, given their prior experiences in the world, than to develop a fully realized continuum of dangers that may leave some situations only ambiguously evaluated.

Using Developmental Psychology: Benefits and Caveats

Feminist conceptualization can carefully utilize the work of mainstream developmental theorists as a source of information about the cognitive and affective capacities of human beings to make sense of their interpersonal and emotional environments. Drawing on this literature, however, requires the caveat that data developed by scholars such as Mahler, Bowlby, Piaget, Inhelder, or Kohlberg is not value-free and often reflects monocultural and androcentric biases and linear models of development. In fact, recent cross-cultural research on child development makes it clear that these supposedly immutable developmental processes proceed quite differently in different cultures, depending on the modes of interaction valued in each (Bradshaw, 1990).

Moreover, much of this body of research assumes the centrality of a nuclear, two-heterosexual-parent family to the normal development of personality. While a careful search of the subtexts of this literature can unearth a less particularistic theme—that is, the importance for children's development of a stable, predictable environment with the presence of loving, attached, and empathic caregivers, a second, less benign and more oppressive metacommunication of this body of knowledge is that development informed by any other sort of familial or social context will be in some manner deviant. Moreover, the normative development of children in social and familial contexts other than those privileged by the mainstream development literature—children raised by one parent, by two same-gendered parents, in extended family systems, in collective child-rearing settings—is often either poorly described, with a biased eye, or simply invisible and not allowed to inform either the research questions posed or the interpretation of findings that emerge from such studies. All these factors must be considered by feminist therapists in evaluating the usefulness of information emerging from the mainstream developmental literature.

These observational data and the accompanying theories of child development arising from them are, however, potential aids in illuminating the phenomenology of childhood and adolescence, which—particularly for the feminist therapist working with adults—is not always immediately accessible via clients themselves. These sorts of data are guides in answering the question, Who learned this lesson? by allowing the therapist to enter the phenomenology of the learner to some degree and evaluate what kinds of cognitive and emotional capacities the person was most likely to have had access to in making sense of experience. The child of three understands her mother's death from cancer differently from the child of ten or the adolescent of fifteen or the adult of thirty. How the experience is processed affects how it becomes a part of self-knowledge. The point in development at which experience occurs can also mediate the degree and manner in which an encounter with loss or oppression might lead a person away from her mother tongue to a more alienating acquired internal vocabulary.

Another model deriving from the edges of the mainstream that can be usefully integrated into feminist conceptualization processes is Lorna Benjamin's Structural Analysis of Social Behavior (SASB) model (Benjamin, 1986). While not explicitly feminist or derived from feminist foundations, Benjamin's model is quite congruent with the feminist emphases on the interplay of interpersonal, social/contextual, and intrapsychic phenomena. And unlike almost every other mainstream perspective on the development of behavior, Benjamin's model attends to the dimension of power, an important facet of a feminist analysis. This model classifies inter- and intrapersonal experience on three matrices, each indicating a different focus of the person's behaviors; this level of analysis goes beyond that provided in some unidimensional systemic models by noting that behavior changes depending upon its intended targets and upon the positions of the actors in various social and interpersonal hierarchies.

While these and other mainstream developmental models are very useful to feminist epistemology of usual and distressed development, there are as yet no schools of human development that are primarily feminist in their assumptions. Consequently, it is necessary for feminists deriving guidance from this source to examine carefully the assumptive models that inform such knowledge claims, not simply to find errors but also to illuminate other meanings of the findings than those ascribed by the mainstream developmental model. As feminist psychologist Sandra Bem has noted (1993), developmental psychologists peer through cultural "lenses of gender" that can and do distort their interpretations of the facts they observe and lead to intentional or accidental reinforcement of sexist, racist, and heterosexist dominant norms. She has pointed to tendencies in the developmental literature to assume the presence of sex differences or to assume that the few that can be observed are evidence of essential, biological differences between the sexes rather than artifacts of powerful and pervasive social and political forces.

One of the best-known examples of such a feminist critique of a dominant interpretive error, one that led to new insights into the various paths of human development, is Carol Gilligan's now famous (1981) reexamination of Kohlberg's models of moral development. Although even Gilligan's model has limits because of its monocultural roots, her critique of Kohlberg's paradigm of moral development provided feminist therapists a strategy for utilizing data from patriarchal sources in order to inform a feminist diagnostic process. Gilligan posed the important feminist question, Says who? to Kohlberg's assertions about the supposedly universally linear nature of moral development, a paradigm in which a detached adherence to the rules of the game is privileged over a more ambiguous and relational strategy of balancing judgments within the interpersonal matrix. While most developmental theories are rich in data, the manner in which mainstream scholars have fashioned their questions needs to be considered along with their findings when feminists utilize these materials diagnostically.

Although feminist psychology lacks developmental theories of the depth and completeness—albeit illusory—of mainstream developmental psychology, feminist models are emerging, some that are of value to the feminist therapist and her clients in the process of conceptual and diagnostic thinking. The recent work of Gilligan and her colleagues regarding girls' and young women's resistance to patriarchy and loss of voice (Gilligan, Rogers, & Tolman, 1992), the writings of the Stone Center theorists on the development of relationality (Jordan, Kaplan, Miller, Stiver, & Surrey, 1992), and the formulations of feminist developmental psychologists like Michele Fine (1992) studying the lives of girls in social context suggest important ways of understanding experience, particularly strongly gendered experience, that are not typically identified by mainstream developmental models. Questions of relationality and resistance, which are currently emerging as themes for feminist models in a manner parallel to the

centrality of separation and individuation in mainstream models, are especially salient when the goal of the diagnostic process is to strategize revolutionary social change from within, because these models highlight those
aspects of development that might lead to such changes. Again, such theoretical formulations must be used with caution, because they have commonly been based only on the lives of white and middle-class girls in the
United States. (Fine's work is a striking and exemplary exception and
stands as a model of how to take race, class, and political context into
account in feminist theorizing.) Because these are feminist theories, feminist therapists have not always been as careful to apply to them the critical
standards used to screen mainstream materials for problems of dominant
normative assumptions.

Using both mainstream and feminist developmental models and continually questioning the assumptions of mainstream scholars undermines
any false hierarchies of value assigned to different cognitive strategies and
instead is primarily tentative and descriptive. For example, one might utilize a cognitive strategy that relies heavily on comprehension of relationships rather than objects, or might symbolically represent experience in
terms of ghosts and ancestors, rather than saying that by the age of three,
any normally developing child will have some particular set of cognitive,
social, and emotional skills only. This sort of information about the ways
in which some human beings are likely to develop and make sense of their
worlds, made available to clients in this sort of nonprescriptive manner,
may be of help to the client in naming and normalizing phenomenology;
for many of the people I work with, it is the "so that's what it means that
this felt this way" experience.

This sort of sharing of the conceptualization between therapist and
client can often serve as a mechanism by which the person gives up self-
criticism and thus becomes less vulnerable to the undermining effects of
patriarchy. For Marnie, a white middle-class bisexual woman in her early
thirties whose mother had died suddenly of a stroke when Marnie was six
years old, it was illuminating and liberating to hear that there was nothing
unusual in the way she had responded, becoming fearful of all losses at
just the point in development when she was faced with learning how to
operate in the environment of school and achievement, away from her
family. Marnie learned that it would be a profound loss for any child suddenly to have no access to her greatest source of support, her mother. She
became aware of the ways in which the culture of radical individualism
represented in her family made it more difficult for her to see the normalcy of those feelings of loss, and led to shame and the loss of "mother
tongue" about her needs to be intimate, as well as her grief over the loss of

her mother. She was able to utilize this knowledge to comprehend how it was that as an adult she was now ambivalent about all intimate attachment and commitments because they contained the potential for loss and the relived experience of being cast into the void without her anchor. She began to see this so-called problem as her attempt to communicate to herself about her loss and grief without naming them directly.

Along with what she called, at the beginning of therapy, her "fear of intimacy" was Marnie's inability to leave her tremendously secure job of many years, although she hated it, because she could not imagine leaving something that was not going to leave her. This, too, she berated herself about, as evidence of cowardice and bad faith. Seeing herself not as cowardly and avoiding intimacy but as operating from the decisions of the grieving child who had promised herself never to feel such pain or show such weakness again transformed Marnie's telling of her own story. Eventually, it also allowed her to reconsider her options and decisions and to take risks that went against the culture, including the decision to name her bisexuality at times and in places where doing so was not fashionable.

It is also important for feminist theorizing of a case to factor in cultural variations in privileged modes of cognitive and affective functioning. For instance, so-called "magical thinking" is devalued in white Western cultures, where rationalism and empiricism are privileged. This bias can be seen in mainstream developmental psychologies, in which the belief in nonrational and unseen forces and phenomena is a cognitive strategy ascribed to children or those "stuck" at a child-like stage of development. In most cultures outside of white Northern European and North American settings, however, such "magical" interpretations of reality reflect normative and valued strategies. For instance, it would be unusual for a traditional person in some American Indian or Asian Pacific groups *not* to believe in the existence of ghosts and their real capacity to do harm. Consequently, a feminist diagnostic paradigm requires a knowledge of the diversity of strands of human development, so that reasonably accurate hypotheses about the client as knower can be generated. The presence of "magical thinking" in a Navajo raised traditionally on a reservation will likely mean something entirely different from the same style of thinking and information processing encountered in an upper-class white Protestant from Shaker Heights.

Thus, the work of coming back to a client's emotional mother tongue, to that capacity to accurately know and name, to leave behind gibberish of so-called pathology, is to utilize this life information to develop a clear image of the client's own ways of strategizing, knowing, and problem-solving. What did this client learn from experience? What shaped the learning? What biological, cognitive, affective, spiritual, and contextual tools were available to mold the learning process? The client and therapist come to learn the client's own methodologies and epistemologies of silence, subversion, and survival as steps toward recovering a full emotional and intellectual vocabulary.

Gradually, value and honor can be ascribed to stigmatized "discourses"; the woman who practices self-inflicted violence learns that she did so in order to feel a sense of control over pain, or to help herself dissociate and escape from terror at times in her development when no other strategy worked so well to achieve that goal. Seeing the behavior in this contextualized manner allows clients to honor their goals (for example, safety, freedom from pain, escape from intolerable situations) without having to conflate those goals with the strategies for achieving them. It allows clients to reclaim these goals, to speak of them directly to themselves and others, and to see those goals as core and central, as "mother tongue."

It also allows clients to make different decisions about what they wish the goals of therapy to be. Rather than compliantly taking on tasks assigned by the dominant culture—for example, "Stop being depressed, become more productive"—a person furnished with this sort of knowledge may develop goals for their therapy that undermine dominant norms because these goals honor and privilege resistances—"Learn to get angry more often and see my connections to other people more clearly." The superficial outcomes may appear similar, but what people can accomplish with those outcomes may vary, because the feminist outcome has attempted to avoid colluding with patriarchal norms and scripts for the client's life.

In tracing the steps taken by a client in learning and losing his or her emotional native language and acquiring the adapted tongues of survival under oppression, the therapist and client must then consider together the lessons taught by life and the context in which they were learned: practica in how to be female and Jewish, advanced coursework in living with cerebral palsy, introductions to life as a powerful white man, seminars in coping with being beaten by a parental caregiver each day. Some lessons are more apparently benign than others; in all, the student does coursework in upholding patriarchal realities.

The job of conceptualizing in feminist therapy includes uncovering these lessons and the form that they have taken. What did the political and sociocultural realities that accompanied the moment of new learning lend to the client's understanding of the experience? Was the lesson hammered home by intense love or intense fear? Was it a lesson learned in isolation or in a group? What factors were present in that social and political context? What was the relative power of each factor to clarify or distort meaning? This set of questions moves the analysis yet another step past mainstream history-taking. It focuses the diagnostic and conceptual inquiry on those variables that are critically important to feminist analysis—gender, race, class, sexual orientation, age, culture, and disability—within the sociopolitical context of experience and personal power and on patriarchal structures as impediments to fluency in the emotional mother tongue.

One way to understand these multiple layers of inquiry in the feminist diagnostic process is to trace the interplay of individual and contextual meanings in one common sort of experience that is a "lesson" for its participants. Being a target of sexual assault is an instructive example of such an experience because it is both extremely common (happening in one form or another to approximately one-third of all girls or women, 16 percent of boys, and unknown numbers of adult men) and yet unique in its meaning for each person who experiences it. It is also an experience likely to set its survivors on a path to a therapist's office. For a feminist therapist with a client who has been sexually assaulted at some point in life, this knowledge of base rates is necessary but not sufficient for the diagnostic and conceptual process. All sexually assaulted persons construct different meanings for their experiences, differ in the degree to which they become lost to self and present with different symptoms that tell this unique story.

The therapist thus begins her diagnostic process with questions for herself and her client. Who was the client when sexually assaulted—how old and with what prior life experiences and expectations of safety, and what prior knowledge of the phenomenon of sexual assault and its cultural meanings? Who was the person developmentally, and what was the context? Children, regardless of their level of cognitive development, usually do not know how frequently sexual assault is perpetrated. They are unlikely to know the ways in which assailants may be more or less protected, depending upon their relationship to their victims as well as their race, class, and position in dominant culture. This isolation of the child from such information, enforced by cultures that silence discourse regarding sexual violence against children, lends certain meanings to the experience, which in turn become aspects of the creation of self-knowledge. The child creates meaning out of the experience: "I was bad, sex is hurtful, being little (or female) in this place is dangerous." The self-descriptions and personal narrative learned by this child will contain certain realities, as well as certain gaps, that cannot be described because they can be named only in the child's mother tongue, silenced by the assault and the failure or inability to listen of those around her. The attempt to speak of these things will therefore emerge as "symptoms," phenomena to be traced diagnostically to the child's attempt to communicate the meanings of the experience. The inability of the child, thirty years later, to experience feeling in her genitals or to be sexual with anyone he loves is a symptom that "speaks" of the meaning of the experience, whether or not that person, now adult, consciously comprehends the meaning of the communication at the onset of therapy or even recalls the circumstances of the violation itself.

In parallel fashion, the knowledge that *is* available to adults will similarly inform and transform the meaning made of this event. Adults' knowledge of the stigma attached to the targets of sexual assault, the presence or absence of support in naming and charging the assailant, the actual and perceived remedies available for redress and amends, the interactive effects of race, class, and sexual orientation upon the social meanings of the assault will all determine, to a greater or lesser degree, the manner in which this sexual assault is likely to affect the victim. (See Scherer [1992] for a first-person account of a heterosexual white middle-class woman rape survivor who experienced strong support and contrast with it Fine's [1992] account of the experience of a poor heterosexual African-American woman whose social network was fragile even before she was raped.) As the African-American feminist psychologist and researcher Gail Wyatt has noted (1985), one of the legacies of racism in the United States has been the tendency of many African-American women to question if it is even possible for them to be raped, given the racist social construction of their bodies as available to all for sexual exploitation (Wyatt, 1985).

A feminist therapist must also consider—and communicate to the client—how a particular experience functions to uphold patriarchy. The more essential a certain common experience may be in maintaining homeostasis in patriarchal hierarchies of power and value, the more powerful and potentially alienating will be patriarchal reactions against change. The resulting social environment in turn profoundly affects the nature of the resources available to the target of an oppressive experience. Sexual assault is an example of an experience that keeps people "in line"; as feminist theorist Andrea Dworkin (1974) has noted, it teaches women "proper" behavior by communicating that only "bad" women, those not under the protection of a man, will be sexually assaulted, by reinforcing women's dependence and their withdrawal from the public sphere. Similarly, sexual assault reinforces male heterosexuality; as profeminist theorist John Stoltenberg (1990) has commented, being "a man" is equated in many powerful cultural subtexts with being the rapist, while being a male target of sexual assault is presumed evidence of non-maleness, homosexuality.

This sort of political metamessage of experience is an aspect of the social context that the client may never have consciously considered, although many clients have a subliminal awareness that sexual assault means more than their own pain and terror. For the purposes of feminist diagnosis, however, knowledge of the political meaning of an experience is essential for understanding its long-term effects. The client's symptoms again "speak" of this larger meaning; the woman sexually assaulted in college who enters therapy complaining primarily of an inability to assert herself and be authoritative in mixed-sex groups is reporting the message of punishment she received about what happens to women stepping "out of line," whether or not she consciously agrees with that patriarchal mandate.

It is of great interest to me that a backlash has emerged against those voices raised in protest against the sexual assault of both children and adults. This backlash has received enormous attention from the mainstream media, with covers on national news magazines and op-ed pieces in major newspapers trumpeting the notion that perhaps things are not as bad as they had begun to seem and that the epidemic proportions of sexual child abuse and date rape were simply the creations of the fevered imaginations of crazed feminists and therapists run amok. The False Memory Syndrome Foundation, founded by the parents of Jennifer Freyd, a well-known cognitive psychologist who recovered memories of incest at the hand of her father, has explicitly singled out feminists and lesbians as the sources of such supposed "witch hunts" against fathers. Both the False Memory Syndrome Foundation and the literature pooh-poohing the existence of acquaintance rape on college campuses are manifestations of attempts within the dominant culture to shore up an eroded tolerance for sexual violations within intimate and familial relationships.

Finally, feminist diagnosis and conceptualization look to sources of strength, resilience, and resistance in the person and the person's contexts. As we saw earlier, the goals of feminist diagnosis are not simply to describe wounds but also to uncover and encourage what is working well; it is a diagnosis of strengths as well as of pain. Detecting strengths and resiliencies may not always be simple, because talent has often been hidden to protect it from direct assaults. Moreover, experiences that may appear on the surface to be wounding may in fact be strengthening and may provide sources of personal power. As Maria Root (1992a) has noted, exposure to certain types of potentially alienating events such as everyday racism or heterosexism may, in the context of a supportive reference group, lead to the development of greater resilience and self-knowledge. To go back to our example of sexual assault, a survivor who has a strongly supportive personal reference group may find that her experience has freed her from her fears of speaking up; she has now experienced "the worst," has found love, healing, and empowerment in response, and has become an ever-stronger advocate for herself in the process.

An example of the feminist diagnostic and conceptual process at work emerged in my work with Paula, a white lesbian, raised in the lower-middle class but now living in the upper-middle class, who entered therapy with a formal diagnosis of "major depression." While this label was technically accurate, in that she met the formal *DSM-IIIR* criteria for this "disorder" (that is, depressed mood, low energy, self-criticism, guilt, self-blame, sleep and appetite disturbances, cognitive distraction and distortion, and suicidality), it was not diagnostically and conceptually useful to me as a feminist. That is, it told me very little about what it was like to be Paula in the world and how she would be in our relationship. I was more curious about the function that this depression had for my client. What were her symptoms telling me about her disconnections and internal silences, her capacity to hear herself contrasted with her vulnerability to being overpowered by the voice of another—including my voice? How had the contexts of her life informed the process by which she had come to sit in my office numb, sad, sleepless, devoid of pleasure, and mostly wishing to die?

As we found ways for her to tell me her story, it became apparent that Paula's depression was, paradoxically, her health and strength speaking to her—yelling, in fact, because she had not been paying attention to herself while a variety of social contexts rewarded her with money, prestige, and power over others in exchange for her assimilation and loss of mother tongue. Paula had been a physician, a specialist in an area where there were almost no women. She had made a lot of money in her work and had the appearance of having a great deal of power over her patients, her staff, and the many people in her life who had less money and social prestige than she did, including her partners and most of her friends. These accoutrements of power and privilege were hard rewards to question; so, as more questions did emerge within herself as the years went on, she tried to will them away and go on with her work.

I learned early in our relationship that Paula had always wanted very much to be a healer. In the years she had worked in medicine, however, she had become disillusioned with the tools of her trade. To go to work each day, she had had to make herself progressively more numb, less attuned to herself, and less in relationship to her inner voice. Paula had strongly held beliefs and feelings about how she wanted her relationship to the world to be; she had a finely tuned spiritual sense and a rich and complex ethic of being in the world. She had a feminist politic that was important to her. Yet in every context in her life, she had been ignoring herself. Her work life, her intimate relationships—every part of her day-to-day existence was a turning away from herself as she attempted to live the role she had chosen, because she had thought it was the only available path to accomplish her goals. Her depression was, in fact, evidence of what feminist scholar Dana Jack has called a "silencing of the self" (1991). Paula was, it appeared, so well tuned in to the needs, imperatives, and feelings of others, and to the cultural mandates of patriarchy that insisted that she fit within certain prescribed parameters in order to pursue her goal of healing others, that she had a supremely difficult time listening to her own channel on her internal radio.

Diagnostically and conceptually this was very valuable information from the first. For example, when I considered how I might integrate self-disclosure into my work with Paula, the feminist diagnostic question Who's on the receiving end? led me to understand that it would be very important not to disclose too much about my own strategies for addressing some of the challenges that we had faced in common, because she was still so unable to hear herself that she would hear such information as a command to act as I had. If I told her my strategies, I would simply be replacing one of Paula's acquired inner languages with another—in this case, my own mother tongue, which would serve her no better than any other acquired inner language that she already had.

On the other hand, it would be very important to disclose to Paula my current affective states, those times when my own equilibrium was disrupted in some way on the days that we met. It became clear as she told me her story that she would tune into me if she sensed even the slightest evidence of distress in me and would proceed to ignore her own needs, assuming her well-learned role as the caretaker of others. I needed to establish with her that I noticed her noticing me, appreciated her skill at this task, and would be taking responsibility for myself so that she could be free to focus on her own well-being rather than mine. This also served as an initial step toward undermining the patriarchal prescription that women are in the world to be handmaidens to others and began to direct Paula's acute attentions toward her own needs and well-being.

Identifying her depression as evidence of resistance to her growing loss of self and voice, as a strenuous last-ditch attempt to get herself to "just slow down and listen," as we came to call it, disrupted Paula's constructions of her past experiences. As she uncovered the ways in which she had been taught to ignore her own voice in family, church, school, and work, she came to marvel at the persistence of her emotional mother tongue, in which she heard her own strong desire to be a healer, at the escalating attempts she had made throughout her adulthood to come back to herself and honor herself. No longer was she a failure at being a doctor in the patriarchal mold; rather, she was a success at being a healer despite the best efforts of her professional socialization to train the healer out of the medical technical expert that her speciality called for.

Paula came to believe that her depression had been her last desperate effort to save her own life by making it impossible for her to continue in the life courses for which patriarchal social and political contexts had rewarded her. She had gotten too depressed to work; so, with her depression she had finally forced herself to stop and painfully weigh the price she was paying for her income and prestige. She discovered how she had been seduced into assimilation and how her depression "exposed" her, as it were, making it impossible for her to pass as comfortable in patriarchy or to pretend that the rewards of her prior life were in any way meaningful to her, when in reality they either meant little or were sources of distress.

This conceptualization of her life as an escalating series of attempts to resist assimilation into patriarchy allowed Paula to become much less fearful of her symptoms, even to prize and cherish them as the first words of her recovered emotional mother tongue. As she became more adept at speaking herself, she also became increasingly capable of sorting out her voice from that of others and more skillful hearing several sources at once without placing her own emotional voice in the background. She stopped assuming that everyone else knew what was best for her in any of her roles and relationships in life; she began to value highly her own opinions, perceptions, hunches, intuitions. This change, in turn, shifted the dynamics of power in our relationship; it became decreasingly necessary for me to tell Paula when I was having a bad day from allergies, for instance, because she became less interested in knowing and attending to the emotional states of other people, myself included.

Today Paula no longer needs to yell "stop" at herself with such force because she is no longer careening headlong from herself. Her use of depression as a strategy to achieve the goal of self-knowledge and self-care has been supplanted by other methods. She has learned to respect her emotional and biological self, instead of constantly violating her own boundaries by attempting to force herself into shapes and forms of existence that in the past would have depressed her. She has been able to sort through her cultural contexts and identify those things that are healing to her and those that collude with the patriarchal mandate for assimilation and self-loss. She is increasingly able to separate her strong internal desire to be a healer from the patriarchal image of the physician and to see ways to heal others that are vastly divergent from her old occupation but entirely consistent with her values, her body's needs, and her feelings. She feels concordant, rather than discordant, with her desires to heal, because the manner in which she offers healing to others no longer wounds her. We continue to uncover and enrich the vocabulary of her emotional mother tongue and to detect the complex and subtle ways in which she, as a capable student, learned to betray herself on behalf of a patriarchal social context; together, we are continuing to conceptualize and "diagnose" her life and her change process.

The diagnostic and conceptual process proposed here for feminist therapy is a dynamic one, proceeding throughout the life of the therapy relationship. A client does not have a diagnostic name from which to recover or be in remission; case conceptualization is not a one-time occurrence. Diagnosis and conceptualization are, instead, the continuing process of personal epistemological exploration by the client, in dialogue with the therapist. This acquisition of self-knowledge is a highly subversive activity, undermining patriarchal silences and distortions and giving voice to the client, which resonates and moves that person to action in the face of patriarchy and oppression.

CHAPTER 7

The Master's Tools: The Dilemma of Dealing with Patriarchy

FINE, ONE MAY SAY. All this theory about subverting patriarchy is well and good. But I work in the real world, the world of psychological tests and psychotropic medications and managed mental health care, agency policies about who to treat and how, outpatient treatment reports to be filed with insurance companies, and mandatory disclosure laws by which to abide. What does any of this have to do with me, my real life and actual clinical dilemmas? How do I deal with the realities of my work setting and still apply feminist principles? I may wish to share power, be subversive, do feminist diagnosis and conceptualization, but I've got to make a living, and if I don't code people from the *DSM*, I won't get to keep my job for very long.

Well, the master's tools may never dismantle the master's house, said the eminently quotable Audre Lorde; but what if a feminist therapist finds herself with these tools in her hands? Does she throw them down? Give them back to the patriarchy they came from? Or try to find ways to beat the swords into plowshares?

When Lorde (1984) refers to "the master's tools," she is describing the strategies, methods, and schemata of patriarchal systems. She and other feminist thinkers (Rich, 1979) have questioned whether it is even possible to participate in patriarchal structures such as academia and, by implication, the mental health system without somehow upholding those structures. A feminist therapist may feel as if she is confronted with a difficult choice: to work in an agency and fill out those mandatory reports while making feminist therapy available at a low fee; or to decide, as some have, that she can only do feminist therapy in the private practice she maintains on the side.

But I do not believe that this choice either can or should be made. I believe that it is not only possible but essential for feminist therapists to bring their analyses of power and gender to their collisions with patriarchal realities of mental health care delivery. The business of practicing, the use of tests and medications, managed care, and inpatient treatment are all issues that lend themselves to such feminist analysis. Feminist practice suffers when these factors are placed outside the feminist analytic framework, overpowered by dominant categories of meaning. How does one understand the strategies for subversion of patriarchy in the administration of a psychological test to a client if this aspect of mental health care has been excused from feminist critique and revisions?

The "master's tools" include those that concern almost every therapist of whatever orientation, and they are often the expressions of dominant attempts to control and define the process of healing so that it does not threaten patriarchal hegemonies. These are the techniques used to classify people, to impose social control, the strategies that see psychotherapy as a form of corporate enterprise in which denial of therapy sessions turns into dividends for shareholders. These are tools that a feminist therapist may find herself required to learn about and use, and simply because a feminist therapist uses these tools to sabotage the system does not mean that she will ultimately be able to bring it down. These tools may even do damage to her. Consequently, feminist therapists' participation in the organized, institutional mental health system has been controversial, and often—like diagnosis—avoided.

If feminist therapists do not understand these tools and learn, if nothing else, how to throw the occasional monkey-wrench into the gears of the patriarchal engine, they will, I believe, succeed only in offering alternative shelter rather than in dismantling the edifice of patriarchy, which is the ultimate goal of feminism. As the feminist psychologist Mary Ballou (1990) has suggested, however the master's tools can be used in a feminist theoretical context to "round off the patriarchal towers" or to drill some holes in the authority of patriarchal structures and let in the light and air of feminist vision.

Informed and Empowered Consent

To make clear to clients that the feminist therapist may still be holding and using some of the tools of patriarchy, it is necessary to provide meaningful, interactive, and freely given informed consent to clients. The idea of obtaining informed consent to treatment in psychotherapy, particularly outside of institutional settings, is relatively new to mainstream mental health care and has faced objections from therapists who fear that informing clients of their rights and privileges will undermine the therapeutic relationship and strip away the mystery from what one unhappy therapist called "simply a helpful conversation."

Even when mainstream practitioners accept the inevitable legal necessity of obtaining informed consent to treatment, which is rapidly becoming a norm in the United States, the information shared is commonly kept to a bare minimum. In reviewing the informed consent statements of nearly fifty therapists applying for inclusion in a therapy referral file, I was struck by the brevity of most of these statements (commonly a page or less) and the paucity of information provided. There was usually an emphasis on such matters as fees, collection of overdue bills, session times, and cancellation policies. Because of the requirements of state law, there was often a description of the limits to confidentiality and the circumstances under which reports to such authorities as Child Protective Services would be mandated. There was rarely information about the therapist, however, her or his therapeutic orientations or perspectives, the way in which diagnoses would be made, the meaning of having bills sent to third-party payors, or the risks and benefits of engaging in the psychotherapy process.

From a feminist standpoint, truly informed consent involves not just information but empowerment. Feminist writers on the rights of psychotherapy consumers have long argued that the empowerment of clients requires far more disclosure by the therapist than the minimal norms (Hare-Mustin, Maracek, Kaplan, & Liss-Levinson, 1979). Even the term "informed consent" becomes suspect when subjected to feminist scrutiny and requires careful analysis and deconstruction to avoid becoming a master's tool in disguise.

Who is being informed? How? By and about what or whom? Under what conditions of freedom or choice or "friendly" coercion is consent being given? The client may not even be aware of such conditions. For example, if I inform a client that my bill to her insurance company must include a *DSM* diagnosis, this statement may appear to fulfill the legal requirement of informed consent. Yet what information have I actually given the client? Only that I will choose some label from a book that is unfamiliar to the client and will share that label with the unseen staff at the insurance company or managed care firm, so that my bill will be paid. Making the statement without context fails feminist tests of informed consent on many dimensions; most importantly, it strengthens the power differences between us, because I know not only the name of the problem and with whom to share it but also the long-term consequences of using that name and sharing it with a third-party payor. Under the guise of sharing information, it reinforces the patriarchal assumption that the ignorance of the client is to be maintained in the therapeutic relationship.

Feminist empowered consent would share adequate information for a client to make decisions about therapy and its mechanics with as much knowledge as is available to the therapist. Such information would communicate not only facts but the value of context in understanding and decision-making, as well as the feminist therapist's respect for the client as choice-maker. In the example just given, a feminist process of informing and empowering might include describing the diagnosis, telling the client the label that is going to be attached to the client in the record; noting what that diagnosis means to other mental health providers; offering to make available to the client a copy of the *DSM*; and offering to discuss the diagnosis with the client and to consider alternatives that the client might suggest.

It would also empower the client to be told of the risks involved in using insurance to purchase psychotherapy: the possible obstacles to future purchase of health insurance because it would establish a preexisting condition; the degree to which this insurance, if it is of the managed mental health care variety, will require intrusion into the confidentiality of therapy in exchange for payment; possible consequences for employment, security clearances, or child custody; and possible risks to confidentiality stemming from relationships between a third-party payor and the client's employer. Instead of making the decision for clients to use their health insurance to bill for psychotherapy, it offers information that will aid clients in deciding whether or not to do so, given all foreseeable risks of that choice.

Feminist therapists also need to make the choice of informing their clients that they practice feminist therapy. While this statement may seem self-evident and even redundant, I have found that it is not the norm for feminist therapists to identify themselves as such to potential clients. In my discussions with colleagues, I have heard several rationales for this decision to withhold important information about the therapist's theoretical orientation, including a concern that the therapist will pigeon-hole herself and not attract clients who might be frightened off by the term "femi-

nist" and a wish to avoid offending clients who have no choice of who
they will be assigned to see and who never would have freely chosen to
work with a feminist therapist.

Although I respect such reasoning, I believe that such statements play
into harmful stereotypes, both about feminism and feminists and about
clients' capacity to process information and make use of it. Researchers on
stereotyping have consistently found that bias is unlikely to persist in the
face of actual personal acquaintance. Clients who know that they are seeing feminist therapists are thus challenged on narrow, patriarchally created definitions of feminism and may come to recognize their own feminist beliefs and analyses, ideas that they had not seen as feminist because
they did not match mainstream media images of what constituted feminist
thought. Clients who come to associate feminist therapy with respect,
empowerment, and relationality are unlikely to feel frightened of their
therapist. The feminist therapist who withholds this information colludes
with patriarchy and undermines herself, as well as the feminist process
and integrity of her therapeutic work. She also communicates that somehow feminist therapy is a dirty secret to be hidden, not a theoretical orientation to be shared as one might share that one is psychoanalytic, or cognitive-behavioral, or gestalt.

As one who does share this information (as if it were possible to obscure
it, given my outspokenness!), first in the form of my telephone directory
listing and then in several paragraphs of my five-page consent-to-treatment
form, I have found that no one has been frightened, but almost everyone
has been curious. In their curiosity, many clients have been emboldened to
ask the sorts of important questions about their choice to be in therapy that
they might never have raised without this stimulus early on in our relationship, which served as an invitation to query.

Most importantly, clients have a right to this information. When they
are sitting with a therapist and revealing their innermost thoughts and
feelings, they are entitled to know something about the values of the therapist that are basic to the work and will color the therapist's reception of
those thoughts and feelings. When this information is an important part of
the therapist's modus operandi and yet unavailable to the client, the risk
of harm to the client increases. An example may serve to illustrate this
point. Diane, a middle-class, white, heterosexual woman in her thirties,
had spent three years in therapy with a woman therapist of about her own
age and background and had come to trust her greatly. The therapist had
never shared information about her own theoretical orientation or biases,
but in the three years of therapy she had never commented on matters in
Diane's life in other than a supportive manner. When Diane shared with

the therapist her carefully thought-through plans to undergo a course of study to convert to Buddhism, however, the therapist shocked Diane by saying that it was her "moral duty as a Christian" to let Diane know that she was putting her mortal soul in jeopardy by embracing this pagan creed; the therapist then suggested that this decision was a symptom of an unconscious desire to wound her and an acting out against Diane's own Presbyterian parents and that it should be explored as a problem in therapy.

Diane was astonished and wounded by her therapist's response, particularly because the therapist had never shared with her that her own Christian beliefs were an important component of her work and that she would treat any deviation from Christianity as a symptom of pathology. Diane felt lied to and betrayed, and implicitly she had been. Similarly at fault is the therapist who strongly does not believe in divorce but fails to share this information with the client at the outset of treatment, misleading the client who believes that therapy will be a safe place to discuss ambivalence about remaining in a marriage. How much more important it is for feminist therapists to inform clients of a theoretical orientation that is as transforming to the process as the feminist perspective.

Identifying oneself as a feminist therapist at the onset of therapy and describing how the feminist approach will affect the work gives clients the power of truly informed and empowered consent, and respects their ability to make choices in their own best interests. It is as important as letting clients know that the managed care firm that pays the bills will want to see copies of the session notes or sharing with them the actual consequences of being reported to protective services for suspected abuse of children. While it is possible to argue that it might be even more subversive of patriarchy to withhold one's identity as a feminist therapist until the client has come to like, trust, and feel empowered by the feminist approach to practice, and while there may be circumstances where the sociopolitical milieu makes this a better option, my own bias is to allow this identifying information to form a part of the entire therapy relationship. Informed consent does not begin and end with the form signed at the onset of treatment. In a feminist model, such informing and consenting constitute ongoing aspects of the sharing of power and the development of the feminist therapeutic relationship.

Finally, the concept of informed and empowered consent, reconfigured through feminist questioning, also includes encouraging potential clients to question themselves regarding their motives for choosing psychotherapy as the strategy for dealing with their problems at this time and suggesting to them that therapy may not be useful for them, and may even be harmful to them. Complete information about therapy—the sort that can lead to empowered consent—includes information about the problems and risks of engaging in this process as well as the presumed benefits. Feminist therapists can afford to be honest about the potentials for harm when people begin to ask deep and subversive questions about their lives. They must be able to let people know that therapy is simply one—and sometimes not the best—strategy for asking those questions or making desired changes. The therapist may suggest that starting therapy simply because one is in a new relationship, or having normal feelings of grief over a loss, may be less helpful than finding a support group of people at a similar developmental step. As Hare-Mustin and her colleagues (1979) noted, feminist therapists need to share information about the alternatives that are available, including political activism (Kitzinger & Perkins, 1993). The feminist questions, Whose information? and Consented to how? are basic to a feminist revision of the informed-and-empowered-consent process.

Psychological Testing

Psychological testing is an unexplored and, to many feminist therapists, mostly invisible locus of possible subversive strategies, appearing as it does to be entirely a patriarchal tool. Tests are used to categorize and pathologize people, and to do so with the voice of actuarial authority, backed by years of patriarchal research. But its capacities to be reshaped to a feminist vehicle for change are quite promising. All feminist thinking on this topic owes a debt of gratitude to the feminist psychologist Lynne Bravo Rosewater, whose pioneering work in introducing feminist episte-mologies and methodologies to psychological testing will be discussed later in this chapter.

Until Rosewater's work appeared in the early 1980s, the use of psycho-logical testing by feminist therapists was almost unknown, with good rea-son. The history of psychometrics is planted firmly in oppression. The original developers of psychological tests were eugenicists and social Dar-winists, who believed that nondominant group peoples should be stopped from reproducing and who were searching for "scientific" means to prove the inferiority of such groups and thus empirically justify discrimination and oppression. Francis Galton, the "father" of psychological testing, con-structed early intelligence tests based upon such assumptions; while the specifics of his work have long been repudiated by mainstream scholars, the inherent assumptions of the testing movement have never changed.

Testing exists to separate the sheep from the goats, the normal from the less-than. Psychological testing is almost always conducted with pro-foundly decontextualized assumptions. There is always a norm group against which the picture of deviance is developed, and in tests of person-ality and intelligence alike, the norm group most commonly reflects domi-nant group membership and values. Thus verbal ability is valued over the ability to sing on pitch, rationality over passion and intensity, because these are norms derived from patriarchy. Testing serves to reify artificial categories that are then defined as the "objective truth" about a person's skills, abilities, pathology, or personality characteristics.

An excellent example of this phenomenon is the original version of the Minnesota Multiphasic Personality Inventory, or MMPI. This test has been probably the most frequently administered test in the psychological arma-mentarium. And because of the rise of computer scoring and interpreta-tion services, it is now accessible to any mental health professional, not just to psychologists, as was originally the case. It has been widely used for such functions as personnel selection, child custody evaluation, and psy-chological assessment in legal settings. (This begs the question of whether the test should even be used in these contexts, given that it was never developed to be applied there; see Pope, Butcher, & Seelen, [1993] for a discussion of validity considerations in psychological testing.) Considered an objective test because it is administered and scored according to prede-termined formulas, the MMPI has been highly touted as reliable and valid.

Yet the group of people who constituted the "normal" population against which everyone else was measured during test development was anything but diverse. The "Minnesota normals," as they have come to be called, were visitors at the University of Minnesota Hospitals during the late 1930s and early 1940s. Representative of the population of Minnesota at the time, they were almost entirely Caucasian, of Northern European back-ground, and most likely to be either Lutheran or Catholic. Their average education was eighth grade. Most lived in rural areas or small communities and worked in trades. No information was gathered from this group—or from any of the other groups used to establish the scales for pathology, for that matter— about histories of violence, trauma, or abuse. Nor were their possible experiences as perpetrators of violence ever assessed.

To the surprise of few feminists, people who were clearly different from the Minnesota normals were likely to be diagnosed as quite disturbed on this test, regardless of whether they were in distress or having difficulties functioning. People of color, especially African-Americans, routinely looked "paranoid." Women and men who did not have the interests and attitudes that, in the 1930s and 40s, were stereotypically assigned to their gender became the targets of questions about their sexual orientation and adjustment. Anyone with dissenting or progressive political views came out looking like a "psychopathic deviate." People with fundamentalist or charismatic religious beliefs often were diagnosed psychotic. And people with post-traumatic and dissociative problems, which were invisible to the psychopathologists of mid-century North America, could receive a number of incorrect diagnoses arising from this "reliable, valid" document. The ecological validity of the MMPI—its capacity to make sense within a diversity of contexts—was a myth.

Computerized scoring services tend to compound the dominant-culture errors of analysis, as well as to extend them to ever-wider audiences. The interpretations generated by these services, for the MMPI and any other computerized psychological test, are commonly no more than quotations from standard texts. The ultimate in decontextualized constructions of reality, such computerized interpretations have the powerful ring of truth, an experience known as the "Barnum effect" in homage to the notion that authoritative language can and will sucker anyone into belief. As one mainstream critic of the scoring services noted, these documents are "all mean and no sigma" (Matarazzo, 1986)—in other words, all normative data, with no contextual information factored in. The computerized interpretations, parallel to the test itself, took no account of the problems of power, oppression, and attempts to resist that are central to feminist analysis, nor of the immense diversity and variability of social settings that mediated the expression of behavior.

The MMPI is not necessarily the most problematic of psychological tests, although until recently it has been the most pervasive. (It has been succeeded by a second edition, in which many revisions were made to make the test more diverse in its normative bases.) Projective testing, such as the Rorschach Inkblot test and the Incomplete Sentences Blank, compounds the effects of dominant-group scoring norms with the extreme risk of bias on the part of the person scoring and interpreting the test findings. Other self-described objective tests, such as the Millon Clinical Multiaxial Inventory (MCMI-II), contain assumptions that are likely to result in the misdiagnosis of victims of interpersonal violence, assigning them to a diagnosis of self-defeating personality disorder.

What can feminist therapists do when faced with the requirement that they utilize or be guided by such testing materials? This is not an idle question; in some agency and hospital settings, standardized tests are given to all clients and become the cornerstones of diagnostic workups and treatment planning. Some managed mental health firms now require the administration of psychological tests at the beginning of and then throughout treatment so that progress in therapy can be tracked on computer models. Feminist therapists operating in any sort of legal setting are likely to find that psychological tests are the foundation for decisions to incarcerate or release persons charged with crimes and are deemed essential in civil cases and in family court. Custody, freedom, payment of damages—all can hinge on the capacity to comprehend and utilize such documents. Unless a feminist therapist is prepared to respond to the tests—at the very least, to raise important feminist questions about such an approach to understanding human behavior—she will be less effective in subverting their potential for further oppression and unprepared to turn them to feminist ends.

A helpful model is provided by the work of the feminist clinical psychologists Lynne Bravo Rosewater (1985a, 1985b) and Mary Anne Dutton (1992), who have studied the uses of personality testing with battered women. Both Rosewater and Dutton have focused on the use of the Minnesota Multiphasic Personality Inventory (and its successor, the MMPI-2) and have created a data base that contextualizes the test findings in terms of violence against women. Their work has involved collecting data on large numbers of battered women and identifying common patterns of response on the testing. In effect, they have noted that the standard mainstream texts and computerized scoring systems for the MMPI do not take into account the possibility that the person taking the test is a woman who currently is, or recently has been, beaten by her spouse or partner. So each of these researchers has asked the question, How do women look on this test when we know that abuse and violence are present in the context?

The results of asking this question have been profound and powerful as illustrations of the potential for transformation of patriarchal tools. As Rosewater first pointed out, without the context, specifically the identification of the presence of violence, battered women look like schizophrenics or borderline personalities on the MMPI. With the context of violence explicitly framing the interpretation of the test findings, however, it is possible to note that the sort of distress indicated on the testing is a reasonable response to events in the test-taker's life. That is to say, when a woman's partner is beating her, it makes sense that she is depressed, confused, scattered, and feeling overwhelmed. It is not necessarily the case that this state of response to life-threatening violence is either usual for the woman in question or a sign of psychopathology. It is then also possible, utilizing the data generated by this feminist transformation of testing, to take the next step and raise questions about all women diagnosed as schizophrenic or borderline. If the feminist reclaiming of psychological testing teaches feminist therapists that the survival of violence is easily mistaken for severe pathology on a test, then we can extrapolate to any woman previously labeled in circumstances where feminist knowledge and contextual data were lacking. This can allow a feminist practitioner to challenge the accuracy of the prior, stigmatizing diagnosis and open a door to the possibility of abuse in the woman's life and its meanings for her functioning.

Thus, the first feminist question is, What do we know about how people with this particular experience respond to this specific psychological test? For mainstream psychometrists, this should actually be a standard question; tests are meant to be used only for those groups and to answer those questions for which they have specifically been normed (Pope et al., 1993). In practice, however, questioning the authority and universal applicability of a psychological test is a radical action. The Millon Inventory is completely valid only when given to people who are just commencing psychotherapy, since such people constituted the norm group on which the test was developed. Yet the test, which has been heavily promoted by its publishers, is frequently found in the context of child custody evaluations, personal injury lawsuits, and other settings that require evaluations very different from those needed in the first few weeks of psychotherapy. Although questioning the ecological validity of this sort of test document is not a strictly feminist maneuver, framing that question in terms of the test's potential to oppress and disempower is. Since most tests available have not been normed with questions of race, class, exposure to violence, cultural difference, and so on in mind, and since there is often little or no data to support the use of most tests with many people from nondominant groups, the addition of feminist analysis to the equation may undermine the authority of the test to categorize or classify a person. Feminists can thus utilize this simple but powerful criticism effectively within our overall analysis of the weaknesses of patriarchal paradigms. The subversive possibilities for educating the psychometrist and debunking the authority of the test provide feminist implements for the therapist in dealing with this particular patriarchal tool.

For example, Alina was a woman of Kurdish ancestry, born and raised in the Middle East, who had immigrated to the United States. She had attended college in Europe and the United States where she had met her husband, Jeff, a U.S.-born Euro-American man, with whom she had had three children. Alina was in the middle of what seemed to be a losing custody battle. Her husband had consistently abused her and the children verbally. He was rarely involved in their care and took no interest in the children's schoolwork or accomplishments. As a native English-speaker immersed in the norms and metaphors of U.S. culture, however, he appeared quite functional when given the MMPI and the Rorschach by the custody evaluator. Alina, by contrast, although functionally fluent in English, was grounded in the metaphors and belief systems of her culture of origin. The computerized interpretations of the standard testing that the custody evaluator relied upon labeled her a mixed personality disorder with histrionic and borderline features. In addition she expressed anger at Jeff for having left her and the children for another woman; Jeff, by contrast, appeared calm and organized in his interactions with the custody evaluator. Largely on the basis of the results of the psychological testing, the evaluator recommended that the father have full residential custody, because the standard tests made him appear healthier mentally, and suggested that the mother be required to be in therapy before she could have unsupervised visitation with the children, whose primary caregiver she had always been.

While the problems in this custody evaluation are likely to be intuitively obvious to the feminist reader (as well as to some mainstream psychometricians), such cavalier use of tests with people for whom they have not been normed, to answer questions that they were not designed to answer, is a frequently encountered and rarely challenged norm in actual clinical practice. Several feminist psychologists (Chesler, 1987; Walker & Edwall, 1987) have documented the alarming trend in which mothers who have experienced abuse or are from cultural minority or marginal populations, are pathologized by standard psychological tests used in custody evaluations and lose custody of children. In Alina's case, had there not been a feminist psychologist on hand, she probably would have lost the custody fight.

But the feminist psychologist consulted by the mother after the custody evaluation raised a number of criticisms of the evaluator's findings that were immediately of use to this woman and her attorney, who had initially counseled her client to give up fighting lest the court become more punitive. Chief among the feminist therapist's critiques was that neither of these tests had been normed on people from Middle Eastern cultures. She noted that the use of such tests carried a high risk of attributing pathology to attitudes and actions that were culturally normative for Alina. She pointed out that research on women with histories of abuse, as was present in Alina's situation, indicated that standard interpretations of such tests would fail to take into account the expectable, short-term effects of abuse on mental health, increasing the risk of misdiagnosis. Finally, the feminist psychologist noted that neither the MMPI nor other standard tests of personality had been designed to measure a person's parenting skills, which are often unrelated to findings on standard psychological tests. She suggested that Alina's attorney request that the court order a more contextualized evaluation, specifically, that the children be observed in long interactions with each parent, to determine how the presumed differences in maternal and paternal mental health played out in context. She also urged that Alina's anger be viewed in the context of events rather than as evidence of pathology; similarly, Jeff's calm was reframed by the feminist psychologist as understandable, given that he had *not* been a target of constant verbal abuse for many years and had chosen to leave his family rather than being left by them.

When the court acceded to this request, an entirely different pattern of results emerged. The custody evaluator noted with surprise that this "mentally healthier" father had no notion of how to interact with his children; he used age-inappropriate language, failed to appreciate that his needs and desires would be different from those of his children, and allowed them to play with objects that might be dangerous. He also became easily angry and frustrated and, even while knowing that he was being observed and evaluated, was unable to control himself and refrain from verbally abusing the children, calling them "stupid" and "clumsy" and frequently adding, "just like your mother." The so-called "personality-disordered" mother, on the other hand, was able to demonstrate her skills as a parent; she was appropriately empathic, challenged her children to grow while offering necessary support, and was able to handle fussiness and tears with equanimity. When her children spoke of their father, she was able to place their feelings in an appropriate context and not voice her anger at him in her interactions with them. The original recommendations for custody were reversed, and both Alina's lawyer and the family court judge received a valuable lesson in asking questions about the validity of testing instead of assuming that psychological tests yield useful results irrespective of with whom they are used and for what purposes.

In another case, Zoe, a woman who had been injured on her job as a groundskeeper for a county park system, was required by the worker's compensation board to undergo intellectual and aptitude testing for a rehabilitation process. She scored very poorly on the Wechsler Adult Intelligence Scale (WAIS-R), the most commonly used standard test of intellectual functioning; the evaluator concluded that her below-average scores predicted poor results of any form of retraining and advised against payment for courses that she was considering because "it would be a poor investment." The evaluator commented that the good grades Zoe had received earlier in community college classes were probably not a valid indicator of her ability to achieve and must have reflected the ease of those courses since, as the evaluator put it, the WAIS-R was the gold standard of intelligence testing.

What the evaluator failed to take into account was that Zoe was a survivor of childhood abuse, with many dissociative symptoms that tended to be triggered in high-stress or time-pressure environments. Both of these elements were present in the testing situation; she was in pain, frightened, and worried about what the testing would mean for her future. When she and her attorney went looking for a second opinion, the feminist psychologist from whom they sought help queried Zoe carefully about her prior history and then asked, as the psychometrist had not, if the woman ever found herself "spacing out" or losing time, common mental health sequelae of the sort of history of abuse given by the client. Zoe, surprised that anyone knew about this sort of experience, which she had always thought to be unique to her, proceeded to describe a long history of dissociating in testing situations, including the most recent one for her vocational rehabilitation. This new, contextual information allowed Zoe's attorney to petition successfully for a new evaluation by a more experienced evaluator, who used a wider range of instruments to assess the woman's aptitudes and intellectual functioning. This second evaluation, by a nonfeminist psychometrist with strong interests in trauma and its effects on intellectual functioning, revealed that Zoe had a broad range of skills; in a low-pressure test setting, she was able to demonstrate them, because the triggers for her dissociation were not present and her concentration improved dramatically. Moreover, having learned serendipitously that she was not alone in her experience of spaciness at times of stress or distress, and that her behaviors made sense, given her life history, Zoe became less self-critical; she came to know that she would not have to live with her dissociation forever, should she choose to take steps to modify that coping strategy.

This powerfully oppressive master's tool of psychological testing is extremely well entrenched in the mental health system, particularly as mental health interacts with the legal arena. Even the feminist therapist who vows to have nothing to do with forensic practice is likely to have clients who eventually have to deal with worker's compensation, family law, or other legal or regulatory authorities. Anyone, no matter how court-averse, can end up with a client who has been arrested for shoplifting or hurt in a car accident and thus comes into contact with psychological testing in the forensic evaluation process. Not every feminist therapist will become expert on the use of such tools, since not all feminist therapists are psychologists or interested in the esoterica of T-scores and F-K ratios. But feminist therapists can sufficiently and potently undermine the hegemony of a test by familiarizing themselves with the critiques of reliability and validity that can be found even in mainstream testing literature, as well as with the data that feminist scholars are continuing to generate about the

performance of marginalized and oppressed peoples on particular popular tests. They can demand that the users of tests take context into account
and hold testers responsible for their errors when they fail to be ecologi-
cally valid in their pronouncements. Most importantly, they can refuse to
cede authority to psychological tests. While such tests provide a source of
information, they are simply that—one source of information, complete
with biases and flaws, and no more authoritative than other sources of
information about a person's intellectual, emotional, or interpersonal functioning. Tests can be a chainsaw, cutting down a person's sense of worth
or value; or they can be turned on the structures of patriarchy, cutting the
latter down to size or nicely remodeling them to be a better fit.

Psychotropic Medications

When I graduated from my doctoral program in 1977, I owned a poster,
sold by a mental patients' liberation group, that followed me around from
office to office until it died of too much masking tape and was recycled to
the bins of memory. It pictured Alice in Wonderland holding one of her
"drink me" bottles and listed the names of the common psychotropic medications of the time, with some of their rather horrible side effects. The
message of the poster was the message of the anti-psychiatry movement:
taking these drugs could make you smaller, like Alice, lost in a not-so-
wonderful-land of memory loss, confusion, disorientation, and tardive
dyskinesia/dystonia. These drugs, legal and often legislated upon people,
could damage brains, minds, and spirits. Both early feminist therapy literature and the writings of the mental patient/inmate movement are full of
stories of the lasting harms done by these medications. Feminist therapists
argued then over whether it would ever be appropriate to place a client on
medication. Few feminist therapists had the power to do so in any case;
then, as now, feminists in psychiatry are rare (and courageous) birds, and
nurse practitioners had not yet seized the power to prescribe that they
now have in many jurisdictions. But they wondered out loud about
whether it was a violation of feminist principles to send clients for medication evaluations.

Sixteen years after the poster was taped to my first professional office
wall, the feminist psychologists Rachel Perkins and Celia Kitzinger wrote
a book (1993) that heavily criticized therapy but praised psychotropic
medication. Meanwhile a report on women and depression (McGrath et al.,
1990), issued by a feminist-informed task force of the American Psychological Association of which I was a member, advised that referral for

medication should be considered by therapists treating depressed women (and recommended referral to feminist therapy!). What has happened in the intervening period? And how does a feminist analysis understand the meanings of psychotropic medications in the social and political context of a world in which the antidepressant Prozac is featured on the cover of a weekly news magazine and becomes the subject of a best-selling book (Kramer, 1993)?

Twenty years ago, in the minds of feminist therapists psychotropic medications stood for attempts by patriarchy to control "inconvenient" people, to silence the wails of the "hysterical" incest survivor described in the introduction to this book, or to numb the rage of the African-American men—all targets of lifelong violence—who were the patients in the state psychiatric hospital where I had my first mental-health-related summer job. In some respects the scene is much the same. Poor people, people of color, people whose symptoms are florid or frightening are still more likely to be "treated," first or only, with medications. This practice often reflects blatant misdiagnosis; one study of psychiatric in-patients in a state hospital found that many of those diagnosed psychotic and dosed to a stupor on antipsychotic medications were actually experiencing multiple personalities or other dissociative disorders, for which such medications are strongly contraindicated (Ross & Norton, 1988).

Then, as now, psychotropic medications are big business, as well. Prozac, that best-selling antidepressant of the 1990s, is steadily going up in price; rather than becoming more affordable as more is sold (which would seem to be the reasonable course for the market to take), it has become further out of reach for anyone without either money or that fast-vanishing phenomenon, good medical insurance. Ads for medications have long served as the frontispiece for the *American Journal of Psychiatry;* more often than not, the patient portrayed in the ads, then and now, is a woman. Drug companies underwrite professional symposia for psychiatrists and (increasingly) psychologists at which they tout the latest drug treatment.

Yet in the face of this pressure to give pills to people, we do know now one thing that was less evident to feminist therapists two decades back: that many of the kinds of distress we observe have biological concomitants. It is useful and necessary to continue to debate whether the neurochemical changes in the brains of people who experience depression or anxiety are the cause or the result of the pain being felt. Research by psychiatrist and trauma specialist Bessel van der Kolk (1992) strongly indicates that trauma makes changes in brain function that can be measured and detected through the use of positron-emission scans, changes that are consistent with some of the kinds of symptoms—for example, sleep distur-

bances or hyperirritability—that are experienced by many trauma survivors. This sort of evidence would appear to argue for interventions that
are themselves directly biological and somatic, rather than psychological
and interpersonal.

Accepting these data regarding brain neurochemistry does not, however, imply automatically including the popular psychotropic medications
in the strategies commonly used by feminist therapists. Rather, it is an
argument for using *somatic* interventions together with interpersonal and
political strategies for change. Bringing feminist methodologies into play
helps, because the universe of possible somatic interventions can be perceived to be far broader than those suggested by the formulary of psychotropic medications. A feminist viewpoint allows for a challenge to the
notion that all biological approaches must rise from the allopathic foundation that has become the province of North American medicine. It also
allows feminist therapists to take a critical look at the current rush to prescribe those medications and to question why this emphasis on the power
of drugs to change personality is emerging now, given current cultural
zeitgeist.

The rebel psychiatrist Peter Breggin has argued in his book *Toxic Psychiatry* (1991) that the hegemony of biological psychiatry in the United States
reflects the overall political trend during the 1980s to search for simplistic
solutions to people's distress that would not entail any sort of social or
political change or challenge growing mainstream cultural trends toward
alienation, disconnection, and social irresponsibility. Breggin comments
that it is much easier to prescribe one of the potent new serotonergic antidepressants, such as Prozac or Zoloft, for the woman depressed by gender
or racial discrimination in her workplace than to take the time to develop a
psychotherapeutic relationship with her in which she will be empowered
to tell her own truths and decide upon a course of action. Such a course is
also less expensive and more congenial to managed care organizations
that require the completion of treatment within twelve, ten, or as few as
two meetings between therapist and client.

The feminist therapist must keep such political realities in mind when
the question of medication is raised by her or by her clients. Is medication
being utilized as a short-cut, a silencer? Or has the relationship of therapy
progressed long and far enough that both parties believe that a somatic
intervention will now make sense by giving the client enough of a sense of
hope and respite from symptoms to go on with the healing process? Does
a somatic intervention fit best with the desires and needs of the client, her
cultural perspectives and understandings of her distress, or does it represent a better match with the desires and needs of the therapist? And, if a

somatic intervention is needed, why psychotropic medication? What other possibilities are available?

The various so-called nontraditional streams of somatic health care provide a variety of alternatives. Naturopathic and homeopathic models of medicine each provide a variety of types of somatic treatment that have proved efficacious in some instances, with less risk of the sorts of side effects that for many people are an unpleasant aspect of psychotropic medications. Oriental medicine also has a variety of approaches to somatic intervention, including acupuncture, Chinese herbal medicine, and Chi Gong, all of which can have some effect on brain neurochemistry, mood, and functioning. Running and other forms of vigorous aerobic exercise have been demonstrated to be as effective in the treatment of depression as have some standard antidepressants.

Presentation of the various alternatives in an open, noncoercive manner allows feminist therapists to honor and respect their clients' choices of somatic interventions while undermining the patriarchal versions of what constitute valuable somatic interventions. Some clients will decide that allopathic medicines are the best strategy for them; van der Kolk's work (1992), for example, suggests that because serotonin transmission is disturbed by trauma, the serotonergic antidepressants may be a useful somatic intervention with some trauma survivors. Other clients will make the choice to utilize nonallopathic methods; still others will decide to use no somatic interventions at this time. The task for the feminist therapist is to learn what options are available without being seduced into thinking that the latest productions of the drug companies constitute the only appropriate or most effective option.

Working Within Institutional Constraints

Typically, a feminist therapist is thought of as working in an independent practice setting, answerable to no one but herself, her clients, and feminist ethical standards. As more people are trained in feminist therapy, however, the diversity of our work settings has broadened as well. The feminist therapist working in an institutional setting, such as a mental health agency, psychiatric hospital unit, school counseling office, or community health clinic, may initially have difficulty seeing how she can apply the principles of feminist transformation and social change to her work. These settings are not usually run with feminist principles and may be characterized by notions of treatment and the proper relationships of therapists and clients that are manifestly antithetical to feminist values and aims. Yet it can be within mental health institutions that the subversive potentials of feminist therapy are most powerfully realized. When work in such a setting is theorized as an opportunity for the development of new strategies for resistance, rather than as the acceptance of a lesser life for feminist therapy practice, then the capacity for feminist practices to transcend the stereotypes of where, how, and with whom feminist therapists work can be broadly actualized and the possibilities for feminist capture of patriarchal institutions from within are increased. Today, domestic violence prevention programs are designed and implemented for the Marines and the Department of Veteran's Affairs by feminist therapists. While not all examples need be so striking, they illustrate how far from the stereotyped field one may find the feminist flower blooming.

Such settings call for creativity on the part of feminist therapists and for asking how they can turn the powers of the institution toward feminist ends. This provides opportunities for the development of strategies and knowledge that may be unavailable in the superficially freer setting of an independent practice. Specifically, by demonstrating the efficacy of feminist epistemologies and methodologies in their work, they can lead mainstream agencies to an awareness of the necessity of feminist perspectives for the achievement of their own goals.

One may wonder at this point who's co-opting whom. In the discourse on this topic, feminist therapists have often acted as though they were the more easily subverted party. There are some valid reasons for this sort of concern. The power inherent in participation as therapists in the institutions of the mental health care delivery system can feel and be quite attractive, and the implied punishments for deviation can be rather frightening. No feminist therapist is so courageous that she will not, in some manner, succumb or wish to succumb to the allure of just going along to get along. Nor should the power of her own internalized domination be underestimated as a factor in this process. Moreover, the manner in which patriarchal strategies are presented may be confusing, difficult at first to deconstruct and analyze through feminist lenses. Sometimes institutional settings that would appear to be feminist, such as sexual assault treatment programs, are no more so, and sometimes less so, than those whose designations, such as group home for adults with developmental disabilities, do not appear to suggest feminist goals.

But feminist therapists have an ace in the hole in their relationships with mainstream institutions. They are acutely aware of and attentive to the potential for being co-opted and for their feminist values and strategies to be subverted by patriarchal institutions. Feminist analysis makes visible how patriarchal paradigms can seem to overpower them and make them temporarily forget who they are and what they know about their own integrity. Thus they are prepared to resist and capable of developing the support they need to be strong and persistent in the task of subversion. Most mainstream mental health institutions, on the other hand, have no such awareness of the possibility that they might be subverted by feminist practices. Their defenses against the subversive possibilities of feminist therapists in their midst are weak or absent altogether.

Consider the example of Filomena, a heterosexual Filipina-American social worker and feminist therapist. After graduation from social work school, she was employed at a community mental health agency. The agency was suffering from financial problems, caused in part by the fact that few people in the local community sought services there. Filomena heard her new supervisor talk about how the local community—a working-class mixture of African-Americans and Asian Pacific Islanders, many of them immigrants—were simply not sufficiently therapy-oriented. Filomena was angered by this attitude, which blamed the community for not using services that had never been shaped to meet their particular needs—a familiar experience for her personally and for many people she knew. She also realized that she had a strange common cause with her new employers. They wanted more clients. She wanted to transform this mainstream, culturally less-than-sensitive agency into a setting that met and empowered the local community where it was and into a place of work that nourished rather than drained her. She discussed her alternatives with her friends in a political action group for social workers of color; she could quit and try to find a more congenial place to work, or she could, with their help and support, make some attempts to undermine the oppressive paradigms that pervaded her new workplace.

Filomena's initial strategy for implementing feminist transformation of her agency was to join the agency's continuing education committee and become an active source of providers of in-service training. Soon the agency staff was being exposed to feminist and antiracist approaches to psychotherapy through her recommended trainers and consultants. The agency director in turn became excited about the possibilities of making services more community-friendly. Filomena seized this opening to suggest that she start a support group for adolescent women. The group, which utilized feminist research on encouraging resistance in adolescent girls, proved popular, and the demand grew for more similar interventions to be provided by the agency. This response from the supposedly apathetic community led to hiring more culturally aware and culturally diverse staff in order to meet the demands for new services.

Today, seven years after starting work at this agency, Filomena is the supervisor of other staff members and interns at an agency that has expanded both its services and its physical quarters because of increased demand. Groups for survivors of family violence, classes on raising resilient children in the face of racism and sexism, a drop-in center for sexual minority youth of color, and outreach liaisons to various community organizations have been established. Filomena's is a particularly successful attempt at transformation, although she also acknowledges that the toll taken on her by years of being at the front edge of a struggle to subvert a patriarchal institution has been heavier than she could have imagined when she first took the task on. Not every feminist therapist will have the capacity, temperament, desire, or necessary social and political support system to engage in this sort of process. But this example illustrates the possibilities that are inherent in any situation where feminist therapists are employed.

Feminist therapists have accomplished similar transformations and liberations in many highly patriarchal institutions. The notion that we might get patriarchy to pay for its own dismantling is an attractive one. Each military or Veteran's Administration program for treating men who beat women, each employee assistance program that offers support groups for oppressed groups in a corporate environment, is evidence of the infiltration of patriarchal mental health institutions by feminist therapy values and principles. Such a strategy requires that we theorize the work of feminist therapy in a broad and complex manner. When feminist therapists work in institutional settings, they are not simply affecting radical social change in the lives of their clients. Rather, they are also confronted with the challenges of subverting the systems in which they work, toward the same liberating goals.

Feminist therapists must also take care not to give away power to patriarchal institutions. As the chapters on diagnosis and case conceptualization described, the knowledge of one's "enemies" is a necessary component of subverting those enemies. Thus feminist therapists, in order to function in patriarchal institutions, must become even more knowledgeable and grounded in the work, and thus the weaknesses, of mainstream mental health than those who accept it as a norm. It is far easier to use the *DSM-IV* when required to do so if one can also critique it skillfully and thus support one's choices of diagnoses that are less tainted by bias or poor research. Ironically, contrary to the stereotypes, the feminist therapist in an institutional setting may be more grounded in feminism and more attuned to feminist epistemologies out of necessity based in survival needs than her sisters in private practice, who may be more easily seduced into accepting some patriarchal notions because they are less confronted with them daily.

While the examples in this chapter speak to specific instances and types of patriarchal manifestations in the lives and work of feminist therapists, there is a central theme underlying all the theorizing: There are few, if any, situations in feminist therapy work that cannot in some manner or another be transformed and put to the services of a liberating process. This is not simply a matter of reframing or learning to put a good face on ugly propositions, any more than is the case when feminist therapists work with clients to transform the meaning of their personal narrative, recover their mother tongues, and take back the grasp of their power. Rather, it is a matter of taking the feminist process as practiced in the therapy hour and appling it to the systems in which therapists work. This application of feminist practice in patriarchal institutions constitutes a refusal to believe the lies of patriarchy that, like the trappings of the Wizard of Oz, act to create the illusion of greater power and invincibility in patriarchal systems of mental health care than may actually exist. Feminist therapy uses the master's tools to reforge, reshape, and transform each possibility for oppression into one of liberation and social change.

CHAPTER 8

Feminism and Ethics

Y OU ARE A THERAPIST practicing independently in a medium-sized town. As a feminist, you have also been an activist in your community on the issue of violence in families. So you are not surprised when you are asked to join the board of directors of a local program for promoting nonviolent conflict resolution skills in adolescents. You know some of the board members from your work over the years, and you look forward to getting to know them better and having some say in the further development of this valuable program. You are flattered and pleased, and you say yes.

You arrive for your first board meeting, a weekend-long retreat at a rural conference center. You are sitting in the common room, chatting, when into the room walks a woman who three days ago was sitting in your office as your client. You know that she is a survivor of beatings from her former husband. You have never before encountered her in your work in the community and never discussed with her what to do if you were to encounter one another in public. Neither of you had shared with the other the news of your invitation to this board. One of the other board members "introduces" her to you as the other new member of the board, telling you that she, like you, has a special interest in reducing violence in families. You feel intense discomfort and confusion and you sense your client's uncertainty; you and she are going to be together all weekend in an emotionally intense and often self-disclosing setting. The ethical code of your profession prohibits dual relationships, and you are on the threshold of having one with this woman. As a therapist, what do you do? As a feminist therapist, does the answer to this question become different? easier? more difficult?

Or imagine a very different situation. You respond to a request from the court to conduct an evaluation in a situation of contested custody. You carefully study each parent in relationship to their two small children, observing their capacities to be empathic, set limits, resonate to the developmental needs of each child. The mother, although genuinely and desperately trying to do well, continues in situation after situation to appear less capable in the parental role than the father, who seems at ease, tuned in to both son and daughter, and able to be present with them rather than anxious about pleasing you, the evaluator.

Your commitment in this process is to the best interest of the children. Yet how do you, as a feminist therapist, make sense of what you have seen? How do you place what you observe into the contextual information that you have gathered? The father has a professional degree; like you, he is verbally fluent, comfortable with being evaluated because he has spent a lifetime in situations where he has been tested and observed. The mother married him after a year at a community college; he was her math instructor. She is fearful of evaluation, deferential to authority, and you are an authority figure to her, because she knows that you will determine who gets to live with these children and who gets to visit. Knowing this background, how do you make sense of what you have seen? How do you interpolate a feminist analysis of this family with your commitment to the children's best interest? Will your answers to the question of child custody be different because you are a feminist? If so, why, and how? And what biases will you be injecting into the evaluation process?

These are questions about ethics, about the value-laden issues that arise in the practice of psychotherapy. Every therapist's work involves grappling with ethical dilemmas; no one is immune. Yet few therapists are well trained in ethics. Research indicates that less than a quarter of all currently practicing therapists have had formal coursework in ethics during their training, and feminist therapists are no exception (Pope & Vasquez, 1991). Yet for the discipline of feminist therapy, ethics has been an abiding, transcendent concern, one that ties together every issue and aspect of our practice. The very core of feminist therapy is founded in a critique of the ethically problematic nature of mainstream mental health practice. Everything I have addressed so far in this book leads inevitably to questions that, in a feminist framework, are those of the ethics of practice. There is no aspect of feminist therapy that cannot be theorized as the core of an ethical stance or the source of an ethical dilemma, the solving of which serves to illuminate and define feminist therapy theory.

As a consequence, ethics is the topic in feminist therapy that has been most thoroughly theorized and subjected to questions and debate. Encounters with the kinds of dilemmas I have just described have moved feminist therapists beyond the parameters of mainstream psychotherapy ethics, because the nature of the ethical questions that they encounter entwine inextricably with feminist politics and subversive intentions. Often the ethical principles of psychology, social work, psychiatry, counseling, or nursing give little or no guidance as to how to answer those questions *as feminists*. Feminist therapists have had to develop their own perspectives on ethics in order to the understand how to balance the disruptive voices of feminist theory with the need for clear boundaries and parameters in psychotherapy practice.

It has also been useful to distinguish how ethical theories in feminist therapy differ from those of mainstream psychotherapies. In the examples with which this chapter begins, for example, there are standards promulgated by all the mental health professions that would guide an ethical nonfeminist therapist in formulating a response to the ethical dilemmas in each story. Yet a feminist therapist encountering each of these situations might perceive entirely different ethical questions and thus require an ethical framework with different assumptions about what is right and of value in the practice of psychotherapy. The outcomes achieved may be precisely the same or may differ broadly from those resulting from mainstream deliberations.

Feminist theory in psychotherapy does more than permit a divergent analysis of common ethical questions, however. For in theorizing the work of a therapist within an explicitly politically informed framework, feminist therapy creates a different set of possible dilemmas from those posed by other, dominant-culture mental health disciplines. The notion that a feminist therapist has a responsibility to change in the larger sociopolitical context and that this responsibility must be discharged in each aspect of her work offers opportunities for understanding the meaning of ethical action—or of ethically problematic action—that are absent in those approaches whose vision of the ethical field is constricted to the decontextualized relationship between professional and client.

Feet in the Concrete: The Dominant Ethical Paradigm

Ethics in the mainstream mental health disciplines in North America derives conceptually from the Hippocratic Oath, which constitutes the ethical foundation of the first official healing art, medicine. While the specifics of each mental health professional code of ethics vary somewhat in response to the special characteristics of the discipline, most reflect the basic notions promulgated by Hippocrates. Some of these notions are entirely compatible with a feminist perspective, at least on the surface. Beneficence, the principle of doing no harm, abstinence from sexual contact with vulnerable populations receiving care, guarding the confidentiality of those cared for—these are concepts that present no problems for feminist therapy on the simplest level.

Yet the Hippocratic Oath and its various modern derivatives also contain patriarchal—and therefore to a feminist problematic—assumptions about the nature of the relationship between the healer and the patient. Foremost is the assumption of hierarchy; the healer is the guardian of mysteries and secrets, the one who makes healing happen, who does healing on the passive recipient. The healer makes decisions about what sorts of procedures are available. The healer is the only expert on what is good and what is not, thereby privileging the opinions of the most powerful actor. As defined by the mental health ethics codes, the relationship of therapist to client is one whose lineaments are essentially legal, those of a fiduciary relationship of responsibility. In fact, the ethical codes of all of the mental health disciplines have become increasingly legalistic documents; the notion of the broader social and political meaning of practice, the importance of looking at questions about power and domination— between therapist and client, between clients and their social and emotional environments, of the therapist as an agent of society—none of these is critically addressed in mainstream codes of ethics. Rather, there is the implicit assumption that the therapist has more power, will act according to the dictates of the dominant culture, and will strive to be benevolent in the wielding of that power.

The most recent revision of the ethical guidelines of the American Psychological Association presents an excellent illustration of the development of patriarchal ethics codes as documents that explicitly theorize a hierarchical, legalistic relationship in therapy as the exemplar of ethical practice (American Psychological Association, 1992). This code provides a useful foil for feminist ethical theorizing. I do not intend to suggest that there is something wrong with the APA code that could not be solved by the thorough subversion of patriarchal values in the discipline of psychology; for a patriarchal ethics code, it is complete, thoughtful, and attentive to a number of details of concern to feminists. But I would argue that *because* it is a code founded in patriarchal assumptions, it will always be deficient in contrast to principles informed by feminist analysis. Its roots are planted in polluted soil, and the plant growing from them will thus always be deformed to some degree by the patriarchal assumptions from which this ethical fruit derives.

The feminist psychologists Hannah Lerman and Natalie Porter presaged the problems inherent in the new APA code in their critique of dominant-cultural ethical standards, written prior to the revision of the code (Lerman & Porter, 1990a). They began by noting that mainstream codes are reactive; they respond to complaints about the behavior of therapists and consequently construct a legalistic framework for ethical thinking, an analysis joined by other feminist ethical commentators (Griffith, 1992). The revised APA code specifically focuses on the problem of therapists being sued or being the targets of complaints or legal cases against psychologists. It is not an aspirational code, with a focus on ideal behavior; it is a minimum standard code, defining what is to be avoided by a psychologist. This legalistic stance raises another problem, in the eyes of feminist therapists. As a patriarchal code, this and all other dominant ethical standards privilege those holding the power—that is, the therapists—rather than trying to educate therapists in how to share power and instructing aggrieved consumers on their right to power. The revised APA code constructs a model of social relationships between therapists and clients that is adversarial at its core; the ethical principles serve to tell therapists how best to protect themselves from clients. The "management of risk" becomes the foremost ethical principle in this document; the power of the therapist both to heal and to harm is obscured in this legalistic framework by a fantasy vision of beleaguered therapists holding off crazed, vindictive clients and regulatory boards. The ways to heal oppressive practices by therapists are obscured by this protectionism.

Reactive codes also create an ethics of the least common denominator. Patriarchal codes proscribe specific behaviors in the presumed best interest of the client, but rarely are the clients asked their opinions on what will help and what will harm. The assumption of such codes is that only the official experts are in a position to make such judgments. As the lesbian feminist theologian Carter Heyward has noted in her description of a painful experience as the client in therapy, there are occasions when the therapist's presumption of having exclusive knowledge of the correct course of action may be profoundly harmful to a client, as it was in her case (Heyward, 1993). This is not to say that the desires of clients are necessarily the sole valuable source, but rather that they have been almost entirely discounted as useful for therapists caught in ethical dilemmas.

But even this standard of paternalism is expressed, not in terms of an ideal to which therapists must strive but rather in terms of a territory of behaviors to be avoided. The list of "thou shalt nots" grows exponentially over time; the list of "thou shalts," meanwhile, is whittled away by the advice from lawyers that one should not imply a promise to do good by including aspirational statements in official ethical documents. As an extreme example of this stance, many mainstream professional associations have, in the past decade, changed their by-laws and ethics documents removing statements about protecting the public because of warnings from legal counsel that a statement of desired virtue will lay the group open to legal action.

This stance of minimalist paternalism in turn generates another problematic aspect of mainstream therapy ethics: the tendency toward notions of ethics that are polarized and dichotomous, describing behaviors as either clearly wrong or clearly right. There are a few behaviors that might fall cleanly into such categories because the empirical evidence regarding the harmfulness of such actions is overpowering in its persuasiveness; the sexual or physical abuse of clients, for example, does not seem to have any other, possibly positive meaning, no matter what lens they are viewed through. There are, however, many behaviors that, in such a system of ethical theorizing, fall squarely between the cracks. As Lerman and Porter (1990a) have noted, dichotomous categories may proscribe blatant, concretely harmful behaviors, such as public expression of bigotry towards oppressed groups, but they do little to educate therapists on the ethical necessities of struggling to subvert one's own internalized domination when its expressions are more subtle. As with the second case described at the beginning of the chapter, where subtle questions of sexism and the interplay of power and privilege are brought out by a feminist ethical model but omitted from dominant ethical paradigms, the potential for therapists working within dominant frameworks to be profoundly oppressive while adhering strictly to the rules of the game is always present.

Such concreteness in dominant ethical standards also gives rise to creative attempts on the part of some therapists to discover the loopholes that would allow them to exploit and disempower clients while remaining officially ethical. Thus, for example, before ethical codes proscribing sexual relationships between therapists and their *former* clients were enacted, some therapists would use the distinction between a present and a former client in order to give themselves access to a vulnerable person. In one case in which I served as an expert witness for a complaining client, the therapist had the client sign a statement to the effect that she was no longer his client. He then immediately commenced sexual contact with her. In numerous other such cases, the therapist's main defense was that the ethics codes were silent on the subject of former clients and that no prohibitions on sexual contact applied. The notion of providing conceptual frameworks that would allow therapists to extrapolate principles for application to unspecified or previously unforeseen ethical dilemmas does not exist in dominant ethical modes, in which the implication is that all possible ethical problems have been identified and spelled out. Ironically, even some current attempts at defining former clients as off-limits for sexual predation by therapists contain similar errors of concreteness, such as specific time limitations that have little or no basis in a theory of what constitutes ethical action. In the first example opening this chapter, a similar confusion of meanings emerges when only dominant-cultural ethical codes are available to guide a therapist. Such codes, as noted, proscribe "dual (or multiple) relationships"—that is, a nontherapy relationship between therapist and client. The possibility that therapist and client might together craft an ethical response to the dilemma of this example that is *not* creative loophole-diving is wholly absent from dominant ethics standards, in which one is either in compliance or wrong.

Dominant-cultural ethical standards also assume dominant norms of social relating. In addition to a vision of disconnectedness in the lives of therapists and their clients, rather than one of shared community, these norms include an assumption of hierarchy and paternalism in the therapist-client relationship. This view is very different from the feminist acknowledgment of the power of the therapist role in relationship to the client that was discussed in chapter 4; the dominant vision is an uncritical gaze, assuming the necessity of power differentials rather than noting them as obstacles that must be addressed in order for therapy to be an empowering and liberating process.

The absence of clear ethical theorizing in dominant-culture codes suggests how the relationship of ethics to practice is perceived in the minds of most nonfeminist therapists: Ethics are a good thing in the abstract, but they are distanced from oneself, not explicitly derived from one's theories of the relationship in therapy or the work of the therapeutic process. Often ethical codes are experienced as external strictures, to be complied with or rebelled against but not central and integral to one's vision, as a therapist, of the nature of the work. Such codes disempower the therapist as an ethical decision maker: Expressing ethics in these terms simply creates the need for more and more concrete rules about what should be and not be done.

The Foundations of Feminist Ethics

In contrast, feminist therapy ethics, as expressed in formal codes (Feminist Therapy Institute, 1990) and in the writings of feminist therapists (Gartrell, 1994; Lerman & Porter, 1990b), derive from an entirely different vision of the ethical therapist-client relationship. Feminist therapy ethics take the stance that practitioner and client are allies in the process of transforming patriarchal oppression and that the liberation of one cannot be found in the oppression of the other. Since every aspect of feminist therapy practice is framed in the struggle for feminist social change, every aspect of practice is thus endowed with ethical meaning and with the potential for movement toward ethical action. Ethics as theorized from a feminist paradigm call upon therapists to examine themselves for possible expressions of oppressive dominance. The process by which an ethical stance is developed by feminist therapists must itself be inherently feminist—that is, it must privilege the voices of the oppressed and decenter the expertise of the therapist, replacing paternalism (or maternalism) with the sharing of power (Rave & Larsen, 1990). Feminist therapy ethics explicitly concern themselves with questions of oppression and domination, defining the political context and power relationships as the rightful domain of ethical struggles and theorizing (Brown, 1991c; Kanuha, 1990b).

The Feminist Therapy Institute Code of Ethics (Feminist Therapy Institute, 1990) is an example of the differences between feminist and dominant-culture ethical theorizing. This document, which I helped to develop over a number of years, reflects the collective wisdom of many feminist therapists and their clients, students, and colleagues, not just the official "ethics mavens" of feminist therapy; the widely inclusive input was integrated into a final draft statement by Carolyn Larsen and Elizabeth Rave (1990). The preamble to the code contains numerous explicit references to the social and political context and to the ethical necessity of "a commitment to political and social change that equalizes power among people" (p. 1). It also defines the code as a document in progress, rather than as a final word or pronouncement, and invites the participation of its readers in the ongoing process of theorizing ethical action in feminist therapy.

The topics addressed by the code are clearly derived from feminist theories: cultural diversities, oppression, power differentials, relationship overlap, therapist accountability, and social change. The political nature of therapy and the potential of the therapist to oppress—and thus her ethical obligation to serve as an instrument of liberation—lie at the conceptual core of this document. The code is written as a series of affirmative, aspirational statements; with the sole exception of the prohibition of sexualized relationships with clients and former clients, the code defines no concrete behaviors to be avoided. Instead, it defines areas of concern for feminist therapists, underscores the need for heightened awareness at points where patriarchal values might intrude, and outlines ways of thinking about ethical dilemmas and ambiguities in a manner that empowers the therapist and those with whom she works to be owners and active participants in the creation of feminist therapy ethics.

This code assumes the human relationship between therapist and client, along with the role-bound dance that is psychotherapy or other professional service delivery. Consequently, it makes it very difficult—as do feminist ethical epistemologies in general—for the therapist to objectify her clients as the existential other, a class of persons whose needs, feelings, and capacities vary greatly from her own. While clearly defining the power of the therapist, feminist therapy ethics also subvert the notion of the therapist as the sole source of power or value in the therapeutic exchange and require of the therapist complex and precise thinking regarding the nature of and solutions to possible ethical dilemmas.

The Challenges of Practicing Feminist Ethics

This authorization of each feminist therapist and the recipients of her services to take part in the feminist discourse on ethics is a profound departure from dominant ethical standards and practices. At times it has intimidated feminist therapists; when I lead workshops on feminist therapy ethics, I continually encounter the desire for the kinds of clear, concrete, and paternalistic rules that all therapists have become used to in their training in the mainstream mental health disciplines. The notion that they are empowered as ethical thinkers, theorists, and decision makers can be terrifying at times, because the possibility of harm is frequently present. If the feminist therapist does not know specifically what to do and what not to do, how will she know with certainty that her actions fall within ethical acceptability? When she believes that she is practicing in the best interests of her clients and then is told that her careful following of rules has been oppressive rather than liberating and empowering, how can she respond? How can she learn to trust her voice, the voices of her professional and political support systems, and the voices of her clients, in place of the official pronouncements of ethics codes or ethics experts?

These questions are challenging partly because of the legacy of stumbles and falls that feminist therapy has experienced in the field of ethical endeavors. There was a period in the early stages of feminist therapy when rebellion against patriarchal values stood in for thoughtful feminist action; any behavior that was antithetical to dominant ethical notions was explored as potentially ethical for feminists. At times the rationale of challenging sexist standards of therapist-client relationships led practitioners to oppress and disempower clients in overt and painful ways. Clients were sexually exploited and used for financial gain and business advancement. Therapy cults were created in collective houses. Training programs became cruising grounds for powerful teachers to find sexual partners. Complexity in ethical theorizing was not a hallmark of early feminist therapists. It did not take long, however, for feminist therapists to realize that they needed to ask of themselves how to be proactively ethical as feminists, rather than simply how to be different from patriarchal therapists.

The first case in this chapter illustrates some of the classic dilemmas of ethical work in feminist therapy. The ethical codes of dominant mental health professions proscribe dual relationships between therapist and client; any time a therapist has a role in a client's life outside the therapy relationship, a dual relationship has theoretically been established. Technically, serving on a board with a client puts the therapist in this instance in violation of such standards, and the only possible solutions would be for the therapist to resign from the board or for her client to be induced to do so. In each of these alternatives, however, something important to feminist political principles would be lost. In the first, the therapist would be required to distance herself from her community and refrain from participating directly in nontherapeutic forms of work toward social change. In the second, the client woudl be excluded as a source of experience, wisdom, and power, and her position relative to the therapist would be devalued. Neither of these communications about client or therapist is inherently acceptable within a feminist theoretical context.

Feminist theories of the relationship in therapy and of the situation of therapy in the larger social and political context offer other possible avenues for attempting to resolve this dilemma. They require that the feminist therapist call upon every aspect of her understanding and theorizing of feminist therapy: her knowledge of power dynamics, her capacity to diagnose and conceptualize, and her willingness to authorize the client as an authoritative voice. One important difference between dominant and feminist strategies for solving this sort of ethical dilemma is that the therapist is not the only decision maker; if the decision is to be rooted in feminist ethics instead of an expression of maternalistic protectiveness, the input of her client is necessary. The principle of egalitarianism, described in chapter 4, calls for attending to the client's thoughts and feelings about how to respond to the problem of shared board membership.

In participating in this shared ethical decision-making process, the feminist therapist also needs to draw upon her capacity to conceptualize her client and think diagnostically about her. The question of who is on the receiving end of the various dynamics of the symbolic relationship between this particular client and the therapist, as well as the meaning derived from the social context of the board and the retreat meeting, are all aspects to be considered. Also to be factored into decision making are the meaning of this different relationship to the therapy relationship and the contribution of this different relationship to the ultimate goals of liberation, empowerment, and social change in the life of client, therapist, and shared society. It is necessary to include the client's voice in this process, and to inquire of her what she wants, fears, and knows about the potential for healing or harm deriving from a particular course of action.

The feminist therapist in this example can also turn to other feminist therapists who have grappled with this sort of ethical dilemma. The feminist therapist Joan Saks Berman (1985) coined the phrase "overlapping relationships" to describe this sort of situation arising from the connection of feminist therapists to their communities, the encounters outside of therapy that may be unavoidable when the lives of feminist therapists overlap with those of the people they serve. Because feminist therapists often live and work in the same social and political worlds as their clients, they sometimes occupy the sociological and psychological equivalents of small towns. Overlapping relationships are consequently among the top two or three paradigmatic feminist ethical dilemmas discussed in the feminist therapy ethics literature (for extensive discussion, of this issue see Adleman & Barrett, 1990; Berman, 1985, 1990; Brown, 1991b; Gates & Speare, 1990; Sears, 1990; Smith, 1990).

Feminist therapists theorize such overlapping relationships as differing from dual relationships in several important ways. They are, for example, not motivated by the therapist's needs but reflect a common interest or concern in the broader social context. In many cases, they are unavoidable. They are not initiated by the therapist; rather they result from the movement of other social forces. Finally, they are potentially beneficial to both parties by bringing another level of meaning to the therapeutic exchange. They are not routinely positive experiences, however, and must be examined carefully any time they emerge, in the context of mutual reflection between therapist and client. No amount of theorizing will give the feminist therapist in this particular case *the* correct answer. She and her client must arrive together at a solution that honors their uniquenesses, their connection, their social and political context, and the frame-work of the therapeutic relationship in which they have engaged. This process may not lead to a comfortable endpoint; a therapist may decide not to do things that a client perceives as essential or important, and a client may experience frustration or disappointment in the outcome of the dialogue. A therapist may find herself requiring constant consultation from colleagues in order to ensure maintenance of a frame for this particu-lar therapy relationship. But because they have struggled together, their discourse does subvert the patriarchal assumptions of a hierarchy of knowledge and value in which the therapist, as the only expert, imposes the solution upon the client.

The shape of their solution may transform with time and experience; it may or may not resemble the outcomes arrived at by another feminist therapist and her client faced with a similar dilemma. This ambiguity of outcome, the allowance for process, and the willingness to respect the diversity of possible factors informing the therapist's decision are all important. The function of ethical standards is not to create new hierar-chies of value, new rules of right and wrong, of political correctness or deviance. Ethical standards exist as stimulants to the process of knowing, thinking, intuiting, and struggling toward actions that reflect feminist val-ues of equality, empowerment, and radical social change. The burden is on the feminist therapist to be an ethical activist rather than a passive recipi-ent of ethical rules. Resistance to premature closure of this discourse, as a means of subverting patriarchal notions of right, wrong, and normative correctness, is inherent to feminist theorizing of ethics.

Core Notions in Feminist Ethical Epistemologies

A feminist theory of ethics in psychotherapy can be expressed in two core notions informing ethical knowing. These are boundaries, boundary main-tenance and boundary violations, including engulfment and absence of protection, and failures of respect and mutuality and the expression of oppressive dominant norms.

BOUNDARY ISSUES

One myth that strongly influences the dominant mental health disci-plines is that there is a universal frame for therapy, with invariant and well-defined boundaries. While the discourse in mainstream theories appears to admit to some variability deriving from specific theoretical per-

spectives (for example, family systems therapists see the frame as encompassing, if not requiring, the presence of family members in the therapy
process, while some psychodynamic approaches argue theoretically
against such inclusions), there are elements of this universal frame for the
ethical boundaries of therapy practice that pervade much of the discussion. Robert Langs (1978), who represents the apotheosis of this perspective, stresses the importance of creating a rigidly decontextualized and
"neutral" frame for therapy, in which any meaning or connection not
strictly deriving from the therapeutic relationship is a violation of the
frame and thus a failure of ethical relating. Langs is specific and concrete
about a number of factors; for example, there must be separate entrances
and exits to the therapy office, referrals to therapists should come only
from neutral and distanced third parties, first names are to be avoided.
Langs is worthwhile reading for feminist therapists, not because his
invariant prescriptions mesh well with feminist theorizing but because he
exemplifies the manner in which patriarchal theorizing of the ethics and
boundaries of therapy gives rise to this way of thinking about the therapeutic frame. Unlike many of his mainstream colleagues, however, he
models a relationship between his theory of therapy and the boundaries
he prescribes; this notion that it is important to mesh ethical action with
therapeutic effectiveness is one shared by feminist theorizing.

Understanding boundaries is somewhat more complex in feminist therapy than in mainstream theories, because, as earlier chapters indicate,
feminist theorizing of the therapeutic relationship admits to a diversity of
interactions of therapist and client, with race, class, culture, sexual orientation, gender, setting, and power dynamics all informing the specific and
unique relational matrices present in any given therapeutic exchange. We
also explicitly acknowledge the importance of affirming to our clients that
we are ultimately only another human being and not some godlike authority figure.

Thus, a particular framework for therapy that may work well and facilitate therapy in one therapeutic relationship may, if applied in a rote fashion to the next relationship, be experienced as engulfing and invasive or,
alternatively, as cold, punitive, and distancing. A rule that says "never
hug a client" or "always hug clients when they ask"—to draw an example
from a common question raised in feminist therapy ethics workshops—is
not useful because it is insensitive to the complexity of the individual symbolic relationship between client and therapist and to the social and political context in which that relationship is played out.

This myth of the invariant, concrete frame for therapy generates
another sort of fiction, akin to the dominant ethical notion of clearly right

and wrong, well-dichotomized modes of action. It is the myth that a boundary violation can always be identified readily because it will be overt and observable in the therapist's behaviors. This image of the boundary violation as clearly contained in the therapist's behaviors ignores the manner in which a client's unique personal symbologies or the specifics of the social and political context, may lend meaning to a particular behavior.

Feminist theorizing of boundaries requires attention to the shared phenomenologies of the client and the therapist. Thea, a client whose capacity to attend to her own perceptions was extremely fragile, would sometimes experience my offering an interpretation as profoundly violating. In our symbolic relationship, respect for her boundaries required a level of sensitive listening and willingness to withhold certain kinds of feedback that was specific to the life experience she brought to our work. Gordon, who struggled with a lifetime of being compliant and rule-bound, experienced as invasive my suggestion that he read a book about coping with growing up with a mentally ill parent. He was able to tell me, many sessions and much immobility later, that he had experienced my remark as a hidden command to him that he live his life as had the author of this book. In each of these examples, I had not attended to some of the specific factors that informed the creation of personal boundaries for Thea or Gordon and to the manner in which those factors had affected the symbolic factors and power dynamics in our work.

It would be foolish to state that these examples teach us that, to avoid boundary violations, a feminist therapy must abstain from making interpretations or suggesting reading material. Rather, these examples illustrate the interactive nature of finding the boundaries and frame for any given therapy relationship. Rather than a concrete behavioral frame (for example, "thou shalt not prescribe books"), feminist ethical epistemologies give rise to focuses for attention, in this case, the necessity of attending to and validating the client's own phenomenological experiences of what constitutes engulfment or intrusion.

It is also important to attend to one's own internal experience of what constitutes a personal boundary. Every therapist has a different sense of what constitutes her own zone of privacy, the kinds of information about self that are shared from a position of strength, well-being, and self-knowledge. At times, these expressions of self will not fit standard definitions of "strong"; there are moments when a therapist's tears in the face of a client's pain are the strongest and most powerful self-expression she can offer, because they challenge the years in which that pain was minimized or silenced by patriarchal norms and they arise from the depth of our connection to our own emotional knowledge. But she needs to respect her own decisions about how and where and with whom to disclose herself; she needs to be willing to know and say when her work threatens to violate those boundaries for herself as well as for her clients.

For example, an important concept in feminist therapy deriving from its consumer orientation is that therapists will share information regarding the sorts of experiences that inform their expertise in working with a particular issue. But in defining and respecting their own zones of privacy, they will vary in their willingness to go beyond the abstract in giving this sort of information. One feminist therapist will be quite comfortable letting clients know that her capacity to work with incest survivors derives in some part from the fact that she is herself a survivor of incest; another will experience this level of sharing as a disrespect of self and will prefer to refer to other sources of knowledge.

In order to cope with the ambiguity engendered by this paradigm for boundaries in therapy, feminist ethical principles construe boundary maintenance in therapy as a continuous, rather than dichotomous, variable (Brown, 1988, 1990a). This notion of the continuum of boundary violations proposes that because of the power of their role, all therapists, feminist and otherwise, will behave at times in ways that violate a client's sense of self, safety, and well-being. This is one of the dilemmas inherent in therapy practice for feminists; the power of our role allows for minor but unavoidable expressions of oppression and dominance in our relationships with our clients. There will be times and circumstances in the life of a therapist, as well as in the progression of a particular therapy relationship, when the level of violations of boundaries occurring in therapy may increase or decrease. Various factors can add to the risk of a therapist's committing possibly avoidable and potentially egregious and genuinely harmful boundary violations. The therapist who is herself in distress or who is professionally or politically isolated is more likely to act in ways that increase her power over her client, as a means of enhancing her comfort and well-being. Such distress or dis-ease may not always be readily apparent, either to a therapist herself or to those around her. The therapist who is giddy, self-important, praised and powerful, who is isolated because she believes she is too experienced to need consultation or who is numb from the overwork of success is as off-balance and at risk of moving toward higher levels of violation and intrusion as the therapist whose distress is defined in more commonly accepted manners, such as sadness or loss. Such moves toward greater imbalancing of power in the psychotherapy relationship tend to be behaviors that are concretely harmful to clients, as well as likely to harm the therapist and others in their shared social context. What is important to note in this model is that *no* therapist is immune from the potential to engage in violations of client boundaries; in patriarchy, every therapist, even one striving for feminist social transformation, may oppress when in a position of power and dominance.

This paradigm moves the problem of boundary maintenance out of the arena of dichotomized images of "good," boundary-maintaining and "bad," boundary-violating therapists. The problem of boundary violation is centered in the power differentials inherent in all therapy. Identifying boundary violations as extant in the work of all therapists makes it possible for feminist therapists to address the effects of patriarchy in the therapy relationship and to recognize themselves as potentially egregious violators of boundaries. They can theorize the problem as learning to identify the risk factors for boundary violations, and making a commitment to seek out such risk factors in themselves. This method of theorizing ethical action reduces the risk of simply acting in rebellion against perceived patriarchal strictures.

This image of the continuum of boundary violations empowers feminist therapists to think more conceptually about boundary problems in therapy, because it decreases the need to create (or rebel against) concrete rules and allows a greater tolerance of the ambiguity of the pluralistic approach to ethical questions. It encourages the grasp of a feminist frame for therapy, in which the power of the therapist transforms the potential to oppress into the responsibility to think, attentively and with discretion, about the presence of the many and complex power relationships between herself and the people with whom she works. It focuses us on the core feminist principle that oppression and the exploitation of power relationships underlie all deviations from the ethical.

A non-rule-bound perspective on ethical decision making necessitates more thorough strategies for understanding boundaries in therapy if therapists are not to rely upon endless lists of what can and cannot be done. In my recent work (Brown, 1994), I have described three thematic characteristics of boundary violations, identifying which strategies can support feminist ethical decision-making processes for therapists wishing to remain on the more benign end of the continuum of boundary violations. This model assumes that most ethical therapists will probably, albeit inadvertently, engage in some low-level violations of boundaries, but that the risk for committing harmful and damaging high-level violations such as sexual exploitation can be predicted and avoided.

One characteristic of boundary violations is that they reflect an *objectification of the client*. The client is no longer met as a human with unique needs and feelings but instead becomes, temporarily or over a long term, an object for the satisfaction of the therapist's needs. The needs being satisfied are not per se problematic ones; they are the usual human desires for power, recognition, affection, intimacy, amusement, comfort. Within the context of therapy, however, and specifically when seen in relation to the therapist's power, objectifying clients to meet these needs constitutes a violation of the feminist frame, because it exaggerates the power of the therapist and increases the oppressive potential of the therapy relationship.

While much of the discourse in both feminist and mainstream therapies has focused on the sexual objectification of clients, it is somewhat more helpful to think about this problem with an illustration of nonsexual objectification. For instance, a therapist may find herself looking forward to her sessions with a particular client because that client always laughs at her jokes and says and does many things to indicate admiration for her. When she finds herself disappointed on the day when no such admiring expression is forthcoming from this client, she may have an indicator that she has made this client into an object of gratification of her need for adulation. If she examines what has been happening in therapy, she may find that the various subtle ways in which the client's power to be unhappy with her or to speak in his or her own voice and not as the object of the therapist's self-esteem-building, have been violated. Emotional role reversals, as described by the feminist therapist Marcia Hill (1990), are another concrete example of the objectification of clients by therapists. In the cases she describes, our clients become the objects of the therapist's envy, leading the therapist to try to obtain direct emotional care from them.

In each case, the question arising for the feminist therapist is whether, and to what degree, her relationship with a client distances her, constructing the person as different than human and blurring her capacity to conceptualize the client's uniqueness. Racist, classist, and other oppressive biased attitudes certainly fulfill the criteria for objectifying of others, yet objectification need not take such overt or clearly negatively valenced forms. The standard here is whether the therapist is transforming the person who is our client into a category called "client," in which the person's humanity begins to disappear. None of this is to say that the therapist should not permit clients to laugh at her jokes or tell her that she is wonderful or be a source of information about their ethnic group or the best place to scuba dive in Maui; rather, it is to point out the need to ask the meanings of these and other exchanges in the framework of power and the liberating process of therapy.

A second characteristic that defines boundary violations is that they serve to *act out* or *gratify the therapist's impulses*. Often such impulses can be quite benign or even helpful and may take the guise of caring or nurturing the client. Yet impulsive action does not take into account the factors described earlier in chapters 5 and 6; when the politics and layers of meaning of an exchange are not assessed, then the behavior, no matter how caring it appears, carries the risk of invading or engulfing a client by increasing the power differential. Not all failures of boundary maintenance constitute invasions; some, particularly those representing benign impulses, are engulfments, overpowering a client by prematurely calming, soothing, or comforting that which needs, for purposes of resistance and liberation, to remain temporarily rough or unsettled.

When I act impulsively, I am privileging my own needs, be they to comfort a crying client, decrease my own feelings of ineffectiveness, reduce my frustration over a client's residence on an emotional plateau, diminish real differences between myself and the person I am working with, or demonstrate my importance in their life. In any case, such privileging of my otherwise perfectly common desires in this manner constitutes a meta-assertion of my greater value in the relationship, and my increased importance and power vis-à-vis the client. It is also a departure from knowing, from acting as a therapist out of theory and conceptualization, and an excursion into thoughtlessness.

There are myriad concrete ways in which the therapist can act in an impulsive and boundary-violating, as opposed to a nonimpulsive and respectful, manner. Here, it is important to conceptualize in terms of the *impulse* for the behavior, rather than the behavior itself, to avoid reifying any particular action as evidence of impulsivity. The tests for this aspect of boundary maintenance are embedded in the phenomenology of the therapist and her willingness to forgo gratification when it fails to respect the client.

Impulsive behavior is thus different from actions derived from intuitive knowing; at times the knowledge that moves us away from impulsivity may at first be intuitive and nonrational, the hunch that this behavior, with this person, in this context, will be problematic. We may later be able to flesh out that hunch cognitively and conceptually and better understand our decision to practice a certain type of boundary maintenance. The embrace of intuitive knowing is an aspect of feminist therapy's pluralistic methodologies and allows for the integration of felt and thought knowledge. Impulsivity, conversely, informs simply that which feels good to the therapist at the moment.

A final characteristic of boundary violations is that they *excessively privilege the needs of the therapist*, thus increasing the therapist's power and exacerbating the possibility for oppression of the client. The place of the therapist's needs in feminist therapy is controversial; clearly if therapists were not gratified in some manner by what they do, they would not be able to persist in it. The challenge here for feminist therapists is to acknowledge their needs and to notice how these can be expressed in ways that do not transform the relationship in therapy to one of domination. For example, as workers, therapists need to have a say in the conditions of their work; the hours that they work, the amount of time that they are available to clients, the wages that they are paid, and the necessity for safe working conditions are all reasonable concerns for therapists to advance in negotiating agreements with their clients or employers. For feminist therapists, as women, the importance of attending to self-care is especially critical, since there are few cultures in patriarchy that instruct women in caring for themselves; when feminist therapists do not acknowledge their needs for recognition, power, and emotional and sexual intimacy in their peer relationships, they are at greater risk of making those needs important in a context where they are in the dominant position in a social hierarchy. Feminist therapy, for all of its liberating emphasis, contains the potential to be such a context; using the power of her role to express her unmet needs may thus constitute violation of a client's boundaries.

These characteristics of boundary violations have in common a failure to attend to the relational and contextual aspects of the therapeutic relationship. In understanding how *feminist* ethics pertain to her work, the feminist therapist must keep fresh her awareness of the oppressive potentials of therapy. The subversion of patriarchal paradigms of relating cannot be supported by the violation of boundaries in a relationship, a process that mirrors oppression in the broader political context.

FAILURES OF RESPECT AND MUTUALITY

Along with attention to the power dynamics in the therapeutic relationship, feminist theories of therapy highlight the importance of the human connection, of caring and relationality in therapy.

But how does this matter of mutuality in relationship, of the capacity, as Janet Surrey and Carter Heyward (1990) describe, for compassion, for "feeling with" another person, translate into an ethical consideration for feminist therapists? The best way to answer this question is to explore situations where such modes of relating, which engender respect and mutuality, break down, leading to the expression of domination by feminist therapists. The most profoundly problematic expression of this breakdown has occurred when white feminist therapists have engaged in overt and covert expressions of racism (Brown, 1991a; Kanuha, 1990a). In those myriad instances where feminist therapists have subsumed women of color into the experiences of white women, silenced their voices by declaring them out of tune with feminist analysis, or excluded their participation in the creation of feminist therapy theory by marginalizing their experiences in some manner, feminist therapists have failed in respect and mutuality and enhanced the power of dominant hierarchies. White women have resisted, in the nonfeminist sense of the word, feeling with, knowing with, women of color because that knowing was disruptive to their comfort and required them to attend to their participation in oppression and domination.

When white women fail to talk together about their racism, they encourage the dishonesty of silence between them as well. This silence has dangerous implications for the work of therapy, in which feminist therapists attempt to integrate the conscious and material world with the nonconscious, embodied experiences to which they aim to give voice. As Adrienne Rich has noted, "Lying is done with words, and also with silence. To lie habitually, as a way of life, is to lose contact with the unconscious" (1979, pp. 186–87). This loss of contact and of voice presents a profound ethical dilemma for feminist therapists; how can they possibly attend to the various aspects of the symbolic and political meanings of their relationships with those they serve when they stifle themselves with lies of silence? Mutuality, which arises from awareness, conscious attention, and uncovering the voice and mother tongue of each participant in the therapeutic exchange, is lost when the diversity of experience is denied.

Because feminist therapy contains a central ethic of advancing feminist social change, failing to acknowledge and respect difference and imposing dominant norms of exclusion present an ethical dilemma that is unique to feminist therapy. Feminist therapists cannot be ethical simply by following the rules; they must also theorize their ethics in terms of active confrontations of their own internalized domination as it might emerge in their work, be it in the form of racism or any other empowerment of the dominant. The implications of this ethical conundrum can be seen when we turn again to the second case example described at the opening of this chapter, the custody evaluation decision.

For a nonfeminist therapist, the issues in this case seem straightforward and not matters for ethical consideration. An evaluation was conducted according to valid and reliable methods; the father appeared to be more capable and competent as a parent, and his custody appeared to be in the children's best interest. Case, it would seem, closed. Yet embedded in this family's story are questions of respect for diversity and the risk of privileging dominant norms. There are matters that should raise the concerns of a feminist evaluator: the educational and power differences between the two parents, the objective variations between father and mother in their experience with being critically evaluated, the preexisting dominance-submission relationship underlying their marriage. To ignore these factors in the evaluation process would be to fail to respect the social and political implications of what this family brings to the evaluation process.

Thus the feminist evaluator has an ethical obligation to ask how these issues might affect the ecological validity of the assessment methods. The question that might arise here is whether the opportunities for mutuality of relationship between the evaluator and each parent are similar or whether the mother may experience a greater sense of disconnection, distance, and disempowerment in relationship to the evaluator, despite their shared gender, because of the other, potentially more powerful factors of class, education, and experience with critical evaluation. The politics of the evaluation process and the appearance of fairness as opposed to the possibility of advancing oppressive dominant norms carry ethical implications for the feminist therapist in this evaluator role.

Again, as with our previous examples, the application of feminist epistemologies regarding ethics will not provide any one correct answer. What will emerge are more questions: Are there strategies for observing the mother that will enhance her sense of power and competence, so as to elicit the best examples of her skills as a parent? Are the standards by which parenting skills are being judged sufficiently diverse and pluralistic, or do they overly privilege certain forms of relating and fail to note and value other ways of demonstrating parent competence? Is the therapist attempting to buy into the notion of "fairness" by demonstrating that even as a feminist she can see the quality of a father's parenting? Are there any subtle expressions of sexist values inhering in the evaluative process in the form of higher expectations of performance by a mother than by a father? Is it necessary to buy into the competitive framework inherent in the referral question by anointing only one parent as the competent, custodial figure? By raising such questions, a feminist evaluator challenges dominant norms and enhances the possibility that she will meet all parties to this dilemma with respect and mutuality. The concrete expressions of her responses to these questions may vary; in the end, even with the inclusion of such questions, she may arrive at the same conclusion as a nonfeminist evaluator who simply follows the standard rules.

Similar questions regarding the ethics of advancing dominant norms can emerge around other culturally accepted modes of oppressive dominance. What does a feminist therapist do, ethically, when her client wishes her support to go on a diet? Feminist therapists are often cognizant of the powerful effects of fat-oppressive attitudes in Western culture (Brown, 1989a), and may be aware of the data regarding the health risks of dieting, as well as the extraordinarily high failure rates in dieting (Brown and Rothblum, 1989). They are also likely to be aware of the profoundly misogynist themes informing fat-oppression and the ways in which the diet industry does covert violence to women. But how best to communicate these concerns to a client without taking the position of power and imposing values regarding body size of a different variety, even when those values are subversive to patriarchal destructive notions regarding weight and eating (Chrisler, 1989)?

For a feminist therapist, grappling with these and similar dilemmas poses ethical problems that require careful attention to the constant opportunities colluding in her client's oppression. But without conscious attention to such questions, she risks failing feminist ethical standards, which require going beyond the rules of avoiding harm to affirmative attempts to find active expression of liberating possibilities in each transaction with clients. Feminist therapist Jeanne Adleman (1990) describes the necessity of self-monitoring for the expression of dominant values and attitudes; she and other writers on the topic of the problematic dynamic of domination disguised as benevolence underscore the necessity for feminist therapists to construe themselves as active, theorizing, knowing, and conscious participants in the process of ethical practice. As Adleman has noted, the feminist understanding of moral, and thus ethical, behavior, arising from the work of Carol Gilligan, is that of the willingness to take conscious responsibility for the exercise of choice at each juncture.

Self-Care as a Feminist Ethical Concept

Self-care is an important issue for the feminist therapist. The FTI Ethics Code stands alone among mental health ethics documents in affirming the importance of self-care, the conscious attention by the feminist therapist to her own well-being, as an ethical standard. While mainstream codes warn against practicing when impaired in some manner, none of them define self-care as an affirmative and essential aspiration of ethical practice. How does this notion arise from feminist theory of psychotherapy?

There are several paths that lead to this formulation. The first can be found in radical feminist critiques of the relationship of people to their work in a patriarchal culture. These perspectives note the degree to which work becomes a source of alienation, devaluation, and disempowerment for the worker and in so doing supports the status quo of power disbursements. The worker who is numb to herself and silences her desires is more likely to be vulnerable to the power of patriarchal persuasions. In this framework, self-care by a therapist in the context of her work is a radical challenge to patriarchy; it is a statement that work must be an aspect of the empowerment of self, the liberation of self from oppression and domination, not simply a contribution to the gross national product.

Self-care in feminist ethics also focuses on women's diverse and complex experiences. As the old saying goes, "A man may work from sun to sun, but woman's work is never done." The stories of many different patriarchal cultures are replete with the images of female self-sacrifice (as distinguished from the manner in which women in some cultures develop an indexical self whose definition is embedded in, and enhanced by, relationship to the community; see Landrine [1992] for a complete discussion of this issue). Consequently, to encourage feminist therapists to care for themselves as women is to undermine patriarchal values that encourage women's self-destruction. For women to give themselves focused attention, nurturance, good food, space, and time are all profoundly revolutionary actions. For feminist therapists, getting the emotional and intellectual stimulation and support they need, attending to their own political aliveness and spiritual well-being, achieving financial stability, and meeting needs for intimacy and play—all these are aspects of the complex process of self-care, as much a part of the work of therapy as diagnosis.

But how is this an ethical issue? These are ethical matters because of the manner in which failures of self-care are likely to emerge as violations of boundaries, disruptions of mutuality and respect, and the desperate assertion of dominant norms in the therapy relationship. One of the more pervasive messages of patriarchy is that it feels good to be the ones in charge. In feminist therapy, this message places at risk the careful construction of the relationship as subversive to patriarchy and potentially liberating to both client and therapist. Denial of self-care emerges as the abusive taking of power by the therapist, the objectification of clients to meet the therapist's unmet needs, the impulsive expression of the therapist's desires. Self-care on a variety of variables is thus fundamental to the feminist therapist's capacity to practice in a manner that is ethical and feminist.

Many mainstream norms for the work of therapists discourage and even stigmatize self-care, construing it as self-indulgence. In agency settings, the most admired employee is often the one who is constantly overcommitted and stretched past all reasonable limits. Therapists in private practice feel pressured to work more hours and earn more money; they may speak enviously of the colleague who puts in a seventy-hour week or can go without taking lunch breaks. Putting work before play and sacrificing self "for the good of others" are both valued in patriarchal societies, including those of mainstream psychotherapists. In the dichotomous reasoning that underpins dominant ethical codes, clients' rights and well-being are to be protected at the expense of the therapist's welfare.

This disregard of the welfare of the therapist may make identifying self-care strategies difficult, both initially and long-term. What is care for me will be very different from what is care for my colleagues, and my needs will change as the situations of my life transform. There is no formula for self-care. What is important for feminist ethical action is not to generate lists of "thou shalts" in the realm of self-care but to continually ask whether and how one is practicing this principle.

Thus self-care as an ethical concept for feminist therapy reflects a theory of ethics in which liberation and transformation cannot come to one person at the expense of others. The inclusion of self-care as an important variable in feminist ethical epistemologies reflects the manner in which feminist therapists construe the nature of their relationship to their clients, students, supervisees, and anyone with whom they work, as well as to the greater social and political environment. Anything that undermines them cannot help but undermine and oppress others as well. Conversely, when they practice subversion of patriarchal values in their own lives by caring for themselves, they enhance their ability to facilitate this process in their work.

Responding to the Ethically Problematic Colleague

Sometimes a feminist therapist moves through the continuum of boundary violations to a point that is both objectively and subjectively problematic, the point at which her actions are likely to do harm to her clients, herself, and her personal and professional communities. The therapist may begin to spend the session telling clients her troubles, or to go out dancing with a client. These are behaviors that teeter on the edge of serious ethical transgressions. Feminist therapy theorizes ethical problems as encompassing not only the primary actors in a scenario but also all those connected to the therapist and her client, including her colleagues, who find themselves wondering how to intervene to bring an end to oppressive practices within their community.

This is a delicate and necessary subject for discussion by feminist therapists. After nearly a decade of writing about ethics in feminist therapy, during which I have been consulted by a number of different communities of feminist therapists and their clients regarding ethical dilemmas in their midst, it is abundantly clear that a feminist analysis is not an absolute preventative for oppressive, ethically problematic behaviors. Many factors can lead the therapist to lose her bearings on the boundary continuum, and some of those factors—illness, loss, emotional distress—can come to anyone in time.

The understanding that all feminist therapists are potentially at risk is fundamental in approaching ethically problematic colleagues. In the words of Holly Near's song, "It could have been me, but instead it was you"; any therapist can potentially be the problem in her community. This awareness of shared risk allows colleagues to approach a problematic therapist in a compassionate manner, a manner that acknowledges that there are reasons for ethically problematic behavior, although there are no excuses.

Sometimes it can be difficult to describe precisely what about the behavior is ethically problematic because of the near-absence of concrete "thou shalt nots" in feminist ethical epistemologies. One is likely to be attending to violations or absences of affirmatively ethical feminist ways of practicing. Abuse, exploitation, and oppression in mental health practice can take a variety of forms; emotional abuse (NiCarthy, 1982) and the absence of necessary responsibility and protection (Hall, 1984) are as likely to be the hallmarks of ethically problematic behavior among feminist colleagues as are overt violations such as sexual contact with clients. At times, the behavior may not seem problematic to a client, who may be comfortable and familiar with certain abusive patterns of relating and may also feel protective of the therapist. Thus questions arise of who has standing to raise concerns about the ethics of a feminist therapist's practice if clients are not subjectively experiencing harm.

Consequently, a central notion in a feminist analysis of ethical behavior in therapy is that the ethical responsibilities of feminist therapists extend to their colleagues and their personal and political communities and that other feminist therapists are therefore empowered to respond affirmatively to possible ethical problems. As I stated at the beginning of this book, the first responsibility of the feminist therapist is to the process of feminist social transformation. Failures to act ethically go beyond the given therapy encounter to spread throughout the social matrix.

Several different communities of therapists have grappled with strategies for responding to ethical problems among feminist therapists. Much of this work has been in the direction of education; for example, in Los Angeles, a group of lesbian feminist therapists who were concerned about a series of sexual boundary violations by colleagues joined together to create a conference on boundary dilemmas, which was followed up by several years of work toward a consensus document on practice standards and strategies for confronting colleagues who violated collective norms (Benjamin et al., 1990). The Feminist Therapy Institute, after formulating its ethical code, has worked to develop an accountability process in which ethically problematic behavior by FTI members could be examined in a nonadversarial manner. In other previous work, I have discussed strategies for personal confrontations with ethically problematic colleagues, focusing on the importance of consultation and collective action aimed at healing both the abused client and the offending therapist (Brown, 1990a). Many feminist therapists have also explored strategies for empowering clients who have been oppressed or exploited by other feminist therapists and for developing alliances between feminist therapists and aggrieved clients (Committee on Women in Psychology, 1989).

All this work has emphasized the avoidance of polarizing or adversarial perspectives. It assumes that an ethically problematic colleague will not transform her behaviors if her first encounter with confrontation excludes her from the community of feminist therapists. Such engagement in the process of ethical accountability requires feminist therapists to ask themselves difficult questions and to seek consultation and collegial support in their dealings with ethical dilemmas. A feminist therapist may, of course, find herself working as an expert or educator in a situation where an aggrieved client has entered an adversarial situation such as a regulatory complaint or a lawsuit. When such mainstream methodologies are either not open to or desired by those involved, however, strategies for dealing with ethical problems can be theorized from feminist principles. The empowerment of injured clients to achieve a healing outcome in such painful situations is a central focus for any feminist response to ethically problematic colleagues; the healing of the therapists' communities of practice is a valued outcome as well.

Ethics in Feminist Therapy: Next Steps

As the practice of therapy in the United States is transformed by social and economic forces, as feminist therapists continue to explore the various subtle ways in which patriarchy expresses itself in their work and the lives of their clients, so the questions and themes that inform their ethical theorizing will change and expand as well. What, for example, are the ethical implications of therapists and clients participating in a computer bulletin board system in which high degrees of self-disclosure are encouraged under the supposed protection of a pseudonym? This is not an entirely hypothetical question for me; as a computer enthusiast, I have debated what it would mean were I to put on a code name and enter the computer bulletin board on which many local women, including some clients, are active participants. For the time being, I have decided that the complications it would introduce into my life would constitute a violation of one of my personal principles of self-care (the one that says "don't make your life any more complex than it is all by itself") and have shaped my forays into cyber-space in other ways.

What feminist ethical principles inform the participation of feminist therapists in managed mental health care? Again, this is not a hypothetical question for most therapists today; in some parts of the United States, managed care, where nonfeminist values and theories constantly intrude into the therapist-client relationship, forms an important part of the social and political context in which some feminist therapists practice, and this may become even more the case if the health-care system is reshuffled by government edict. How will it be possible to be ethical and feminist in a service delivery context in which decisions are made by neither therapist nor client, but by an anonymous, corporate third party interested in profits and the bottom line? Simply opting to go outside of the system, as some therapists have proposed, will not solve the problem for feminists, because this may then create loss of access to care for those clients who only have managed care with which to pay. Creative solutions for responding to the managed care dilemma continue to be few and far between. However, the guiding principles for feminist therapists attempting to develop their answers need to remain the same; how do we subvert patriarchy in this therapy relationship, and in this relationship to the managed care corporation? How do we use the power of our role as therapist to empower our clients and increase access and choice for therapy? Ethical theorizing in feminist therapy is truly the opportunity to boldly go, to imagine the ways in which we can expand our understanding of what constitutes ethical practice, and how patriarchy can be subverted through the healing process.

CHAPTER 9

Emerging from the Wilderness

I N THE END, we go back to the beginning, to the Passover story of liberation. In the Haggadah, the tale of the liberation of the Jews from slavery is in reality only the beginning of the story. The exodus from Egypt—the emergence from overt oppression, from daily experiences of pain and genocide—was an utterly necessary first step. Without this episode, the one in which the overt chains of slavery were thrown off, the story of liberation cannot continue. "We were slaves in Egypt; today we are the children of free people," says the chant in the Haggadah. But learning to live as the children of free people involves complexities beyond simply leaving slavery and oppression. After the Haggadah comes the wandering in the wilderness; according to the biblical story, the Jews spent forty years in what today is still a forbidding desert, time enough for the generation of slavery to pass and new ways of knowing how to live as free women and men to develop among the people. Before they could enter the land of promised nourishment, freedom, and self-determination, their liberation needed to deepen, mature, grow over time. The freed people needed to understand how to live in their freedom.

This is a fitting analogy for the end of my tale of theorizing the liberating process of feminist therapy. I am at the younger end of a generation of therapists who were schooled in the strategies of oppression by our training in mainstream programs before the time that feminist consciousness and concepts began to creep into the curriculum. We have been the generation between oppression and liberation, who have struggled to free ourselves from internalized and external patriarchy in order to discover and theorize feminism in psychotherapy. Like the prophet Miriam, a woman whose name and contribution to the process of liberation often vanished in patriarchal Jewish and Christian theologies but who has been reclaimed by feminists in the present day (Broner, 1993), we have sung songs of liberation, celebrating aloud our transformation and the possibilities it has offered us. Our scholarly work, our writings, our day-to-day practice of feminism as therapists, supervisors, teachers, trainers, researchers, and expert witnesses have all been an exultation at discovering that liberating possibilities could be derived from our healing craft.

As the rejoicing quiets down, as we no longer are utterly amazed to find our sisters, as we immerse ourselves in the nitty-gritty of feminist practice within hostile social and political realities, we confront the necessity of reconstructing our disciplines so that we will sustain ourselves into the future. We now find ourselves, not so much wandering in the wilderness (although there are moments at every meeting of feminist therapists when this metaphor applies too aptly to the continued confusion of trying to blend feminist politics with patriarchal systems of psychotherapy) but certainly inhabiting a sometimes foggy middle place betweeen where we began and where we wish to be. We, our clients, and the work that we do are no longer directly enslaved by patriarchal reasoning, but we are clearly not yet in a promised land, if such exists outside of speculative fiction. We are in the midst of attempting to understand how our work is feminist; in the practice of feminist therapy, all feminist therapists embody theory in process. So we stumble, and at times we backtrack, as we attempt to see what constitutes the territory of "not-in-the-wilderness."

Where does feminist therapy go from here? How does the development of theory in feminist therapy contribute to the continuing subversive conversations between feminist therapists and the people who receive our work into their lives? How do we refine our capacity to be the agents of feminist revolution and social transformation? One answer to these questions that is emerging powerfully from every corner of our practice involves the need to develop organized training facilities for feminist therapists (Brown & Brodsky, 1992). The First National Conference on Education and Training in Feminist Practice (a broad term that encompasses therapy, consultation, supervision, and training), organized by feminist psychologists Norinne Johnson and Judith Worell and sponsored by the Division of Psychology of Women of the American Psychological Association, took place in July of 1993. For most of the women present, experienced feminist therapists and feminist therapy graduate students alike, the energy impelling us toward the development of clear and intentional models for the training of feminist therapists at all levels and in all modalities was so powerful that we could hardly bear to take the time away from our deliberations to sleep.

One of the wildernesses in which feminist therapists do wander on our journey of developing liberating theory and practice is the desert of our professional education. While there have been intermittent attempts to develop training programs in feminist therapy since the mid-1970s, few of them have survived, and even fewer have offered doctoral-level training. Most of us, including feminist therapists currently pursuing their formal education, must still bootstrap our training and strain to find the time to fit that coursework into the curriculum of a mainstream, malestream, dominant-culture education in mental health. Some training programs in the mental health disciplines welcome feminist therapy as an elective focus for students, but others continue to be actively hostile to inclusion of feminist epistemologies and scholarship in the mental health curriculum (for example, a pro-feminist man was fired from the faculty of an "alternative" graduate school because he wanted to teach feminist personality theories; he called me because it was a book I had edited that was banned from the classroom when he was fired). Not suprisingly, training sites where there is a strong feminist faculty presence (commonly freestanding schools of professional psychology, counseling psychology programs, and schools of social work and nursing) are those that currently offer the most by way of formal training in feminist practice.

Yet the demand for such training is strong, and the desire to offer it equally powerful. Most visible feminist therapists—those of us who write and teach and get on lists—receive scores of letters yearly from students looking for a program where they will not have to sneak feminist topics into their curriculum. Both the subversion of the mental health training apparatus to feminist therapy purposes and the development of programs founded from inception on feminist theories of practice are necessary tasks for the future of feminist therapy, if we are to nourish the next generation and provide fertile opportunities for their professional development. One of the truly exciting documents emerging from the conference on education and training was the proposed curriculum for a complete doctoral-level training program in feminist therapy. The complexity and depth of the program and the manner in which feminist theories of psychotherapy are inherent in each course topic and each strategy for experiential training represent a vision of what can and will be for feminist therapy in the future. It is also clear that feminist therapists need to continue to provide postgraduate training for themselves, each other, and other therapists wishing to learn about feminist theory in therapy practice. None of us knows as much as she wants; each of us at that conference, selected because we were visible contributors to the scholarship in this field, hungered for more, for the wisdom that every other conference participant had to offer. (People interested in finding out more about what is being done with these recommendations may contact APA Women's Programs, 750 First Street NE, Washington DC 20002-4242 for further information.)

In order for this movement toward the training of feminist therapists to succeed, the theory of feminist therapy must grow and develop. If we cannot describe how each act we take is feminist, there will be no point in offering training, because such courses will risk regressing toward the woman-therapist-woman-client model that I have criticized throughout this volume. We must be able to answer, with clarity and specificity, how each action we take in our work is feminist. Thus I am eagerly anticipating the dialogues and debates with colleagues, readers, clients, and friends that may be provoked by this volume, because that conversation will make our theory grow. What is set forth here is my vision of what constitutes theory for feminist therapeutic epistemologies; I am aware at each moment of writing that it is not complete.

But again returning to my roots as Jew, I am reminded that the sages sat together for centuries developing the interpretations of basic concepts in Jewish law; to some degree, we still debate the meanings of such concrete phenomena as cars, computers, and electric lights that could not be foreseen but could in some manner be theorized theologically, by our ancestors two thousand years past. At times in the writing of this book, I have awakened in the middle of the night, wondering if I had said enough about a particular topic, been clear enough about my meaning, or included everything that needed to be said. Then I remind myself that this book is simply one more step toward the creation of theory in feminist therapy; that this step need not take me, nor my discipline, the whole journey. Feminist political theories continue to develop, and therefore the ways in which feminist therapists apply political insights and analyses to their work will change as well. The scholarship in feminist mental health opens new doors for speculation; the continuing discourse regarding the dynamic tensions between constructivist and essentialist perspectives on gender is beginning to yield intellectual and emotional riches for our theory development (Fine, 1992; Hare-Mustin & Marecek, 1990).

There are many directions in which this expanding feminist therapy theory can go. The theorizing has just begun to be truly multicultural and inclusive, and the work of feminist therapists of color is emerging fast and furiously, continually transforming current understandings of feminist therapy theory. The implications of integrating multicultural and anti-oppressive perspectives into feminist therapy are at times quite stagger-ing, as some of these ways of knowing challenge the assumptions and the-ories of white feminist therapists (Brown, 1990d). As I write this, an explo-sion of feminist therapy scholarship on women of color is being published, including Julia Boyd's volume on African-American women and self-esteem (1993), bell hooks's work on self-help and self-care for women of color (1993), Lillian Comas-Diaz and Beverly Greene's edited volume on the mental health of women of color (1994), and Karen Wyche's review of empirical research on African-American women and mental health (1993). My collection, edited with Maria Root, on diversity in feminist therapy is only a few years old and is just now starting to bear conceptual fruit (Brown & Root, 1990). Jeanne Adleman and Gloria Enguidanos have just sent to press their edited collection on feminist therapists' struggles to integrate antiracist and other anti-oppressive perspectives in their work (in press). With this emerging direction in feminist therapy come new views of what we mean by oppression, resistance, power, and gender. This diversity of viewpoints will continue its powerful transformative effect on our practice and consequently on our theorizing. I believe that it will become impossible for any feminist therapy theorizing of the future to ignore the centrality of diverse epistemologies; our embrace of this mater-ial has helped return feminist therapy to its political feminist roots.

Another direction that continues to call for development is integrated feminist theory of personality development. Many scholars have taken important steps in this direction; Ellyn Kaschak's revisioning of the gen-dered themes of women's and men's lives (1992), the contributions of the Stone Center group to a comprehension of diverse paths for human devel-opment through the lives of middle-class white women (Jordan et al., 1992), and, of course, Hannah Lerman's explication of criteria for a femi-nist personality theory (1986), which formed the nucleus of my thinking about feminist therapy theory in general, are all steps in the direction of such an integrated feminist paradigm for human development. Yet a femi-nist embrace of pluralism in methodology may in the end preclude the sort of all-inclusive theory that we now find in the psychoanalytic litera-ture; it is difficult to promulgate "the" theory of human development when one's basic operating assumptions have to do with the diverse and complex parameters of human experiences.

But I believe that we can continue to borrow from mainstream develop-mental theories only at our peril. The feminist clinical psychologist and theoretician Rachel Hare-Mustin has aptly noted that feminist personality theorists continue to "stand on the bellies of dead white men" in building our theories (personal communication, July, 1993); our models are still derivative of object relations or Jungian psychology or some other model that is centrally patriarchal in its assumptions. A feminist theory of personality requires starting afresh, departing from the patriarchal universe of knowledge, standing on our own feminist feet, and allowing our politically oriented way of knowing to represent good personality theorizing. I do not pretend to know how we are going to accomplish this feat. I can only state with certainty that if the future does not hold this piece of work, feminist therapy theory in general will be weakened by its absence.

Still more work needs to be done in theorizing the applications of feminist therapy theory beyond *our* dominant norm of women therapists working with women clients. Feminist therapy with men (Bograd, 1991; Ganley, 1988), with children, and with families are facets of our practice that are only just emerging. The ways in which feminist therapists work in rehabilitation, in primary medicine, and with physically ill or dying persons have yet to be explored. Feminist perspectives on work with chronically mentally ill women are just now being proposed (Mowbray, 1993; Perkins, 1991b). Feminist forensic psychology is growing in leaps and bounds, and must be the focus of our theoretical analyses, integrated with feminist legal theories (Robson, 1992; Walker, 1990). Feminist therapeutic responses to managed mental health care have been invisible to date, yet for U.S. feminist therapists it may present some of the most difficult ethical and conceptual challenges that can be handed to us by the patriarchal structures that affect our practices. As the settings of feminist practice expand, our theories and epistemologies will have to reflect the new "data of clinical experience" to which Hannah Lerman (1986) has admonished us to remain true in our theorizing.

Finally, the cultures and sociopolitical climates informing our work are anything but static; we are confronted with questions of whether and to what degree our feminist political theories apply in the world of increasingly visible violence against and among the oppressed, portrayed daily in the media for our viewing distress. What meaning does feminist therapy have for the child wounded in a gunfight over a coat at school? What actions do we take in the face of mass rapes in the former Yugoslavia, serial murders of women in the United States, or death squads in Haiti? Patriarchal culture presents us with new horrors daily; can feminists continue to support the notion of psychotherapy as a useful way to spend time in the face of external political realities? It is entirely one thing to theorize feminist therapy as an instrument of feminist revolution in my quiet office in the middle of a progressive, tolerant city; but is it a particularly powerful instrument of global social change, one worth thinking about, expanding, and exploring, when other methodologies for feminist revolution, such as direct action, social organization, or on-site crisis intervention with victims of violence, are available?

To some degree these difficult questions also point to the necessity for further feminist therapy theorizing to encompass that realm defined in patriarchal cultures as "spiritual" or existential. Beyond material political realities are questions of the meaning of life and the capacity to resist despair and feel hope in the face of the seemingly unending barrage of violations and oppression that feminists notice all too clearly. Because the mainstream mental health disciplines in general have dismissed or rejected the spiritual realm, the notion that spirituality and politics lie within the same domain is a very revolutionary, and thus potentially feminist, understanding. Some steps toward this weaving together of questions of spirit and meaning into feminist therapy theorizing are beginning to emerge, particularly in the collaborative work of Janet Surrey and Carter Heyward (1990), in which the shared epistemologies of feminist liberation theologies and feminist therapies are viewed in a manner encouraging theoretical inclusiveness. Other feminist theologians—particularly Marie Fortune (1983)—who address questions of power, dominance, and violation in the pastoral relationship have also posited ways of knowing and understanding these problems that enrich feminist therapy theorizing.

These questions and future challenges constitute the steps in our passage through the wilderness, our continued process of divesting ourselves of the patriarchy inside ourselves so that we may more clearly see and, as healers and activists, respond to the patriarchy that surrounds us. We will then begin to see the so-called wilderness of our temporary confusion for what it truly is: not a barren place, but one rich in resources that we could not see when we defined worth and value only in patriarchal terms. In the fleshpots of Egypt, so the story goes, the people were well nourished, but they were enslaved; in the wilderness, nourishment was more difficult to find but present in sufficient amounts to generate the strength needed to continue the movement to liberation.

Maria Root, in reading a draft of this manuscript, has repeatedly challenged and encouraged me to imagine what therapy will look like in the time and place when we are no longer in the struggle to divest ourselves of patriarchal modes of thinking, feeling, and relating. As I, no visionary, attempt to imagine this reality, I think of moments in the work I do now, and try to see them expanded across all the hours of my working life. In those moments, I do not have to consciously remind myself of how to share power, how to listen and respect, how to draw from a diverse and multicultural knowledge base, or how to conceptualize from an anti-oppressive paradigm. In those moments, it becomes intuitively obvious how to engender the subversion of patriarchy; and for a brief space of time, patriarchy is not the system operating in my office. That image is the closest I can come; my vision of our future is, in this regard, as myopic, as blurry and uncertain, as my own terrifically nearsighted eyes. But central to that image is that the world outside the therapy office will and must have changed as well; we cannot develop feminist therapy completely if we continue to live only within the milieu of oppression and domination.

It is first terrifying, and then exhilarating, to disconnect our epistemologies from the givens and authorities of our dominant cultures and to attempt to center our authority within ourselves, in terms that resonate to feminist understanding. To do so, to persist in our subversive dialogues, is to make possible the vision of the end of our journey of liberation—in our theories of psychotherapy, in the lives of our clients, and ultimately in the patriarchal societies that we struggle daily to transform. That vision, of the just society in which oppression and domination are no longer the norm, is the image formed by theories of feminist therapy, and ultimately the future that lies before us.

References

Adleman, J. (1990). Necessary risks and ethical constraints: Self-monitoring on values and biases. In H. Lerman & N. Porter (Eds.), *Feminist ethics in psychotherapy* (pp. 113–122). New York: Springer.

Adleman, J., & Barrett, S. E. (1990). Overlapping relationships: The importance of the feminist ethical perspective. In H. Lerman & N. Porter (Eds.), *Feminist ethics in psychotherapy* (pp. 87–91). New York: Springer.

Adleman, J., & Enguidanos, G. (Eds.). (In press). *Racism in the lives of women: Testimony, theory, and guides to anti-racist action*. New York: Haworth.

American Psychiatric Association. (1987). *Diagnostic and statistical manual of mental disorders* (3rd ed., rev.). Washington, DC: Author.

American Psychiatric Association. (1993). *Practice guidelines for major depressive disorder in adults*. Washington, DC: Author.

American Psychological Association. (1992). Ethical principles of psychologists and code of conduct. *American Psychologist, 47*, 1597–1611.

Ballou, M. (1990). Approaching a feminist-principled paradigm in the construction of personality theory. In L. S. Brown & M. P. P. Root (Eds.), *Diversity and complexity in feminist therapy* (pp. 23–40). New York: Haworth.

Ballou, M., & Gabalac, N. W. (1985). *A feminist position on mental health*. Springfield, IL: Charles C. Thomas.

Becker, D., & Lamb, S. (1994). Sex bias in the diagnosis of borderline personality disorder and post-traumatic stress disorder. *Professional Psychology: Research and Practice, 25*, 55–61.

Belenky, M. F., Clinchy, B. M., Goldberger, N. R., & Tarule, J. M. (1986). *Women's ways of knowing*. New York: Basic.

Bem, S. L. (1993). *The lenses of gender: Transforming the debate on sexual inequality.* New Haven: Yale University Press.

Bem, S. L., & Bem, D. J. (1970). Training the woman to "know her place": The power of a nonconscious ideology. In S. Cox (Ed.), *Female Psychology: The emerging self* (pp. 180–191). Chicago: SRA.

Benjamin, L. S. (1986). Adding social and intrapsychic descriptors to Axis I of DSM-III. In T. Millon & G. Klerman (Eds.), *Contemporary directions in psychopathology: Toward the DSM-IV* (pp. 599–683). New York: Guilford.

Benjamin, S., Brotsky, J., Butler, K., Goldberg, L., Grady, Hayden, M., Holtz, J., Johnson, M., Levy, B., Moss, L. E., Nevius, L., Retter, Y., Schreiber, S., Siegel, S., & Weinrich, D. (1990). *Ethical standards and practice in the lesbian therapy community.* Los Angeles: Author.

Berman, J. S. (1985). Ethical feminist perspectives on dual relationships. In L. B. Rosewater & L. E. A. Walker (Eds.), *Handbook of feminist therapy: Women's issues in psychotherapy* (pp. 287–296). New York: Springer.

Berman, J. S. (1990). The problems of overlapping relationships in the political community. In H. Lerman & N. Porter (Eds.), *Feminist ethics in psychotherapy* (pp. 106–110). New York: Springer.

Bernard, J. (1981). *The female world.* New York: Free Press.

Bograd, M. (1984). Family systems approaches to wife battering: A feminist critique. *American Journal of Orthopsychiatry, 54*, 558–568.

Bograd, M. (Ed.). (1991). *Feminist approaches for men in family therapy.* New York: Haworth.

Boyd, J. (1990). Ethnic and cultural diversity: Keys to power. In L. S. Brown & M. P. P. Root (Eds.), *Diversity and complexity in feminist therapy* (pp. 151–168). New York: Haworth.

Boyd, J. (1993). *In the company of my sisters: Black women and self-esteem.* New York: Dutton.

Boyd-Franklin, N. (1987). Group therapy for black women: A therapeutic support model. *American Journal of Orthopsychiatry, 57*, 394–401.

Boyd-Franklin, N. (1989). *Black families in therapy: A multisystems approach.* New York: Guilford.

Bradshaw, C. K. (1990). A Japanese view of dependency: What can amae psychology contribute to feminist theory and therapy? In L. S. Brown & M. P. P. Root (Eds.), *Diversity and complexity in feminist therapy.* New York: Haworth.

Breggin, P. (1991). *Toxic psychiatry: Why therapy, empathy and love must replace the drugs, electroshock and biochemical theories of the "new psychiatry."* New York: St. Martin's.

Brodsky, A. M. (1973). The consciousness-raising group as a model for therapy with women. *Psychotherapy: Theory, Research, and Practice, 10*, 24–29.

Brody, C. M. (Ed.). (1984). *Women therapists working with women: New theory and process of feminist therapy.* New York: Springer.

Broner, E. M. (1993). *The telling.* San Francisco: HarperCollins.

Brown, L. M., & Gilligan, C. (1993). Meeting at the crossroads: Women's psychology and girls' development. *Feminism and Psychology, 3*, 11–36.

Brown, L. S. (1984). Finding new language: Beyond analytic verbal shorthand in feminist therapy. *Women and Therapy, 3*, 73–80.

Brown, L. S. (1985). Ethics and business practice in feminist therapy. In L. B. Rosewater & L. E. A. Walker (Eds.), *Handbook of feminist therapy: Women's issues in psychotherapy* (pp. 297–304). New York: Springer.

Brown, L. S. (1986). From alienation to connection: Feminist therapy with post-traumatic stress disorder. *Women and Therapy, 5*, 13–26.

Brown, L. S. (1988). Beyond thou shalt not: Thinking about ethics in the lesbian therapy community. *Women and Therapy, 8*, 13–26.

Brown, L. S. (1989a). Fat oppressive attitudes and the feminist therapist: Directions for change. *Women and Therapy, 8*, 19–30.

Brown, L. S. (1989b). New voices, new visions: Toward a lesbian/gay paradigm for psychology. *Psychology of Women Quarterly, 13*, 445–458.

Brown, L. S. (1990a). Confronting ethically problematic behaviors in feminist therapist colleagues. In H. Lerman & N. Porter (Eds.), *Feminist ethics in psychotherapy* (pp. 147–160). New York: Springer.

Brown, L. S. (1990b). Ethical issues and the business of therapy. In H. Lerman & N. Porter (Eds.), *Feminist ethics in psychotherapy* (pp. 60–69). New York: Springer.

Brown, L. S. (1990c). Feminist therapy perspectives on psychodiagnosis: Beyond DSM and ICD. In I. Foeken (Ed.), *Feminist diagnosis and therapy* (pp. 45–66). Amsterdam: Stichting De Maan.

Brown, L. S. (1990d). The meaning of a multicultural perspective for theory-building in feminist therapy. In L. S. Brown & M. P. P. Root (Eds.), *Diversity and complexity in feminist therapy* (pp. 1–22). New York: Haworth.

Brown, L. S. (1990e). What's addiction got to do with it: A feminist critique of codependence. *Psychology of Women Newsletter, 17* (1), 1, 3–4.

Brown, L. S. (1991a). Anti-racism as an ethical imperative: An example from feminist therapy. *Ethics and Behavior, 1*, 113–127.

Brown, L. S. (1991b). Ethical issues in feminist therapy: Selected topics. *Psychology of Women Quarterly, 15*, 323–336.

Brown, L. S.(1991c). Not outside the range: One feminist perspective on psychic trauma. *American Imago, 48*, 119–133.

Brown, L. S. (1991d). Therapy with an infertile lesbian client. In C. Silverstein (Ed.), *Gays, lesbians and their therapists: Studies in psychotherapy* (pp. 15–30). New York: Norton.

Brown, L. S. (1992a). A feminist critique of the personality disorders. In L. S. Brown & M. Ballou (Eds.), *Personality and psychopathology: Feminist reappraisals* (pp. 206–228). New York: Guilford.

Brown, L. S. (1992b, June). Trauma within the range of usual experience. In L. S. Brown (Chair), *Feminist therapy perspectives on trauma*. Symposium presented at the First International Congress of the International Society for Traumatic Stress Studies, Amsterdam, The Netherlands.

Brown, L. S. (1992c). While waiting for the revolution: The case for a lesbian feminist psychotherapy. *Feminism and Psychology, 2*, 239–253.

Brown, L. S. (1993). Anti-domination training as a central component of diversity in clinical psychology education. *The Clinical Psychologist, 44*, 83–87.

Brown, L. S. (1994). Boundaries in feminist therapy: A theoretical formulation. *Women and Therapy, 15*, 29–38.

Brown, L. S., & Ballou, M. (Eds.). (1992). *Personality and psychopathology: Feminist reappraisals.* New York: Guilford.

Brown, L. S., & Brodsky, A. M. (1992). The future of feminist therapy. *Psychotherapy: Theory, Research, Practice, Training, 29*, 51–57.

Brown, L. S., & Root, M. P. P. (Eds.). (1990). *Diversity and complexity in feminist therapy.* New York: Haworth.

Brown, L. S., & Rothblum, E. D. (Eds.). (1989). *Overcoming fat oppression.* New York: Haworth.

Caplan, P. (1991). How do they decide who is normal? The true but bizarre tale of the *DSM* process. *Canadian Psychology, 32*, 162–170.

Caplan, P. (1992). Driving us crazy: How oppression damages women's mental health and what we can do about it. *Women and therapy, 12*(3), 5–28.

Cardea, C. (1985). The lesbian revolution and the 50-minute hour: A working-class look at therapy and the movement. *Lesbian Ethics, 2*, 5–22.

Cermak, T. (1986). *Diagnosing and treating co-dependence.* Minneapolis: Johnson Institute.

Chesler, P. (1972). *Women and madness.* Garden City, NY: Doubleday.

Chesler, P. (1987). *Mothers on trial: The battle for children and custody.* Seattle: Seal Press.

Chodorow, N. (1978). *The reproduction of mothering: Psychoanalysis and the sociology of gender.* Berkeley: University of California Press.

Chrisler, J. C. (1989). Should feminist therapists do weight loss counseling? *Women and Therapy, 8*, 31–38.

Cole, E., Espin, O. M., & Rothblum, E. D. (Eds.). (1992). *Refugee women and their mental health.* New York: Haworth.

Collins, P. H. (1990). *Black feminist thought: Knowledge, consciousness, and the politics of empowerment.* Boston: Unwin Hyman.

Committee on Women in Psychology. (1989). If sex enters into the psychotherapy relationship. *Professional Psychology: Research and Practice, 20*, 112–115.

Comas-Diaz, L., & Greene, B. (Eds.). (1994). *Mental health and women of color.* New York: Guilford.

Daly, M. (1978). *Gyn/Ecology: The metaethics of radical feminism.* Boston: Beacon Press.

Denny, P. A. (1987). Women and poverty: A challenge to the intellectual and therapeutic integrity of feminist therapy. *Women and Therapy, 5*, 51–63.

Dutton, M. A. (1992). *Empowering and healing the battered woman.* New York: Springer.

Dutton-Douglas, M. A., & Walker, L. E. A. (Eds.). (1988). *Feminist psychotherapies: Integration of therapeutic and feminist systems.* Norwood, NJ: Ablex.

Dworkin, A. (1974). *Woman hating.* New York: Dutton.

Dyer, L. A. (1992). If only resistance counted as forbearance on student loans. *Sinister Wisdom, 17*(48), 74–78.

Enns, C. Z. (1992). Toward integrating feminist psychotherapy and feminist philosophy. *Professional Psychology: Research and Practice, 23,* 453–466.

Espin, O. M. (1987). Issues of identity in the psychology of Latina lesbians. In Boston Lesbian Psychologies Collective (Eds.), *Lesbian psychologies: Explorations and challenges* (pp. 35–55). Urbana: University of Illinois Press.

Espin, O. M. (1993). Giving voice to silence: The psychologist as witness. *American Psychologist, 48,* 408–414.

Espin, O. M., & Gawelek, M. A. (1992). Women's diversity: Ethnicity, race, class and gender in theories of feminist psychology. In L. S. Brown & M. Ballou (Eds.), *Personality and psychopathology: Feminist reappraisals* (pp. 88–110). New York: Guilford.

Essed, P. (1991). *Everyday racism.* Newbury Park, CA: Sage.

Faludi, S. (1991). *Backlash: The undeclared war against American women.* New York: Crown.

Faunce, P. S. (1990). Women in poverty: Ethical dimensions in therapy. In H. Lerman & N. Porter (Eds.), *Feminist ethics in psychotherapy* (pp. 185–194). New York: Springer.

Feminist Therapy Institute. (1990). Feminist Therapy Institute code of ethics. In H. Lerman & N. Porter (Eds.), *Feminist ethics in psychotherapy* (pp. 37–40). New York: Springer.

Fine, M. (1992). *Disruptive voices: The possibilities of feminist research.* Ann Arbor: University of Michigan Press.

Fodor, I. G. (1992). The agoraphobic syndrome: From anxiety neurosis to panic disorder. In L. S. Brown & M. Ballou (Eds.), *Personality and psychopathology: Feminist reappraisals* (pp. 177–205). New York: Guilford.

Fortune, M. M. (1983). *Sexual violence: The unmentionable sin.* New York: Pilgrim.

Fredlund, T. (1992). How we decide. *Sinister Wisdom, 17*(48), 6–12.

Ganley, A. L. (1988). Feminist therapy with male clients. In M. A. Dutton & L. E. A. Walker (Eds.), *Feminist psychotherapies: Integration of therapeutic and feminist systems* (pp. 186–205). Norwood, NJ: Ablex.

Gartrell, N. (Ed.). (1994). *Bringing ethics alive: Feminist ethics in psychotherapy practice.* New York: Haworth.

Gates, K. P., & Speare, K. H. (1990). Overlapping relationships in rural communities. In H. Lerman & N. Porter (Eds.), *Feminist ethics in psychotherapy* (pp. 97–101). New York: Springer.

Gearhart, S. (1979). *The wanderground.* Watertown, MA: Persephone Press.

Giddings, P. (1984). *When and where I enter: The impact of black women on race and sex in America.* New York: Morrow.

Gilligan, C. (1981). *In a different voice.* Cambridge: Harvard University Press.

Gilligan, C., Rogers, A., & Tolman, D. (1992). *Women, girls, and psychotherapy.* New York: Haworth Press.

Goldner, V. (1985). Feminism and family therapy. *Family Process, 24,* 31–47.

Goodman, L. A., Koss, M. P., & Russo, N. F. (1993). Violence against women: Mental health effects. *Applied and Preventative Psychology, 2*, 123–130.

Grahn, J. (1984). *Another mother tongue: Gay words, gay worlds.* Boston: Beacon Press.

Green, G. D. (1990). Is separation really so great? In L. S. Brown & M. P. P. Root (Eds.), *Diversity and complexity in feminist therapy* (pp. 87–104). New York: Haworth.

Greene, B. (1990). What has gone before: The legacy of racism and sexism in the lives of black mothers and daughters. In L. S. Brown & M. P. P. Root (Eds.), *Diversity and complexity in feminist therapy* (pp. 207–230). New York: Haworth.

Greene, B. (1992). Still here: A perspective on psychotherapy with African-American women. In J. C. Chrisler & D. Howard (Eds.), *New directions in feminist psychology: Practice, theory and research* (pp. 13–25). New York: Springer.

Greenspan, M. (1983). *A new approach to women and therapy.* New York: McGraw-Hill.

Greenwald, D. (1992). Psychotic disorders with emphasis on schizophrenia. In L. S. Brown & M. Ballou (Eds.), *Personality and psychopathology: Feminist reappraisals* (pp. 144–176). New York: Guilford.

Griffith, R. S. (1992). The new APA Code of Ethics: Long on legalism, short on spirit. *National Psychologist, 2*, 4–6.

Hacker, H. M. (1951). Women as a minority group. *Social Forces, 30*, 60–69.

Hacker, H. M. (1976). Women as a minority group. In S. Cox (Ed.), *Female psychology: The emerging self* (pp. 156–170). Chicago: SRA.

Hagan, K. L (1989). Codependency and the myth of recovery: A feminist scrutiny. *Fugitive Information, 1*, 1–12.

Hall, M. (1984, May). *Counselor-client sex and feminist therapy: A new look at an old taboo.* Paper presented at the Third Advanced Feminist Therapy Institute, Oakland, CA.

Hare-Mustin, R., & Marecek, J. (Eds.). (1990) *Making a difference: Psychology and the construction of gender.* New Haven: Yale University Press.

Hare-Mustin, R., Marecek, J., Kaplan, A. G., & Liss-Levinson, N. (1979). Rights of clients, responsibilities of therapists. *American Psychologist, 34*, 3–16.

Herman, J. L. (1992). *Trauma and recovery.* New York: Basic.

Herman, J. L. (1993). Sequelae of prolonged and repeated trauma: Evidence for a complex posttraumatic syndrome (DESNOS). In J. R. T. Davidson & E. B. Foa (Eds.), *Posttraumatic stress disorder: DSM IV and beyond* (pp. 213–228). Washington, DC: American Psychiatric Press.

Heyward, C. (1993). *When boundaries betray us: Beyond illusions of what is ethical in therapy and life.* San Francisco: HarperCollins.

Heyward, C., Jordan, J., and Surrey, J. (1992). *Mutuality in therapy: Ethics, power and psychology.* Colloquium presented at the Stone Center, Wellesley, MA.

Hill, M. (1990). On creating a theory of feminist therapy. In L. S. Brown & M. P.

P. Root (Eds.), *Diversity and complexity in feminist therapy* (pp. 53–66). New York: Haworth.

Ho, C. K. (1990). An analysis of domestic violence in Asian American communities: A multicultural approach to counseling. In L. S. Brown & M. P. P. Root (Eds.), *Diversity and complexity in feminist therapy* (pp. 129–150). New York: Haworth.

Hoagland, S.L. (1988). *Lesbian ethics: Toward new value*. Palo Alto, CA: Institute for Lesbian Studies.

hooks, b. (1989). *Talking back: Thinking feminist, talking black*. Boston: South End Press.

hooks, b. (1993). *Sisters of the yam: Black women and self-recovery*. Boston: South End Press.

Jack, D. (1991). *Silencing the self: Depression and women*. Cambridge: Harvard University Press.

Johnson, S. (1989). *Wildfire: Igniting the shevolution*. Albuquerque, NM: Wildfire Books.

Johnson, S. (1991). *The ship that sailed into the livingroom*. Albuquerque, NM: Wildfire Books.

Jordan, J. V., Kaplan, A. G., Miller, J. B., Stiver, I. P., & Surrey, J. L (1992). *Women's growth in connection: Writings from the Stone Center*. New York: Guilford.

Kanuha, V. (1990a). Compounding the triple jeopardy: Battering in lesbian of color relationships. In L. S. Brown & M. P. P. Root (Eds.), *Diversity and complexity in feminist therapy* (pp. 169–184). New York: Haworth.

Kanuha, V. (1990b). The need for an integrated analysis of oppression in feminist therapy ethics. In H. Lerman & N. Porter (Eds.), *Feminist ethics in psychotherapy* (pp. 24–36). New York: Springer.

Kaplan, M. (1983). A woman's view of the *DSM-III*. *American Psychologist, 38,* 786–792.

Kaschak, E. (1992). *Engendered lives: A new psychology of women's experience*. New York: Basic.

Kennedy, E. L., & Davis, M. D. (1993). *Boots of leather, slippers of gold: The history of a lesbian community*. New York: Routledge.

Kilpatrick D. G., & Resnick, H. S. (1993). Posttraumatic stress disorder associated with exposure to criminal victimization in clinical and community populations. In. J. R. T. Davidson & E. B. Foa (Eds.), *Posttraumatic stress disorder: DSM IV and beyond* (pp. 113–146). Washington, DC: American Psychiatric Press.

Kitzinger, C., & Perkins, R. (1993). *Changing our minds: Lesbian feminism and psychology*. New York: New York University Press.

Kramer, P. (1993). *Listening to Prozac: A psychiatrist explores mood-altering drugs and the new meaning of self*. New York: Viking.

Kravetz, D. (1978). Consciousness-raising groups in the 1970s. *Psychology of Women Quarterly, 3,* 168–186.

Landrine, H. (1992). Clinical implications of cultural differences: The referential versus the indexical self. *Clinical Psychology Review, 12*, 401–416.

Langs, R. (1978). *The listening process*. New York: Jason Aronson.

Lasky, E. (1985). Psychotherapists' ambivalence about fees. In L. B. Rosewater & L. E. A. Walker (Eds.), *Handbook of feminist therapy: Women's issues in psychotherapy* (pp. 250–256). New York: Springer.

Lerman, H. (1986). *A mote in Freud's eye: From psychoanalysis to the psychology of women*. New York: Springer.

Lerman, H., & Porter, N. (1990a). The contribution of feminism to ethics in psychotherapy. In H. Lerman & N. Porter (Eds.), *Feminist ethics in psychotherapy* (pp. 5–13). New York: Springer.

Lerman, H., & Porter, N. (Eds.). (1990b). *Feminist ethics in psychotherapy*. New York: Springer.

Lerner, G. (1993). *The creation of feminist consciousness*. New York: Oxford University Press.

Lerner, H. G. (1993). *The dance of deception*. New York: HarperCollins.

Lorde, A. (1984). *Sister outsider*. Trumansburg, NY: Crossing Press.

Lorde, A. (1992). *Undersong: Chosen poems old and new*. New York: Norton.

Luepnitz, D. A. (1988). *The family interpreted: Feminist theory in clinical practice*. New York: Basic.

Mander, A. V., & Rush, A. K. (1974). *Feminism as therapy*. San Francisco: Random House/Bookworks.

Margolies, L. (1990). Cracks in the frame: Feminism and the boundaries of psychotherapy. *Women and Therapy, 9*, 19–36.

Masson, J. M. (1993). *Against therapy*. New York: Common Courage.

Matarazzo, J. (1986). Computerized clinical psychological test interpretations: Unvalidated plus all mean and no sigma. *American Psychologist, 41*, 14–24.

McGrath, E., Keita, G. P., Strickland, B. R., & Russo, N. F. (1990). *Women and depression: Risk factors and treatment issues*. Washington, DC: American Psychological Association.

Mednick, M. T. S. (1989). On the politics of psychological constructs: Stop the bandwagon, I want to get off. *American Psychologist, 44*, 1118–1123.

Miller, D. (1994). *Women who hurt themselves: A book of hope and understanding*. New York: Basic Books.

Miller, J. B. (1976). *Toward a new psychology of women*. Boston: Beacon Press.

Moraga, C., & Anzaldua, G. (Eds.). (1983). *This bridge called my back: Writings by radical women of color*. Watertown, MA: Persephone Press.

Moss, L. A. (1985). Feminist body psychotherapy. In L. B. Rosewater & L. E. A. Walker (Eds.), *Handbook of feminist therapy: Women's issues in psychotherapy* (pp. 80–90). New York: Springer.

Mowbray, C. T. (Chair). (1993, August). *Seriously mentally ill women: Does a feminist perspective apply?* Symposium presented at the 101st Convention of the American Psychological Association, Toronto.

NiCarthy, G. (1982). *Getting free: A handbook for women in abusive relationships*. Seattle: Seal Press.

Noble, K. (1994). *The sound of a silver horn*. New York: Viking.

Norwood, R. (1985). *Women who love too much*. New York: Pocket Books.

Panzarino, C. (1994). *The me in the mirror*. Seattle: Seal Press.

Perkins, R. (1991a). Therapy for lesbians? The case against. *Feminism and Psychology, 1*(3), 325–338.

Perkins, R. (1991b). Women with long-term mental health problems: Issues of power and powerlessness. *Feminism and Psychology, 1*, 131–140.

Pheterson, G. (1986). Alliances between women: Overcoming internalized oppression and internalized domination. *Signs: Journal of Women in Culture and Society, 12*, 146–160.

Pope, K. L., Butcher, J., & Seelen, J. (1993). *The MMPI, MMPI-2 and MMPI-A in court*. Washington, DC: American Psychological Association.

Pope, K. S., & Vasquez, M. J. T. (1991). *Ethics in psychotherapy and counseling*. San Francisco: Jossey-Bass.

Protacio-Marcelino, E. (1990). Towards understanding the psychology of the Filipino. In L. S. Brown & M. P. P. Root (Eds.), *Diversity and complexity in feminist therapy* (pp. 53–66). New York: Haworth.

Rave, E. J., & Larsen, C. C. (1990). Development of the code: The feminist process. In H. Lerman & N. Porter (Eds.), *Feminist ethics in psychotherapy* (pp. 14–24). New York: Springer.

Raymond, J. (1986). *A passion for friends*. Boston: Beacon Press.

Rich, A. (1979). *On lies, secrets, and silence: Selected prose, 1966–1978*. New York: Norton.

Rich, A. (1993). *What is found there: Notebooks on poetry and politics*. New York: Norton.

Robson, R. (1992). *Lesbian (out)law: Survival under the rule of law*. Ithaca, NY: Firebrand.

Root, M. P. P. (Ed.). (1992a). *Racially mixed people in America*. Newbury Park, CA: Sage.

Root, M. P. P. (1992b). Reconstructing the impact of trauma on personality. In L. S. Brown & M. Ballou (Eds.), *Personality and psychopathology: Feminist reappraisals* (pp. 229–266). New York: Guilford.

Root, M. P. P. (1992c, June). Reconstructing the impact of trauma on personality development: A feminist perspective. In L. S. Brown (Chair), *Feminist therapy perspectives in trauma theory*, Symposium presented at the First International Congress of the International Society for Traumatic Stress Studies, Amsterdam, The Netherlands.

Rosewater, L. B. (1985a). Feminist interpretation of traditional testing. In L. B. Rosewater & L. E. A. Walker (Eds), *Handbook of feminist therapy: Women's issues in psychotherapy* (pp. 266–273). New York: Springer.

Rosewater, L. B. (1985b). Schizophrenic, borderline, or battered? In L. B. Rosewater & L. E. A. Walker (Eds.), *Handbook of feminist therapy: Women's issues in psychotherapy* (pp. 215–225). New York: Springer.

Rosewater, L. B., & Walker, L. E. A. (Eds.). (1985). *Handbook of feminist therapy: Women's issues in psychotherapy*. New York: Springer.

Ross, C. A., & Norton, G. R. (1988). Multiple personality patients with a past diagnosis of schizophrenia. *Dissociation, 1*, 39–42.

Rothblum, E. D., Solomon, L., & Albee, G. (1986). A sociopolitical perspective of the *DSM-III*. In T. Millon & G. Klerman (Eds.), *Contemporary directions in psychopathology: Toward the DSM-IV* (pp. 167–192). New York: Guilford.

Schechter, S. (1982). *Women and male violence: The visions and struggles of the battered women's movement.* Boston: South End Press.

Scherer, M. (1992). *Still loved by the sun: A rape survivor's journal.* New York: Simon & Schuster.

Sears, V. L. (1990). On being an "only one." In H. Lerman & N. Porter (Eds.), *Feminist ethics in psychotherapy* (pp. 102–105). New York: Springer.

Siegel, R. J. (1990). Turning the things that divide us into the strengths that unite us. In L. S. Brown & M. P. P. Root (Eds.), *Diversity and complexity in feminist therapy* (pp. 327–336). New York: Haworth.

Skodol, A. E., Oldham, J. M., Gallaher, P. E., & Bezirganian, S. (1994). Validity of self-defeating personality disorder. *American Journal of Psychiatry, 151*, 560–567.

Smith, A. J. (1990). Working within the lesbian community: The dilemma of overlapping relationships. In H. Lerman & N. Porter (Eds.), *Feminist ethics in psychotherapy* (pp. 92–96). New York: Springer.

Smith, A. J., & Siegel, R. F. (1985). Feminist therapy: Redefining power for the powerless. In L. B. Rosewater & L. E. A. Walker (Eds.), *Handbook of feminist therapy: Women's issues in psychotherapy* (pp. 13–21). New York: Springer.

Starhawk (1993). *The fifth sacred thing.* New York: Bantam Books.

Stoltenberg, J. (1990). *Refusing to be a man.* New York: Meridian.

Surrey, J. L. (1987). Relationship and empowerment. *Work in Progress, 30.* Wellesley, MA: Stone Center Working Papers Series.

Surrey, J. L., & Heyward, C. (1990, August). Toward an ethic of mutuality for the therapy relationship. In L. S. Brown (Chair), *Ethics in feminist therapy: Next steps.* Symposium presented at the 98th Convention of the American Psychological Association, Boston.

Szasz, T. S. (1970). *Manufacture of madness: A comparative study of the inquisition and the mental health movement.* New York: Harper & Row.

Szasz, T. S. (1978). *The myth of psychotherapy: Mental healing as religion, rhetoric, and repression.* New York: Doubleday.

Tavris, C. (1992). *The mismeasure of woman.* New York: Simon & Schuster.

Unger, R. K. (Ed.). (1989). *Representations: Social constructions of gender.* Amityville, NY: Baywood Publishing.

Unger, R. K. (1990). Imperfect reflections of reality: Psychology constructs gender. In R. Hare-Mustin & J. Marecek (Eds.), *Making a difference: Psychology and the construction of gender.* New Haven: Yale University Press.

Unger, R. K., & Sanchez-Hucles, J. (1993). Integrating culture: Implications for the psychology of women. *Psychology of Women Quarterly, 17*, 365–372.

van der Kolk, B. A. (Ed.). (1987). *Psychological trauma.* Washington, DC: American Psychiatric Press.

van der Kolk, B. A. (1992, June). *Fluoxetine and the role of the serotonin system in PTSD*. Lecture presented at the First International Congress of the International Society for Traumatic Stress Studies, Amsterdam, The Netherlands.

van der Kolk, B. A., & Roth, S. (1992, June). Defining posttraumatic stress for DSM IV and ICD-10. In J. Davidson (Chair), *Posttraumatic stress for the DSM IV and ICD-10: The introduction of a new diagnosis, Disorder of Extreme Stress (DESNOS)*. Symposium presented at the First International Congress of the International Society for Traumatic Stress Studies, Amsterdam, The Netherlands.

Walker, L. E. A. (1989a). Psychology and violence against women. *American Psychologist, 44*, 695–702.

Walker, L. E. A. (1989b). *Terrifying love: Why battered women kill and how society responds*. New York: Harper & Row.

Walker, L. E. A. (1990). DSM-III-R and violence against women. In I. Foeken (Ed.), *Feminist diagnosis and therapy* (pp. 11–29). Amsterdam: Stichting De Maan.

Walker, L. E. A., & Edwall, G. E. (1987). Domestic violence and determination of visitation and custody in divorce. In D. J. Sonkin (Ed.), *Domestic violence on trial: Psychological and legal dimensions of family violence* (pp. 127–154). New York: Springer.

Weise, E. R. (Ed.). (1992). *Closer to home: Bisexuality and feminism*. Seattle: Seal Press.

Weisstein, N. (1970). Kinder, kuche, kirche as scientific law: Psychology constructs the female. In R. Morgan (Ed.), *Sisterhood is powerful* (pp. 205–219). New York: Vintage.

White, E. (Ed.). (1990). *The black women's health book: Speaking for ourselves*. Seattle: Seal Press.

Wilkinson, S., & Kitzinger, C. (Eds.). (1993). *Heterosexuality: A feminism and psychology reader*. London: Sage Publications.

Williams, P. J. (1991). *The alchemy of race and rights*. Cambridge: Harvard University Press.

Williams, W. P. (1987). *Spirit and the flesh: Sexual diversity in American Indian culture*. Boston: Beacon Press.

Wyatt, G. E. (1985). The sexual abuse of Afro-American and white American women in childhood. *Child Abuse and Neglect, 9*, 231–240.

Wyche, K. F. (1993). Psychology and the African-American woman: Findings from applied research. *Applied and Preventative Psychology, 2*, 115–121.

Wyckoff, H. (1977). *Solving women's problems through awareness, action, and contact*. New York: Grove Press.

Index

Adleman, J., 210, 221, 231
Adult child movement, 138
African-Americans: family therapy and, 90; lessons in survival learned by, 76; models of family structures for, 78–79; psychological testing and, 185
Ageism, and diagnostic usages, 126
Albee, G., 130
Alcoholism, and diagnostic categories, 139–40
American Indian clients, 82, 140
American Psychiatric Association, 132, 135, 138
American Psychological Association (APA), 80, 192; ethics codes of, 203–4
Androgyny, in reformist models of feminism, 55
Anxiety neurosis, as diagnostic category, 130
Anzaldua, G., 60
Assertiveness training, 56–57
Authority: analysis of, in feminist therapy theory, 23, 52; diagnostic categories and, 138; egalitarian relationship in feminist therapy and, 104–5; formulation of theory and, 7; nurturance as source of, 109; radical models of feminism on, 57; role of therapist and, 52;

therapist-client relationship and, 94–95, 96, 104–5, 109, 111
Autonomy, of client in feminist therapy, 114

Ballou, M., 11, 49, 64, 179
Barrett, S. E., 210
Becker, D., 127
Behavior: feminist therapy theory and concepts of, 49; importance of gender in, 51; reformist models of feminism on learning of, 55
Behavioral psychotherapy, and reformist models of feminism, 55
Belenky, M. F., 51, 66
Bem, D. J., 54
Bem, S. L., 54, 146, 167
Benjamin, L. S., 166, 225
Berman, J. S., 210
Bernrad, J., 140
Bezirganian, S., 135
Biaggio, M., 151
Bias: in diagnostic models, 130–31, 133–34; in research on diversity, 89
Biology: distress and pathology influenced by, 142–43, 193–94; gender and, 65–66

Oppression *(continued)*
survival and, 75–76; multicultural
analysis of, 74–75; patriarchy and,
18–19, 70; reaction to membership
in dominant groups and, 87–88;
therapist-client relationship and
model of, 103, 107, 117

Outcome: in feminist therapy, 39; power
in therapist-client relationship and, 108

Panic disorder, as diagnostic category,
130–31

Panzarino, C., 147

Paraphilic coercive disorder, as proposed
diagnostic category, 133–34

Patriarchy: analysis of, in feminist therapy theory, 23; client's awareness of,
118; conceptualization and understanding of experiences in, 172–73;
costs to men of, 19, 118; cultural stereotypes in, 70; development of paradigms for "normal" that challenge,
77–78; diagnostic categories and,
135–36, 143; dilemma of dealing with,
178–79; ethical issues for feminist therapist involving advancement of,
220–21; ethics codes and, 203–4; examples of institutional constraints in dealing with, 197–98; feminist approach to
diagnosis and, 125; feminist therapy
and confronting, 17, 18–21, 29–30, 45,
70–71, 196–97; knowledge among marginalized and oppressed groups about,
75–77; power and concept of "patriarchal reversals" in, 114; racism and, 84;
radical models of feminism and, 57–58,
62–63; range of cultural manifestations
of, 18–19; reformist models of feminism on, 55–56; relationships among
women and, 42–44; resistance in feminist therapy and, 25–26; revictimiza-
tion of victims of violence who resist,
28–29; therapist-client relationship and
dominance-submission hierarchy in,
84–85; therapy and adjustment of
women to, 21; therapy as tool of, in
dominant culture, 31; usefulness of
feminist therapy in, 21; work of thera-

pist valued in, 41

Pearse, M., 151

People of color: cultural stereotypes of,
70; psychological testing and, 185;
research literature on, 90

Perkins, R., 21, 29, 32, 33, 34, 39, 69, 142,
184, 192, 232

Personality development, 231

Pheterson, G., 85

Political issues: body in feminist biopsychosocial model and, 147; conceptualization process influenced by, 154, 164,
173; diagnostic categories influenced
by, 130–31, 133–34; distress and, 149,
151–52; feminist ethics and, 209; feminist therapy and perspective on, 37–39;
linking of approach to psychotherapy
with, 31–34; personal action and, 50;
psychological testing and, 186; therapist-
client relationship and, 103–4. *See also*
Feminism and feminist political
philosophies

Pope, K. L., 185, 188

Pope, K. S., 201

Porter, N., 204, 205, 207

Post-traumatic stress disorder (PTSD), as
diagnostic category, 136–37

Poverty, and cultural stereotypes, 70

Power: analysis of, in feminist therapy
theory, 23, 51–52; boundary issues and,
214–15; claiming of false equality by
therapist and, 106–7; client in feminist
therapy and, 113–17; conceptualization
and balance of, 162; consciousness-
raising reframed as therapy and
dynamics of, 36; culture and mainstream constructions of, 107; dependency as hidden form of, 114–15; diagnosis and, 126, 127, 137–38; egalitarian
relationship in feminist therapy and,
104–5; example of use of, 110–11; feminist therapy as a disruptive force and
effects on, 30; gender and, 67; informed
consent in therapy contract and balance of, 35; money as signifier of,
39–40; oppression and, 73; radical
models of feminism on, 57, 62;
reformist models of feminism on, 53;
resistance in feminist therapy and,

258

Index